THE NUMEROLOGY WORKBOOK

Provides methods of numerological analysis which can be used to
solve the enigmas of our existence.

THE
NUMEROLOGY
WORKBOOK

Understanding and Using the Power of Numbers

by

JULIA LINE

Sterling Publishing Co., Inc.
New York

The author wishes to thank Bernard Stringer for permission to
use the Prediction Tarot deck to illustrate this book.

Published by Sterling Publishing Company, Inc.
387 Park Avenue South, New York, N.Y. 10016
Originally published in Great Britain by Thorsons
An imprint of HarperCollins*Publishers*
© 1985 by Julia Line
Distributed in Canada by Sterling Publishing
% Canadian Manda Group, One Atlantic Avenue, Suite 105
Toronto, Ontario, Canada M6K 3E7

2   4   6   8   10   9   7   5   3   1

Sterling ISBN 0-8069-9763-X

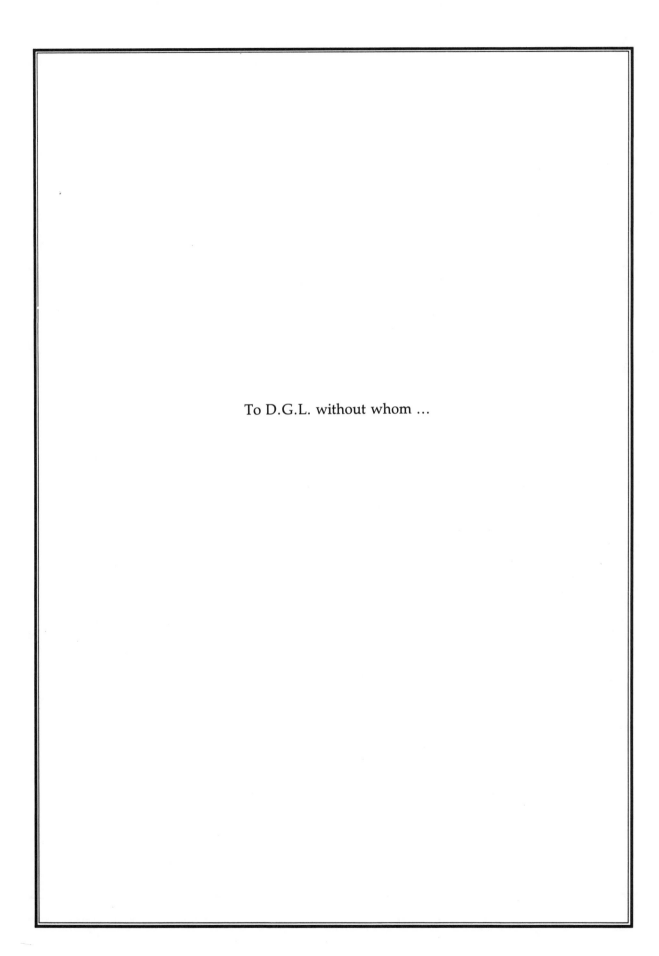

To D.G.L. without whom ...

CONTENTS

INTRODUCTION

Evolution is the law of Life.
Number is the law of the Universe.
Unity is the law of God.

— Pythagoras

It was Honoré de Balzac (1799–1850), the French realistic novelist who, during a conversation on the subject of numbers, said, 'without them, the whole edifice of our civilisation would fall to pieces'. Numbers affect our daily lives in a host of different ways and one of the oldest is the occult science of numerology. No one can be exactly sure when numerology evolved as a method of forecasting the future. The ancient Chaldeans, Egyptians, Assyrians, Babylonians, Greeks, Hindus and Hebrews all developed numerological systems of their own and to this day numerology is constantly being updated, and expanded by various experts and cultures who embrace its doctrines.

The Qabalistic Gematria, a profound magico-philosophical art which uses the twenty-two letters of the Hebrew alphabet, and their corresponding numbers, to decode hidden meanings in the scriptures or to discover a person's essential character and destiny by name analysis, is certainly a major contributory factor to present-day numerology. So with the Gematria providing the cipher, and the Pythagoreans a method of interpreting numbers by the qualities assigned to them, plus a few additional contributions from Judaism and Christianity, numerology was created.

Numerologists believe that we are born at a certain date, hour and minute not merely by chance, but in order to learn important lessons and to perform specific tasks during our lifetimes and that the conditions and vibrations prevailing at the precise moment of our birth must be favourable if we are to fulfil our mission in life. Some also believe that the transmigration of souls and the possibility of reincarnation plays an important role in their philosophy of life. Numerology is also a method of character analysis which uses the numbers of names and birthdates in an attempt to solve the age-old question

'Who am I?' Its study enables us to take an objective, unbiased look at ourselves and to discover our innate talents and abilities.

Through numerological analysis we can not only recognize our limitations but can also discover what we are best qualified to do, and how to fulfil our destiny. We are able to look forward into the future at our 'Cycles of Life' in an attempt to gain advance knowledge of what could be in store for us. All this and more is possible through numerology. Once we have discovered our personal numbers we can, with patience and understanding, use them as clues to solve the enigma of our existence.

Numerology incorporates the Pythagorean belief that 'all things can be expressed in numerical terms because all things are ultimately reducible to numbers'. Numerologists generally work with the numbers one to nine, plus the master numbers eleven and twenty-two — together their meanings encompass all the experience that life can present. Symbolically they represent the stages through which an idea must first pass before it can become a reality. Understanding, and practical application, of the meanings of these numbers will bring a greater personal understanding of life. It is not necessary to possess powers of extra-sensory perception and clairvoyance to practise numerology — just simple arithmetic.

There are two generally recognized methods of converting letters into their numerical values. The first, and certainly the oldest, originates from the Hebrew system of numbering as follows:

1	2	3	4	5	6	7	8
A	B	C	D	E	U	O	F
I	K	G	M	H	V	Z	P
Q	R	L	T	N	W		
J	S		X				
Y							

This conversion table is based on correspondences between our alphabet and the Hebrew, with a little extra assistance from the Greek. You will notice that there are no letters assigned to the number nine. One school of thought claims that the Hebrew letters which stood for the number nine have no equivalents in our alphabet while another believes there were no letters associated with nine because it was the number of finality in Hebrew mythology. Nothing could ever be truly final in the Hebrew philosophy and they had no letter sounds which would convey the concept of finality or totality. To them only one thing could ever be perfect and complete — their God. Some occultists regard nine as the numerical equivalent to the nine-lettered name of God and believe that it is omitted from the above correspondence table for this reason.

The other system of conversion adopts a more modern approach and simply assigns the numerical values for each letter by putting the alphabet in its normal order beneath the numbers one to nine inclusive as follows:

1	2	3	4	5	6	7	8	9
A	B	C	D	E	F	G	H	I
J	K	L	M	N	O	P	Q	R
S	T	U	V	W	X	Y	Z	

These more recent number/letter correspondences are used throughout this book in calculations and examples but the Hebrew system can also be used with equal success. It is up to the individual student of numerology to decide for himself which of the foregoing systems he prefers to use — the method of finding personal numbers remains the same whichever his ultimate choice may be.

Numerologists *always* reduce names and dates from their double-digit numbers to single ones by left to right additions. The single numbers arrived at by this process are then interpreted according to the qualities and characteristics assigned to them.

Throughout history many famous (and some infamous) individuals and societies have been involved in, or become associated with, the science of numerology. The most notable example is Pythagoras (sixth century BC), the Greek philosopher and mathematician who taught his followers that the entire world is built upon the power of numbers. He made such a great contribution to the development of numerology that an entire chapter is devoted to his life and teachings later in this workbook.

Centuries later the Renaissance philosopher-magician Henry Cornelius Agrippa of Netterheim (AD 1486–1555) listed the significance of the numbers one to nine:

1. action, ambition, leadership
2. balance, passivity, receptivity
3. gaiety, versatility, brilliance
4. endurance, steadiness, dullness
5. sexuality, adventure, instability
6. domesticity, harmony, dependability
7. mystery, knowledge, solitariness
8. worldly involvement coupled with material success
9. spirituality, inspiration, great achievement.

They appeared in a treatise on occult philosophy which he published relatively late in life. From existing Pythagorean philosophies he calculated complex

Figure 1 Agrippa's Correspondences.

relationships between the harmony and proportions of man and the numbers which were associated with them. He led an extremely colourful life and was at one time cast into prison when he fell into debt. He taught throughout Europe and had an enormous influence on Western occultism. In his work entitled 'On the Vanity of the Arts and Sciences' he finally repudiated his earlier theses.

Giuseppe Balsamo Cagliostro (1743–1795) appeared on the numerological scene towards the end of the eighteenth century in the guise of magician/miracle-healer/spiritualist. He was reputed to use the Hebrew number/letter correspondences and a system of numerology based on the work of Agrippa and Pythagoras. He took Paris by storm in the year 1785 when he won vast sums of money at the gaming tables and showed off his ability to forecast winning numbers in the lotteries. He achieved his greatest notoriety however for making, allegedly by alchemy, a diamond which he offered to the Cardinal de Rohan. Cagliostro also had quite a reputation as a faith healer and was believed to have effected 15,000 cures in the city of Strasburg over a period of three years. He made some remarkably accurate predictions during a private gathering at the house of a friend, where he demonstrated his skill as a numerologist.

Having analysed the names of King Louis XVI of France and his queen, Marie Antoinette, he foresaw that Louis was 'condemned to lose his head before his 39th year for being guilty of war'. For the queen, he predicted that she would be 'unfortunate, unhappy in France, a queen without a throne or money, wrinkled prematurely through grief, kept on a meagre diet, imprisoned and beheaded'. Surely these must rank as two of the most accurate prognostications ever recorded — and both accomplished with numerology.

Cagliostro was finally condemned to death by the Inquisition and imprisoned in the Bastille where his sentence was later commuted to one of life imprisonment.

Alphonse Louis Constant, an Abbé of the Roman Church who translated his name into Hebrew (Eliphas Levi Zahed, generally known as just Eliphas Levi) was a great Qabalist and scholar although he could never be described as a numerologist, and was the man responsible for relating the twenty-two cards of the Tarot Major Arcana to the twenty-two letters of the Hebrew alphabet and the twenty-two paths of the Tree of Life. His correspondences indirectly gave a whole new dimension to numerology. His books included *Dogma and Ritual of High Magic* which was in two parts. Each part had twenty-two chapters — one for each of the twenty-two Tarot trumps.

The Order of the Golden Dawn, a magical society flourishing in the 1890s which was Rosicrucian in inspiration, expanded Levi's theories even further by classifying colours, precious and semi-precious stones, plants, perfumes and so on. The members also incorporated in their classification system the gods and spirits from many religions and mythical beliefs, particularly those of the Greek, Egyptian, Roman, Christian and Jewish cultures.

Aleister Crowley (1875–1947) must surely be included as an indirect contributor to the growth and expansion of twentieth century numerology. A former member of the Hermetic Order of the Golden Dawn he later founded his own secret society, the 'Astrum Argentinum' which believed that 'existence was pure joy' and that sorrows were only 'passing, artificial clouds'. In the early 1920s at the Abbaye de Thélème in Sicily Crowley instructed his disciples in his own peculiar brand of sexual magic during which vast amounts of opium, cocaine and hashish were consumed. The mysterious death of a child and the hospitalization of several of his 'followers' finally brought this chapter of his life to an end. Crowley poured the entire contents of his magical mind into the Tarot deck which he designed, but never saw published, towards the end of his life and it is from his system of correspondences that numerology most benefits.

Final mention should go to Count Louis Hamon (1866–1936) better known as Cheiro — a popular and influential seer of the present century and regarded by some as the foremost exponent of palmistry — chiromancy. He was also an eminent astrologer and numerologist. The list of people for whom he read during the course of his lifetime is both long and distinguished and includes such famous names as Sarah Bernhardt, Dame Nellie Melba, the Infanta Eulalia of Spain, Mark Twain, Sir Arthur Sullivan and Sir Austen Chamberlain.

It is the aim of this workbook to present as many different methods, styles and numerical correspondences as possible. This will leave students free to explore the subject at their own pace and should enable them to discover exactly what numerology is all about and what it ultimately sets out to achieve. Through first-hand experience, experimentation and personal involvement they should be able to use this occult science in a way which suits not only their needs but also their personalities. Remember the Latin phrase, *Omnia in numeris sita sunt* — Everything lies veiled in numbers.

Chapter 1

NUMBERS AND RELIGION

The Old Testament Book of Genesis tells how the Universe was created by the 'Word of God' — God caused things to exist simply by pronouncing their names. It is most important to note that for 'Word' we can substitute 'Voice' or better still 'Sound'. The ancients believed that sound was a potent force which could be used constructively (as in the Genesis creation story) or destructively, and today it is a proven scientific fact that sound, at certain frequencies, can kill; even a soprano's high note is capable of shattering glass. The ancients also believed that it was possible to discover and apply this 'word power' for their own ends. Special words and music were used for invocations and the successes achieved from these supplications were thought to depend largely upon the vibration and pitch of the sound chosen because music, as well as words, can be related to numbers.

Words were of great importance and so too were the twenty-two letters of the Hebrew alphabet. They were looked upon as divine instruments of creation and each letter was assigned with a numerical equivalent which became established by tradition.

The symbolism of numbers features prominently in religious creeds and doctrines throughout the world. Many passages and occasionally whole books in the Old and New Testaments of the Bible can be interpreted numerically. Religious truths were hidden within the texts from the eyes of the unbeliever while still allowing the encoded Christian message to be understood by the chosen few. Examples of this use of numbers to maintain secrecy can be found in many other religious works including the Books of Creation and Splendour of the Qabala.

Gematria is the name given to the profound magico-philosophical science of reducing words to numbers in order to decode the information believed to be implicit within them. The numerical value of any word can be found simply by adding up the numbers of the letters of which it is composed. It also becomes possible to link words, phrases and names with others of the same value, or multiples thereof. All the names which occur in the Bible are believed to have deeper, hidden meanings concerning the person or place to which they apply and these hidden meanings can be found by the application of Gematria. Even the esoteric reason for the construction of a particular building or object can be found by analysis of its measurements.

Hebrew is just one of the alphabets whose letters have been assigned with numerical values — these letter/number correspondences also occur in the Greek, Latin and Arabic alphabets. The correspondences for the Greek alphabet are shown in Figure 2 below.

A	B	Γ	Δ	E	Z	H	Θ	I	K	Λ	M	N
1	2	3	4	5	7	8	9	10	20	30	40	50

Ξ	O	Π	P	Σ	T	Y	Φ	X	Ψ	Ω
60	70	80	100	200	300	400	500	600	700	800

Figure 2 The Greek Alphabet and its Number Correspondences.

Our present-day science of numerology probably derived much from the ancient system of Gematria which is very much controlled by Hebrew orthography in which vowel sounds are, as a rule, omitted. During the Middle Ages when Jewish theologians began to travel widely across Europe, their teachings were eagerly embraced by Western occultists who formulated numerical systems of their own based on the Arabic numerals from one to nine. Was this twentieth century numerology in embryo?

Perhaps the most famous or infamous number to be found in the Bible occurs in Revelation 13 — it is 666, the Number of the Beast, or the Apocalyptic Number as it is sometimes called. He that hath understanding, let him count the number of the beast; for it is the number of man; and his number is Six hundred and sixty and six.' The beast is regarded by some to be the Antichrist who will one day gain dominion over the whole world only to be finally overthrown by the angels of God.

The number 666 was thought to represent the numerical value of some proper name, written in either Hebrew or Greek letters. Divers attempts have been made to identify the beast with historical characters including Mahomet, Luther and Napoleon I. The most popular identification, however, is with the Roman Emperor Nero. The historian Macaulay described the House of Commons as the Great Beast because it had 666 members and permanent officials at the time of his writing, while Aleister Crowley, the twentieth century occultist, saw himself as the personification of the beast. The number 666 also represents the 'yang', the positive charge of solar energy, which can be associated with the rule of either an emperor or a tyrant. It represents activity and rational intellect too. The sum of the numbers from 1–36 inclusive, which appear in the magic square of the sun, equals 666. The Book of Revelation also states that 144,000 are to be saved. This number when reduced equals nine ($1+4+4+0+0+0=9$) as does 666 ($6+6+6=18/9$) which could imply that the Beast of Babylon and Man are really both one and the same.

Another prominent Gematric number is 1080 which represents the negative, receptive side of nature — the 'yin' — and is linked with the moon, prophecy and intuition. When applying the rules of Gematria to a phrase it is, on occasion, permissible to add or subtract one numeral (colel) without detracting from its meaning. Bearing this rule in mind, the following all correspond with the number 1080 — the Holy Spirit, the Abyss and the radius of the moon in miles. 108 is the atomic weight of silver and the number of the beads on a Buddhist rosary, while there are 10800 bricks in an Indian fire altar and 10800 stanzas in the Rig-Veda. Jesus (888) + Mary (192) = 1080.

When 666 is added to 1080 we get a total of 1746 — the number of fusion or the coming together of the two opposite principles in nature. The ancient alchemists believed that life was created from the fusion of mercury (1080) and sulphur (666) the total of which is, yet again, 1746 and the result of yet another 'union' of opposites — the Alchemical Wedding.

The gnostics referred to Jesus as 'the Ogdoad' because in His aspect as the Redeemer of the World his number was 888. When reduced we are left with 24/6 which represent Venus and Love. This is the direct opposite of the Number of the Beast which reduces to 18/9 — the number of Mars, war and destruction. Qabalists also occasionally used Adam (9) as a synonym for Man (666/18/9). Jesus Christ reduces to nine when the Hebrew number/letter correspondences are used — JESUS (1+5+3+6+3=18/9) CHRIST (3+5+2+1+3+4=18/9) JESUS CHRIST (18+18=36/9) and there must be some deep, significant reason why the Beast, Man, Adam and Jesus all ultimately vibrate to the number nine which still lies hidden within other passages of the Bible just waiting to be discovered.

The name Nebuchadnezzar, which appears in the Book of Daniel, is an example of the use of Gematria to hide the identity of a person, in this case King Antiochus Epiphanes — great care had been taken to see that both names add up to 423. Qabalists thought that the three men who stood by Abraham on the plains of Mamre were the archangels Michael, Gabriel and Raphael because both the phrases in their original language 'and lo three men stood by him' and 'these are Michael, Gabriel and Raphael' totalled 701. There are many, many more examples of this occult science too numerous to mention here which alone could fill a book.

In the near East, long before the year 3000 BC, astronomy, mathematics and many other sciences had made significant progress. As far as religion was concerned, the stars and the planets were regarded as deities and also as personified numbers, which is interesting from a numerological point of view. The Assyrians and Babylonians, for instance, named the planet Venus 'Ishtar' and assigned to it the number fifteen while the Moon became their lunar god Sin and bore the number thirty. Many Muslim legends and stories are constructed around the mystical value of numbers and each number and day of the week was attributed with special qualities by the Prophet himself. Muslim pious thought played a strong part in the importance given to each letter of the Arabic alphabet. The interpretation of the letters was developed by a sect called the Hurufis and came to be looked upon as almost a substitute for

Islamic mythology. The first letter of their alphabet — the straight alif with a numerical value of one — was a symbol for the uniqueness and unity of Allah while their 'B' with its numerical value of two was the first letter of the Koran and represented the creative power by which everything came into existence, and so on.

The numbers from one to ten and their religious symbolism and meanings are as follows:

One — *Our Father, which art in heaven, hallowed be Thy name.*
The first Commandment: Thou shalt have no other gods before me.
One represents God, Jehovah of the Old Testament, and beginnings.
To the Babylonians the divine 'One' was Anu, the god of heaven.
It was the most perfect number which represented the Creator, the Prime Mover of the Universe. To the Egyptians Ra was known as 'the one One'. The Hebrews also viewed the number one as symbolic of the Creator — a point illustrated by their prophet Zechariah (14:9) when he said 'on that day the Lord will be one and his name one' and in the Muslim faith the number one represents the unity of Allah. Kether, the Crown, of the Tree of Life.

Two — *Thy kingdom come.*
The second Commandment: Thou shalt not make unto thee any graven image.
In a Biblical sense the number two represents opposites, duality and pairs — Adam and Eve; heaven and hell; light and dark; good and evil. In Matthew 6:24 he says 'No man can serve two masters — ye cannot serve God and Mammon'. It is the numerical value of the first letter of the Koran which represents, to many mystics, the creative power by which all things came into existence. Hokmah, Wisdom, of the Tree of Life.

Three — *Thy will be done on earth as it is in heaven.*
The third Commandment: Thou shalt not take the name of the Lord thy God in vain.
The number three is symbolic of trinities — Father, Son and Holy Ghost; body, soul and spirit; light, life and love. Three is an important number in the story of Jesus — three kings; three shepherds; He rose again on the third day; He was denied three times by Peter; there were three crosses at the Crucifixion; He was betrayed by Judas for 30 pieces of silver (30/3). Binah, Understanding, on the Tree of Life.

Four — *Give us this day our daily bread.*
The fourth Commandment: Remember the sabbath day, to keep it holy.
There are many references to the number four in the Bible. The river which flowed out of Eden and parted into four heads symbolized spirit (fire), mind (air), body (earth) and soul (water). The cross, a universally sacred symbol, is also associated with the number four. Christ was not the only spiritual leader to have been crucified; so too were Thamus of Syria, Mithra of Persia, Krishna of India and Hesus of the Druids. In the Apocalypse there is also mention of four Horsemen, the four winds of earth, four beasts and four angels. Hesed, Love, of the Tree of Life.

Five — *Forgive us our trespasses, as we forgive them that trespass against us.*
The fifth Commandment: Honour thy father and thy mother.
In the story of David and Goliath 'David chose five smooth stones out of the brook' for his ammunition. In the parable contained in Matthew 25:3 there were five wise and five foolish virgins, and Christ suffered five wounds at the Crucifixion. In the Muslim faith, five is the symbol of Huwa, He, the formula for God's absolute transcendence. Din, Power, of the Tree of Life.

Six — *Lead us not into temptation.*
The sixth Commandment: Thou shalt not kill.
According to ancient records the manna which fell from heaven for six days in the desert was marked with the Hebrew vau — six. Jesus changed six pots of water into wine for his first miracle. Tifereth, Beauty, of the Tree of Life.

Seven — *Deliver us from evil.*
The seventh Commandment: Thou shalt not commit adultery.
Seven represents the mysterious God force in Nature in many religions throughout the world. The best known example of the occurrence of the number seven is in the story of Joshua when he used the power of the number to bring down the walls of Jericho. He marched his army around the city for seven days, accompanied by seven priests carrying seven trumpets and on the seventh day they circled the walls seven times, shouted, and the vibration which they had set up caused the walls to fall. Other instances of the number seven are as follows:

- The seven days of Creation in Genesis.
- The seven Archangels of Revelation and the seven spirits of God sent forth into all the earth.
- There were seven generations from David to the coming of Christ.
- The seven Sephiroth of the Hebrew Cabbala.
- The seven Amschaspands of the Persian faith.
- The seven Angels of the Chaldeans.
- The seven spirits in the Egyptian religion.
- The seven Devas of the Hindu's Bible.

Seven represents Netsah, Victory, of the Tree of Life.

Eight — *For thine is the kingdom, the power and the glory.*
The eighth Commandment: Thou shalt not steal.
The Jews practised circumcision on the eighth day after birth and at their Feast of Dedication which lasted for eight days they kept eight candles constantly burning. There were eight sects of Pharisees and eight prophets descended from Rahab. Triple eight (888) is the number of Christ the Redeemer. Hod, Majesty, of the Tree of Life.

Nine — *For ever and ever.*
The ninth Commandment: Thou shalt not bear false witness.

Nine is a mystical number. In the ninth hour — the hour of prayer — Christ on the cross said 'It is Finished'. (John 19:30). On the ninth day the ancients buried their dead and the Romans held a feast to commemorate their dead once every nine years. The First and Second Temples of the Jews were destroyed on the ninth day of the Jewish month Ab. There are nine orders of heavenly powers such as cherubim, seraphim and so on. In some Hebrew writings it is alleged that God has descended to earth nine times:

1. in the Garden of Eden
2. at the confusion of tongues at Babel
3. at the destruction of Sodom and Gomorrah
4. to Moses at Horeb
5. when the Ten Commandments were given on Sinai
6. to Balaam
7. to Elisha
8. in the Tabernacle
9. in the Temple at Jerusalem.

Nine represents Yesod, Foundation, of the Tree of Life.

Ten — *Amen.*
The tenth Commandment: Thou shalt not covet thy neighbour's house, nor thy neighbour's wife, nor his manservant, nor his maidservant, nor his ox, nor his ass nor anything that is thy neighbours'.
At the tenth coming of God the world is supposed to end and a new one be created from the rubble of the old. Malkhuth, the Earthly Kingdom, of the Tree of Life.

Chapter 2

PYTHAGORAS AND THE PYTHAGOREAN SCHOOL

Man know thyself; then thou shalt know the
Universe and God.

— Pythagoras

Parthenis was told by the oracle, during a visit to Delphi with her husband Mnesarchus, that she would bear a son who would outshine all men in beauty and wisdom, and who would be a benefactor to mankind. The prophesied child, Pythagoras, was duly born sometime between 600 and 590 BC at Sidon in Phoenicia, although his parents' home town was Samos. After his birth Parthenis changed her name to Pythasis in honour of the Pythian priestess who made the prophecy.

Many beliefs exist concerning the conception and birth of Pythagoras — he was thought by some to be a god in mortal form. His natal story is similar to that of Jesus — both were believed to be divinely conceived (the God Apollo was rumoured to be Pythagoras' father), both were born in Syria, both births were prophesied and both were born when their parents were journeying away from home. Because of these similarities, Pythagoras was often known as 'the son of God' and was thought to be under the influence of divine inspiration.

Pythagoras travelled widely during his early years and visited many countries including Greece, Egypt, Phoenicia, Syria, Babylon, Media, Persia and Hindustan. In the course of his travels he acquired great knowledge and wisdom; he was initiated into the Eleusinian Mysteries, the Mysteries of Isis at Thebes, the Mysteries of Adonis and the secret teachings of the Chaldeans. He was, in fact, the first man to use the word 'philosopher' when describing himself; wise men had previously been known as sages.

Pythagoras finally settled at Crotona in Southern Italy about 525 BC where he founded a religious/philosophical society, better known as the Italic or Pythagorean School, in order to pass on his arcane wisdom to a select group of followers. He actually married one of his pupils when in his early sixties. The marriage produced seven children. Physically, he was described as being over six feet tall with a perfect body like that of the god Apollo. He was an

Figure 3 Pythagoras.

awe-inspiring figure who, unlike most, grew stronger and more powerful with age, and was considered to be in the prime of his life at the time of his assassination. Pythagoras was believed to have lived for approximately one hundred years and, as with his birth, there are various accounts concerning his death. It is, however, generally assumed that he was trapped and burned alive by his enemies in Crotona somewhere between the years 500 and 490 BC.

The doctrines of Pythagoras were always closely guarded by his followers and after his death they managed to preserve a great deal of his work which was to exert tremendous influence upon subsequent speculative thought. Indeed, the Greek philosopher Plato (c.429–346 BC) owes much to Pythagoras and his teachings.

Pythagoras, like the philosophers of the Ionian school who were preoccupied with determining what the basic cosmic substance was, also attempted a scientific explanation of the universe in terms of some one thing. In contrast with the Ionian naturalism (Thales believed that all substances were variants of water and Heraclitus that they were variants of fire), Pythagoras took a rather more Orphic approach and found his first principle of the universe in number.

The Pythagoreans had a proverb which stated 'all things are assimilated to number' and were taught that number determined the harmonies of music and of the spheres, the movements of the sun, moon and stars and the proportions of architecture. Pythagoras believed that the world was built on the power of numbers and that it was easy to identify number with everything that is good, beautiful, orderly, right and proper. In his 'Sacred Discourse' he states that 'number is the ruler of forms and ideas, and the cause of gods and demons'.

Members of the Pythagorean society were expected to observe secrecy and strict loyalty to their order; the belief in the transmigration of souls provided a basis for their way of life. Pythagoras was able to remember previous incarnations and for this reason was thought to know more than others knew. Students were challenged to 'be like your Master and so come nearer to the gods'. They never referred to, or addressed, Pythagoras by name but always as 'The Master' or 'That Man'. This may have been because his name was believed to consist of a certain number of specially arranged letters which had great sacred significance or because students were initiated by means of a secret formula concealed within the letters of his name.

His followers were bound by very strict rules of conduct and their religious life was largely ritualistic; they wore white clothing and were required to observe sexual purity. They thought that if their souls were purified with music and mental activity they could reach higher incarnations. The God of Pythagoras was the Monad — the One that is Everything. He described God as the Supreme Mind, the Cause, Intelligence and Power within all things. He saw the motion of God as circular with a body made of light and a nature composed of truth. The students were trained in gymnastics and the study of geometry, music and astronomy was considered essential to a rational understanding of God, man or Nature. Pythagoras taught moderation in all things and he and his students, while they did not totally abstain from eating meat, followed an essentially vegetarian diet.

Aristotle referred to a Pythagorean 'Table of Ten Opposites' which were arranged as follows:

limit/unlimited	odd/even
one/many	right/left
male/female	rest/motion
straight/curved	light/darkness
good/evil	square/oblong

They believed that the odd and even numbers also formed pairs of opposites in the universe. Odd numbers were thought of as male (because they have a generative middle part), active and creative. The even numbers were assigned female (because they have a receptive opening and a space within), passive, receptive characteristics. The division of odd and even numbers is based on the ancient method of representing numbers by arrangements of dots. The odd numbers, regarded as dominant because when odd and even numbers are added together the result is always an odd number, were represented as follows:

3. ● ● ●   5. ● ● ●   7. ● ● ● ●   9. ● ● ● ● ●

and the even ones like this:

2. ● ●   4. ● ● ● ●   6. ● ● ● ● ● ●   8. ● ● ● ● ● ● ● ●

The sacred decad had a particular cosmic significance to the Pythagoreans. It is called the Tetraktys which, when roughly translated, means 'fourness' and implies that the sum of 1+2+3+4 equals 10 or a 'perfect triangle'.

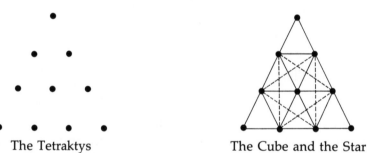

The Tetraktys   The Cube and the Star

One and two were not considered as numbers because they typify two super-mundane spheres, the point and the line, but when added to three, the triangle, and four, the square, the total produced is ten — the archetype of the universe and the great number of all things. It was found that the first four numbers were essential in the construction of solid objects. When the dots of the Tetraktys are connected nine triangles are formed — six are involved in the forming of the cube. They also reveal the six-pointed star with its central dot. The seven dots used to form the cube and the star represent the spirits of the seven creative periods — the Elohim and the central dot the Sabbath. The three corner dots stand for the threefold invisible universe.

Speculative thought on number and proportion led to an appreciation and greater understanding of the harmonia (fitting together) of the cosmos (the beautiful order of things) and when the Tetraktys was applied to musical theory a hidden order in the range of sound was discovered. During the numerical speculations which were a characteristic feature of Pythagoreanism, they employed gnomones (a Greek word meaning carpenters squares) as a means of representing numbers with dots or small stones. Gnomon numbers were arranged as follows:

```
0    0    0    0              0    0    0    0    0
 ┌─────────────┐               ┌──────────────────┐
0    0    0 │ 0              0    0    0    0 │ 0
 ┌──────┐   │                  ┌───────────┐   │
0    0 │ 0 │ 0              0    0    0 │ 0 │ 0
 ┌──┐   │   │                  ┌──────┐   │   │
0 │ 0 │ 0 │ 0              0    0 │ 0 │ 0 │ 0
```

Square Numbers   Oblong Numbers

When odd numbers are expressed in this manner they always form squares so numbers of the series 4, 9, 16, 25 and so on are known as 'square numbers'. 'Oblong numbers' are the result of even numbers being depicted in a similar way, as in the series 2, 6, 12, 20 and so on. 'Triangular numbers' formed from an extension of three dots are 6, 10 (the Tetraktys), 15, 21 and so on. The Pythagorean idea of gnomon numbers was expanded by students of the Platonic Academy in their thoughts on 'polygonal numbers'.

Figure 4 The 47th Proposition.

Pythagoras is regarded as the real founder of the science of geometry and also the discoverer of the musical octave. The famous theorem of the 47th proposition is stated in the following manner: 'In a right-angled triangle the square described on the hypotenuse is equal to the sum of the squares described on the other two sides'. It is an important Masonic symbol and because of its close connection with the builder's art is often called the 'carpenter's theorem'. There is a close correspondence between the three Grand Masters of the Masonic Lodge of Jerusalem and the three squares involved in the 47th Problem. It is also believed that the complicated mathematical details of the Great Pyramid were based upon long forgotten applications of this theorem.

The famous symbol Υ used by the Pythagoreans was probably borrowed

Figure 5   Pythagoras and Jubal (the Biblical father of music) experimenting with musical tones.

from the Egyptians. It represented the power of choice and was emblematic of the Forking of the Ways. The central stem signified Youth on the Path of Life reaching the dividing point where he must choose between Divine Wisdom on the right or Earthly Wisdom on the left.

Pythagoras is usually credited with the discovery of the relationship between sound and numbers. Popular legend has it that when passing a forge he noticed that the four different sized anvils produced different notes when struck with a hammer. Upon further investigation he found that their weights were in the proportion 6, 8, 9 and 12. When he later suspended four weights of the same proportions on strings he discovered, to his immense satisfaction, that when he plucked the strings he could reproduce the same four notes that he obtained from the anvils. When the lengths of the strings were doubled the new notes produced were an octave above the original notes. Therefore the octave could be expressed numerically as a ratio of 2:1. The other musical intervals were ratios of 3:2 and 4:3 — once again only the first four numbers are required to express these facts.

Pythagoras saw the universe as a harmonious whole and believed that everything in it emitted a sound or 'vibration'. He viewed the earth and the planets as globes orbiting around a central luminary. Following his discovery that strings of different lengths produced different notes when plucked, he believed each planet had a note of its own which depended upon its distance from the centre. When combined these planetary sounds should produce a 'harmonious cosmic octave' more commonly known as the 'music of the spheres'.

He believed that if sounds could be expressed in terms of numbers this would provide the key to the mysteries of the universe. The vibration or 'tone' of the universe at the exact moment of an individual's birth was believed to influence both his character and his destiny in life.

Pythagoras often employed aphorisms, which contained concealed meanings, in the instruction of his students. Iamblichus gathered and interpreted thirty-nine of these symbolic sayings which were translated from the Greek by Thomas Taylor. Three examples are given below:

Receive not a swallow into your house. This was meant as a warning to shun idle thoughts and mindless people. A Pythagorean student should always seek the company of conscientious workers who were capable of rational thoughts.

Assist a man in raising a burden; but do not assist him in laying it down. In a nutshell, the message implied here was — help by all means but never encourage a person to evade their responsibilities.

Declining from the public ways, walk in unfrequented paths. Those who desire wisdom should look for it in solitude.

The Golden Verses of Pythagoras contained a synopsis of his teachings and philosophy. Plato was said to have paid a high price for some of these verses which escaped destruction in Crotona.

The following is a brief outline of the ten Pythagorean numbers:

1. The Monad

The Pythagoreans revered the monad. A hermaphroditic number neither all masculine nor all feminine; when added to an even number it produces an odd, and when added to an odd number it produces an even. It is called the mind because the mind is stable and also God because it is the beginning and end of all. A symbol of wisdom. Sometimes known as chaos, the father, germinal reason, Apollo, Prometheus, geniture, substance, Jupiter, Vesta, love, piety, ship, chariot and Proteus.

2. The Duad

Often referred to as audacity because it was the first number to separate itself from the Divine One. A symbol of ignorance and despised by the Pythagoreans as a symbol of polarity. It was also known as genius, evil, darkness, matter, division, marriage, the mother, Isis, Lydia, Ceres, Diana (because the moon is forked), Maia and Juno.

3. The Triad

The first odd number. Its keywords are friendship, peace, justice, prudence, piety, temperance and virtue. It was associated with Saturn (the ruler of time), Ophion, Hecate, Pluto, Triton, the Fates, Furies and Graces. It was called wisdom because men benefit from the past, organize the present and foresee the future. The number of knowledge — music, geometry and astronomy. Pythagoras taught that the cube of this number has the power of the lunar circle. Its symbol is the triangle. It represents the primary colours and the major planets.

4. The Tetrad

Esteemed by the Pythagoreans as the primogenial number, the root of all things, the fountain of Nature and the most perfect number. Also an intellectual number and the first geometric solid. Pythagoras believed that the soul of man consists of a tetrad — its four powers being mind, science, opinion and sense. Its keywords are impetuosity, strength, the key keeper of Nature and harmony. It is often associated with Hercules, Mercury, Vulcan and Bacchus and the secondary colours and the minor planets.

5. The Pentad

The pentagram, to the Greeks, was a sacred symbol of light, health and vitality. It was the number symbolic of ether, the fifth element, because it is free from the disturbances of the four lower elements. Also symbolic of Nature. The Pythagoreans called it equilibrium because it divides the perfect number, ten, into equal parts. The keywords are reconciliation, alteration, cordiality, sound, providence, marriage and immortality. The deities associated with this number were Nemesis, Bast and Venus.

6. The Hexad

The Pythagoreans referred to this number as 'the perfection of all points'. It was called the form of forms, the maker of the soul and the articulation of the universe. Its keywords are time, panacea, the world, omnisufficient and unwearied and its associated deities are Orpheus, the Muse Thalia and the Fate Lachesis.

7. The Heptad

A number worthy of veneration by the Pythagoreans. The number of religion because man is controlled by seven celestial spirits to whom he should make offerings. The number of life because the Pythagoreans believed that human babies born prematurely during the seventh month of pregnancy usually survived whereas those born during the eighth month very often died. Its keywords are fortune, custody, control, occasion, government, judgement, dreams, voices and sounds. It was often associated with Osiris, Cleo (one of the Muses) and Mars. The Pythagorean number of law because it is the number of the Seven Spirits before the Throne, the makers of Cosmic Law.

8. The Ogdoad

The number of the first cube which had eight corners. The keywords for this number are love, counsel, prudence, law, convenience and its associated deities were Rhea, Cibele, Orcia, Neptune and Themis. A mysterious number which was associated with the Eleusinian Mysteries and the Cabiri. Also called the little holy number.

9. The Ennead

The first square of an odd number (3×3). Because it fell short of the perfect number ten by just one, it was associated with failure. The number of man because of the nine month gestation period. A limitless number because there is nothing beyond it but the infinite number ten and therefore it was associated with the ocean and the horizon which the Pythagoreans viewed as boundless. Its associated gods and goddesses are Prometheus, Juno, Vulcan, Prosperine and Hyperion. The number nine was sometimes regarded as evil because it is an inverted six.

10. The Decad

The greatest of all the Pythagorean numbers because it is the Tetraktys and comprehends all harmonic and arithmetic proportions. Pythagoras viewed ten as the nature of number. The keywords are age, power, faith, necessity, memory and tirelessness. Its deities are Urania, Phanes, the One God and Atlas (because it carried the numbers on its shoulders).

Pythagoreanism brings together and unites rationalism and irrationalism better than any other school of Greek thought. It manages to combine a rationalistic theory of number with a mystic numerology and a speculative cosmology with an understanding of the deep, enigmatic regions of the soul.

Chapter 3

THE NUMBERS
1-9

Pythagoras taught that numbers are much more than just a medium of measurement — they represent qualities — it is figures which represent quantities. The principle single numbers from 1 to 9 have been ascribed with specific characteristics which together encompass all the experiences of life. The compound numbers from 10 onwards (when reduced) are merely a repetition of the first nine. Viewed on a universal scale the single numbers stand for principles while on a more personal level they represent characteristics and abilities. The meanings of the single numbers from 1 to 9 are as follows:

Figure 6 The Unicorn from a gold coin of James III of Scotland 1451–1488.

The Number 1

Universal meanings: the number of God, the Prime Masculine Number, the Yang, God/Man, Adam or the Paradise State. The number of consciousness, unity, light, Genesis, Creation, Ego, Being, the Active Principle, the Father, Jehovah in the Old Testament. Energy in a state of perpetual motion. Sometimes the number of egoism, eccentricity and tyrants. It is the beginning — that by which all the other eight numbers were created. One can be divided into any number leaving it unaltered and so represents the spirit which can enter all things without changing their outer forms. It is immoveable and unalterable because whether multiplied or divided by itself one remains the same — this does not happen with any other number.

Symbols: the Sun, the Unicorn.

Sign: the Point.

Personal meanings: Ones are pioneers, explorers and innovators, powerful individuals capable of great achievement. Their tenacity and aggression enables them to rise to positions of power and authority where they are respected and looked up to by others. They are popular. One is the number of aim, ambition and action and if these qualities are used positively ones can be very successful in life. They have dynamic personalities, are prepared to work hard and get things done. They are also prepared to encourage and advise others less courageous than themselves.

Ones are decisive, born leaders, single minded and totally in control of themselves and any situation they may happen to be in. They rarely turn to others for help and prefer to handle problems in their own way. Once a One has chosen a particular course of action, even if it leads to disaster, their obstinacy makes it almost impossible to divert them. Negative Ones can be lazy, lacking in confidence and indecisive. At the other extreme they can also be too positive when they become egotistical, intolerant, domineering and eccentric. The number one, when connected with future events, indicates a time to be determined. Also it's a time for fresh starts, launching new projects and ideas, and to leave the past behind — if you want to succeed. In their personal life Ones have a great sense of responsibility for those they love, and are often over-generous to their partners. They are not jealous by nature but should they discover that their partner has been unfaithful they can be totally ruthless in the way they handle the situation. Generally they dislike arguments and are usually prepared to compromise. Ones are loyal, sincere, charming, affectionate and good company. They are also extremely self-controlled.

Key Words:

Positive — Pioneering, powerful, masculine, aggressive, creative, independent, original, dominant.

Negative — intolerant, obstinate, tyrannical, egotistical.

The Number 2

Universal meanings: this is the Prime Feminine Number, antithesis, polarities, opposites, pairs, complements, partners. A sign of duality and change, because One can only be fulfilled through Two producing Three. The Yin, the Eternal Female. The number of T'ai Chi (a Chinese symbol which represents the motion of all things). Passivity, subordination, a desire for peace and harmony, conciliatoriness. Good/Evil. The beginning of intellect, perception and consciousness of some one/where/time/thing. Negative/Positive. Male/Female.

Symbols: the Moon, two of anything.

Figure 7 The Lion and Lioness who together represent fidelity in love. Detail from sixteenth century set of tapestries entitled 'The Hunt of the Unicorn'.

Sign: Parallel Lines.

Personal meanings: Twos are gentle by nature, artistic, imaginative and romantic. Their qualities are more mental than physical. They are inventive but not forceful enough when trying to carry out their ideas. Twos collect and assimilate. They were not born to lead but to follow, co-operate and harmonize. Some are deeply intuitive and many possess occult powers. Twos are subject to changes of mood and emotion and are often hurt by unkind remarks or criticism. They like beauty and order in their lives, are good natured and kind but can be shy and rather self-conscious. Negative Twos can suffer from depression and can also be cruel, deceitful and malicious at times. They can become extremely possessive over people and objects.

When the number two is connected with future events it signifies a need for caution and means that this is not the right time to make a decision. You should wait and see what develops before making any positive actions.

In personal life Twos are devoted parents who like to provide comfortable homes for their families. They are also very careful with money as it represents security. They hardly ever overspend. They like their partners to demonstrate their love physically, and are constantly seeking reassurance and encouragement. Twos are very faithful and affectionate and must not allow their over-active imaginations to give them groundless reasons for jealousy. Twos dislike arguments and are always the first to want to kiss and make up.

Key Words:
Positive — feminine, parental, emotional, receptive, submissive,
    understanding, gentle, balance.
Negative — deceitful, cruel, malicious, self-conscious.

The Number 3

Universal meanings: the number of time and fate — past, present, future. The number of the family — father, mother, child. Birth, life, death. Heaven, earth, hell. Trinities generally. Creation and procreation representing both spiritual

Figure 8 The Serpent on The Tree.

and sexual creative power. The answer to the conflict posed by One (male) and Two (female). The World on the Seventh Day.

Symbol: Jupiter.

Sign: the Triangle.

Personal Meanings: Threes are ambitious, dislike being in subordinate positions and always ensure that they are one jump ahead of everyone else. They have a strong desire to rise in the world and usually achieve this because they are shrewd, original, observant and willing to work hard. They are prepared to take orders, but dislike doing so, and when giving orders themselves can often be dictatorial. Threes are extremely lucky people and even misfortunes have a habit of working out well for them in the end.They are versatile, clever, satirical and able to outwit ponderous, slow-thinking people with ease.

Negative Threes can often be too outspoken and are easily angered if they suspect that anyone is taking advantage of them. They can also be sycophantic and insincere, wasteful and frivolous. The number three when connected with future events promises luck and gives the go ahead for any proposed schemes. In personal life Threes are neither jealous nor possessive. They are generous, impulsive, warm and loyal. They are extremely good company, witty, entertaining and fun to be with. However, once a Three has decided that a relationship is over he or she will end it without further ado.

The number three has always been regarded as the sublime number and this is evident in the Greek word 'Trismegistos' which means thrice greatest or eminently great. To the Pythagoreans it was the number of excellence because it has not only a beginning but also a middle and an end. Spells are often repeated three times, fairy stories are full of instances of the number three in the form of wishes, guesses or riddles and, in mythology, Neptune carried a triple-pronged staff. The Delphic Oracle held the tripod in great esteem.

Key Words:

Positive — versatile, artistic, witty, energetic, lucky, brilliant, sociable, expansive.

Negative — frivolous, wasteful, sycophantic, outspoken.

The Number 4

Four has always been considered a sacred number and many ancient cultures had four-lettered names for God — Allh (Arabian), Adad (Assyrian), Amun (Egyptian), Itga (Tartar) and Esar (Turkish).

Universal meanings: the world, the Earth, the Establishment, the number of foundation and solid matter. The points of the compass, the seasons, the elements (earth, air, fire and water), the winds. A 'safe' feminine number. A sacred number of the Pythagoreans representing completion, solidity, stability and equilibrium. Four is not an inspiring number and is sometimes referred to as the most primitive among numbers. Four points are needed to construct the tetrahedron. There are four aspects of self: physical body, astral body, soul and spirit. Four functions: sensation, feeling, logical thought and intuition. Four aspects of matter: mineral, gaseous, animal and vegetable.

Figure 9 The Cardinal Points.

Symbols: Uranus, the Tarot suits which correspond in Celtic legend to the Unconquerable Sword, the Magic Spear, the Cup from which an entire army could be sustained and the Stone of Destiny. Also the Menorah (Candelabrum), Aaron's rod, the stone tablets of the Law and the Urn that held the Manna from Heaven.

Sign: the Square, and by implication the Cube and the Tesseract.

Personal meanings: Fours are builders. They are life's organizers. They are efficient, industrious and extremely practical. They are often considered to be rather dull because they are so down to earth, stolid and respectable. Fours are also absolutely trustworthy, tenacious, precise and calm. They seldom allow anything to upset them and deal with their problems both carefully and systematically. Negative Fours can be slow-witted and very boring. Also stubborn, weak and careless. They develop repressive natures and become suspicious of everything and of everyone. Bouts of severe depression are not uncommon in a negative Four. The number four when connected with future events indicates a time to slow down and take life more seriously. It can also mean a period of hard work with little or no spare time for leisure activites. In personal life, Fours are homelovers. They manage their financial affairs well and never live beyond their means. They also have many friends who often seek their advice. Fours are devoted to their partners and would go to any lengths to make them happy. They are thoughtful, considerate and faithful.

Key Words:
Positive — steady, calm, practical, industrious, stable, respectable, efficient, enduring, a builder.
Negative — dull, joyless, gloomy, melancholic, careless, suspicious, repressive.

The Number 5

Universal meanings: the number of chance: considered by some to be most holy or propitious and by others as uncertain, discouraging and hazardous. The five senses (sight, hearing, smell, touch, taste). The Pentagram/Man — man has two arms, two legs and a head and so can be likened to a five-pointed star. The four cardinal points plus the centre. The five elements of Chinese philosophy. Quintessence (an alchemical term meaning the four elements plus that which encompasses them — a fifth quality of physical consciousness).

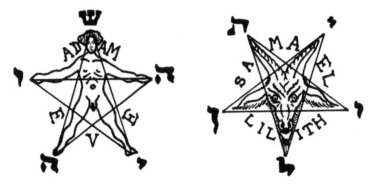

Figure 10 The 5-Pointed Star showing Man and Goat.

Nature/natural man — the sensualist. On a higher level the magician, the controller of Nature's power, the adept. Five frequently occurs in nature and is linked with sexuality. This number is lacking in stability but it brings together the opposites — the first feminine number which is two and the first masculine number which is three. One is primarily considered to be the number of God and therefore not the first true masculine number. Five is also a masculine number. The midpoint in the cycle 1 to 9 — the pivotal point where past and future are both visible at the same time.

Symbols: Mercury, Hermes the Magician, the hand, the body, the Pentagram.
Sign: the Keystone of the Arch.
Personal meanings: Fives are adventurers who love to try anything which is new and exciting. They have many talents and are clever, original, resilient, creative people. They are secretly afraid of failure but are careful not to communicate their fears to others. Fives are industrious and both physically and mentally alert. At times they may appear critical but this is only a reflection of their own inner struggle for perfection and success. Fives are sensual, earthy people. They possess great elasticity of character and never remain down for long. They can bounce back quickly from even the heaviest

blows of life. They are born gamblers and always ready to take chances if they can see an opportunity to make money quickly. Negative Fives are sarcastic and often hurt peoples' feelings. They can also be conceited and spend much time admiring themselves. Some are promiscuous and lustful when seen from a negative viewpoint. Others may be restless, quick tempered or even mentally unstable.

The number five when connected with future events indicates many lucky breaks and the time to take a chance. It can also mean that a change of house or job is on the way. This is a period to communicate and promote your own ideas.

In personal life Fives are loving and show their affections. They are loyal and sympathetic. They are also generous with their time and money although they find it difficult to accept help from others in any form. They can be jealous and suspicious but only when given cause.

Key Words:

Positive — adventurous, clever, resilient, resourceful, sexual.

Negative — conceited, sarcastic, lustful, unstable, restless, nervous.

The Number 6

Universal meanings: the Human Soul because six is symbolic of the union between Fire and Water. The number of ambivalance and effort. A 'perfect number' because it equals the sum of its divisors (1+2+3=6) and is divisible by both a 3 (odd) and a 2 (even) thus harmoniously combining the elements of each. The number of the days of Creation and therefore symbolic of the cessation of effort. The number of love, marriage and domestic happiness. A hermaphroditic number.

Symbols: Venus, Diana, Janus, the heart.

Sign: a double triangle or circle divided into six representing unity of spirit and body and harmony between man and God.

Personal meanings: Sixes are romantically inclined and lean to the ideal in all matters of the heart. Their outlook on life is very Venusian because they love their homes and beautiful objects around them. They can also derive much pleasure from art, music and poetry. Sixes are imaginative and creative, have excellent colour sense and are at their best when involved in some form of artistic expression. These people are most likely to succeed as painters, musicians or writers because they have double the creative ability of a number three (3+3=6). Sixes are intelligent, open-minded and well-balanced. They are also dependable, peaceloving and domesticated. They like their lives to run smoothly with the least possible stress and unpleasantness. Everything for a Six must be harmonious. Negative Sixes can carry their desire for pleasant surroundings too far and become fussy and trivial. They can also become complacent, arrogant and selfish. Some negative Sixes are inclined to gossip.

The number six when connected with future events indicates an urgent need to put matters right in the home without further delay. Because the number six

Figure 11 The Family Home.

rules divorce as well as marriage the adjustments necessary may be between marriage partners.

In personal life Sixes are loyal, faithful and very affectionate. They make loving parents and will do anything they can to help their children prosper and learn. They prefer the company of their partner when married to that of friends and spend much of their leisure time improving their homes. Sixes dislike rows and arguments because they find them distasteful and disruptive. They are fair, considerate and generous to those they love.

Key Words:

Positive — domesticated, reliable, harmonious, idealistic, loyal, creative, honest, parental.

Negative — complacent, trivial, selfish, gossipy.

The Number 7

Universal meanings: the Magic Number which rules occult mysteries, magical ceremonies and clairvoyance. It is a sacred and mystic number in almost all societies including Hindu, Egyptian, Greek, Hebrew and Chinese. Seven stands for the mysterious 'God force' in Nature. It is an indivisible number and therefore compared to God. Seven is also the only number capable of

Figure 12   The 7-Branched Candelabrum.

dividing 'the number of Eternity' and continuing in itself for as long as the number representing Eternity exists, and yet capable, at every addition of itself, of producing the number nine. This means it produces the basic numbers that all material calculations are built upon and which man depends upon and through which thought is expressed. On the Seventh Day God rested and all things rest under the influence of the number seven because they need time to reflect and contemplate. It represents the last step before completion and is closely associated with man's life span of three score years and ten. The eighth step completes the cycle with death and the unknown.

Seven is the number which governs the rhythms of life. In antiquity there were seven planets which had an influence upon events on earth and which are also linked with the seven days of the week. The Moon, the planet which has the greatest influence upon the rhythms of our lives, has a four-phased cycle (a lunar month). Each phase lasts seven days — our week.

Seven occurs frequently in the Bible, when it is often associated with magical powers. Other recurrences of the number seven are the seven colours in the spectrum, seven notes in the musical scale, seven features on the human head, seven vowels in the Greek alphabet, seven principles in man. The seventh son of a seventh son is believed to have occult powers.

Seven is very closely linked with the development of a human child from the moment of birth to almost two-and-a-half years old, a discovery made by Dr Wynn Westcott. The seventh hour after birth will decide whether the child will live or die. On the seventh day the remainder of the umbilical cord comes off and on the 14th day ($2 \times 7 = 14$) the child's eyes follow a light. By the 21st day the baby is able to turn its head ($3 \times 7 = 21$) and by seven months it begins to get its teeth. At fourteen months old ($2 \times 7 = 14$) it should be able to sit steadily and by twenty-one months old ($3 \times 7 = 21$) it should have begun to speak. Finally at twenty-eight months ($4 \times 7 = 28$) the child should be walking strongly.

This number represents the triumph of spirit over matter, the union of three plus four, of heaven and earth and of life and substance. The Great Bear pointing to the one fixed star (sometimes called the pivot of the Universe) is a celestial manifestation of the fundamental truth of the number seven.

Seven occurs frequently in Nature. Flowering plants of a pure strain have seven outside petals. These are plants which have never been cross-pollinated with other plants, either intentionally or unintentionally, and which are becoming increasingly more difficult to find. The Lotus is one such pure type which never loses its individuality. Buddah is often represented sitting in the centre of a Lotus flower — the emblem of the religion he taught. He chose the Lotus because its seven petals, always clearly visible, represent his teachings. He believed that the creative spirit was the origin and foundation of all things and that the seven petals represent the creative action of the seven planets from which all religions have had their origins.

Symbols: Neptune, the seven-branched Tree of Life, the seven-branched Candelabrum, the Chakras, the Ziggurat (ladder) to Heaven with seven steps, the triangle above the square which represents cyclic time in the cosmos and in the life of man and together represent the Masonic apron.

Sign: the Seven-Pointed Star.

Personal meanings: Sevens are deeply interested in all aspects of mysticism and the occult. They are often clairvoyant and/or gifted with powers of extra-sensory perception. Usually they have fantastic dreams. They are solitary people who need to spend a great deal of time alone to meditate and think. Some Sevens become so wrapped up in their thoughts that they become dreamy and impractical and tend to live in a fantasy world of their own. Their ideas about religion are often unorthodox and occasionally they create religions of their own based on mystical beliefs. Sevens are highly intuitive and imaginative — this is the number of poets, philosophers and scholars.

They need to achieve a degree of success and recognition in order to fulfil themselves or they become frustrated and are bitterly disappointed with life. Sevens love to travel because the constantly changing scene appeals to their restless natures and gives them the opportunity to experience different cultures and life-styles first-hand.

Negative Sevens can be depressive or moody while others are aloof, sarcastic and inclined to be lazy. Occasionally they become totally confused and rambling in their speech.

The number seven when connected with future events implies self-deception. Emotionally this will be a testing period in life and financially not a time to enter into any new agreements. You must learn to face the facts and take responsibility for your actions both in the past, now and in the future.

In personal life, Sevens are passionate people with great depth of feeling. They are understanding, good-natured and sincere in all they say and do. They have little or no money sense and often live beyond their means much to the horror and annoyance of their partners. They are magnetic and very individual people.

Key Words:

Positive — mystical, intellectual, philosophical, secretive, solitary, contemplative.

Negative — lazy, aloof, dreamy, depressive, moody, impractical, confused.

The Number 8

Universal meanings: the number of material success and worldly involvement. It has four-fold balance because when halved its parts are equal (4 and 4) and when halved again they are still equal (2 and 2, 2 and 2). The Greeks called it the number of justice because of its equal divisions of equally even numbers. It represents the solid and the complete. Eight represents cycles of time — the four seasons sub-divided once more by the two solstices and equinoxes. In Christian symbolism it stands for the afterlife. It is the number of regeneration and of the Gods who accompanied Thoth. The figure eight is believed to represent the joining of the two spheres of heaven and earth. It is the number of the force which exists between terrestial order (the square) and external order (the circle). Associated with the Serpents of the Caduceus, the balancing of forces, the equilibrium of different forms of power and with infinity (the mathematical symbol for which is an eight on its side). Eight also has a dual nature (evident from the figure itself — one circle on top of another) and sometimes stands for degeneration and regeneration. Complete reversals are always a possibility with this number.

Symbols: Saturn, Demeter, the Caduceus, the figure of Justice with a sword pointing upwards and a balance in her left hand (the symbol of human justice).

Sign: the Double Square.

Personal meanings: This is the number of struggle, tenacity and materialism. Eights are either great successes or great failures, they have no shades of grey and their failures can be just as spectacular as their successes. They are ardent,

Figure 13 The Caduceus (the Wand of Mercury).

zealous and have the ability to see matters in broad terms. These qualities give them the ambition and drive to aim for material goals which they often achieve.

This is not a fortunate personal number and people who possess it are often required to face sorrows, losses and humiliations during their lifetimes. Their motives are also often misunderstood and some Eights experience great loneliness. However, when their strong individuality and deep, intense nature is coupled with a relentless application to work they are often able to establish themselves in positions of authority and power. They are wise, adaptable, tenacious and exceptionally tough characters.

Negative Eights can be ruthless, obstinate and unscrupulous in their lives. Some appear to be haughty while others become the guilt-ridden playthings of Fate with tragedy woven into their Destiny. The number eight when connected with future events indicates a period to take great steps forward but only for those who are prepared to work hard and accept responsibility. Anyone contemplating marriage should consider this move very carefully and pay special attention to their financial security.

In personal life Eights can become eaten up with jealousy and demand constant reassurances of fidelity. They often experience difficulty in expressing their affections but prove to be loyal and devoted partners, albeit undemonstrative. Eights are not the easiest of people to live with as they regard quarrels as a normal component of everyday life. They are people who experience great extremes of emotion — sometimes offhand and detached while at others gentle, kind and understanding.

Key Words:
Positive — materialistic, tough, tenacious, eccentric, capable of concentrated effort.
Negative — obstinate, ruthless, unscrupulous, haughty, guilt-ridden, ill-fated.

The Number 9

Universal meanings: the last and greatest of the series of numbers 1 to 9 which are the root of all things. The Hebrew system of numbering does not assign any letters to the number nine. In their mythology it was associated with finality and there are no Hebrew letter sounds which correspond with the idea of finality or totality. They believed that nothing could ever be truly final and that only God could be complete, lacking in nothing and perfect. The triad of triads and therefore a number of great power which is frequently associated with the occult. Also associated with triple synthesis or disposition on the corporal, intellectual and spiritual levels simultaneously. The greatest of all primary numbers because it contains the qualities of all the others. It reduplicates the creative power of three and stands for completeness. When multiplied by any other number, the sum of the digits making up the final number is always nine, e.g. $5 \times 9 = 45$ $(4+5=9)$, $7 \times 9 = 63$ $(6+3=9)$, $9 \times 9 = 81$ $(8+1=9)$ which signifies a tendency towards egotism. Nine is the pinnacle of mental and spiritual attainment. A masculine number and the number of consciousness and psychism.

Nine represents the eight steps around the cycle of life plus the still centre. The Egyptians saw the still centre as Ra, Lord and Ruler of the Nine Gods at Anu. There are nine Muses who may number in accord with the nine months of pregnancy — a period of preparation for inner creative work. It represents man and everything to do with the physical and material plane. An emblem of matter. In Freemasonry there is an order of 'Nine Elected Knights' who include nine roses, nine lights and nine knocks in their rituals.

Symbols: Mars, the nine white, winged horses of Helios, the Greek Sun God.
Sign: the Sceptre and the Orb.
Personal meanings: Nine is the highest of the single numbers and those ruled by it are courageous and selfless with a genuine regard for humanity. Nines are capable of great spiritual and/or mental achievement. Their greatest dangers lie in impulsiveness of word or action and many are accident prone. Under the strong rulership of Mars, Nines are fighters who pursue their ambitions with grit and determination. They often make many enemies during their struggle to the top. They are both inspired and inspiring. Some Nines are exceptionally gifted artistically while others are brilliant in other fields of endeavour. They are enterprising, imaginative and quick-thinking.

Negative Nines are impatient and often forget to think before they speak. They can also be uncharitable, intolerant and capable of deception. They resent criticism in any form and are conceited, self-opinionated bores.

When the number nine occurs in connection with future events it is

Figure 14 A Branch of Nine Tudor Roses.

interpreted as the end of a cycle and as a time to tidy up your affairs in preparation for the beginning of a whole new phase in your life. When it occurs in the context of relationships it has a slightly different meaning which is, quite simply, the end.

   The private life of a Nine is often punctuated with quarrels and strife. Nines particularly rebel against any kind of interference whether from relatives, in-laws or friends. They are, however, trusting and loyal and usually try hard to fit in with their partner's wishes. Some crave affection and will do almost anything to get it even to the extent of making fools of themselves.

Key Words:

Positive — humanitarian, impulsive, unorthodox, successful, spiritual.

Negative — intolerant, deceptive, uncharitable, very impulsive, conceited, self-centred.

Chapter 4

OTHER IMPORTANT NUMBERS

Beyond the number nine all numbers become mere repetitions of the first nine — these are called the 'compound' or 'double digit' numbers which run from ten onwards. Numerologists generally use only the numbers one to nine for analysis but there are two notable exceptions to this rule — the numbers eleven and twenty–two. In this chapter we will be looking at these two exceptional numbers in depth. The numbers, ten, thirteen and zero, have also been included because although seldom, if ever, used for numerological analysis they are, nevertheless, important numbers, each with its own significance and meaning.

Zero

Zero represents nought, nil, nullity, nonentity, no number or quantity — nothing. It represents the void, or the empty abyss which existed before creation. It has four component parts which can be likened to negative elements — nothing, nowhere, infinite and dark. The zero can also mean invisibility.

On a personal level zero may be likened to a self-emptying process, particularly of the ego. It can also be symbolic of death. Zero represents the point in the scale of a graduated instrument from which quantity, either positive or negative, is reckoned. Also the point of time from which the start of each movement in a timed programme is at a specified interval. The moment of birth.

Zero, when viewed in relation to the number one, represents the gulf between non-existence and existence or between the unconscious existence of an inanimate object and conscious existence. Symbolically, it is closely related to infinity and so becomes symbolic of the infinite value of existence when contrasted with non-existence.

Zero is the circle of pre-conscious totality, the Ouroboros (Gnostic) Serpent with its tail in its mouth encircling the entirety of all things and living perpetually off itself — as does the universe. It is a closed system.

Symbol: the Lemniscate — the symbol for infinity in mathematics and Eternity/Infinity in occult studies (an eight on its side).

Figure 15 The classical Greek alchemists' representation of Uroboros, the World Snake.

Number Ten

When one, the first number which represents God, has a zero, representing Infinity, placed beside it we get not only the number ten but the numerological statement that 'there is only one God without end who knows no bounds'.

Now place as many more zeros as you like after the ten and you could arrive at a figure such as one million. When this is divided by the 'magic' number seven you arrive at the number 142857. Now add as many more zeros as you choose and continue dividing by seven as before. You can only get repetitions of 142857 which is known as the 'sacred number' or the 'number of Eternity'. When this number is reduced to its root it becomes 27 (1+4+2+8+5+7) and when further reduced it equals 9 (2+7). This sacred number contains the full range of numbers from 1 to 9 on which all human calculations can be built. (The numbers 3 and 6 are contained within the final 9).

Ten is often thought of as the number of completion but could also possibly be viewed as the number of over-completion, decadence or death. It is the first of the 'compound' or 'double digit' numbers, which provides vibrant and creative originality. Ten and all numbers above it repeat the one to nine cycle on a higher level of consciousness. It is considered to be a particularly fortunate number and holds the promise of victory in difficult situations. Ten not only represents the end of one cycle but also marks the beginning of another. It is a number which can be viewed from three angles — completion, beginning/end, and inclusive of all other numbers — so it represents the One and the Many.

Ten has often been regarded as a 'holy' number and surrounded in mystic beliefs. These beliefs stem from antiquity when the Godhead 'Io' was believed to be both masculine and feminine. The 'I' represented the male phallus and

Figure 16 The Ten of Clubs.

the 'o' the female womb through which all creation was projected.
Symbol: the Ten Sephiroth of the Qabalah.

Number Eleven

The numbers eleven and twenty-two are only used by numerologists in exceptional circumstances when the assessments of numbers two or four do not seem to apply to the character under analysis. People to whom these higher numbers apply are always extraordinary individuals. Both the numbers eleven and twenty-two are delicately poised between spiritual/material, good/evil, positive/negative.

Universal meanings: Eleven is the number of revelation, transcendental enlightenment and martyrdom. It represents the combination of God (1) plus the World (10).

Personal meanings: Elevens are born to help others by using their skills and knowledge to promote better standards of living for the more unfortunate. Some become teachers, evangelists, missionaries and politicians while more artistically inclined Elevens become great musicians, writers and painters. They can be likened to the eleven 'true' apostles of Christ (Judas being the twelfth) because they all have an important task to perform for the good of mankind. They are idealists who have a genuine regard for humanity. Elevens often become so involved in their efforts to benefit people on a worldwide scale that they fail to notice the needs of their immediate families, to whom they appear cold and uncaring. They are energetic, perceptive, intuitive and

Figure 17 The Pentagon and The Hexagon together representing the union of the numbers 5 and 6.

powerful characters. Eleven is a precariously balanced number and the physical manifestation of its negative side can be quite disturbing. Elevens who are neither wholly good or totally bad find their dual personality confusing, frightening and difficult to cope with. Negative Elevens often channel their unlimited energy into foolhardy schemes but if their sense of right and wrong should become completely distorted they can be dangerous individuals who are malevolent, debauched, perverted and evil. In private life Elevens are emotionally cool and undemonstrative. They need to spend a great deal of time on their own and often seem to be distant and detached from their immediate environment. They are neither jealous, possessive nor argumentative. They can be very secretive.

Key Words:

Positive — morally courageous, visionary, humanitarian, energetic, intuitive, powerful, talented, inspired, prophetic.

Negative — unfeeling, uncaring, malevolent, debauched, evil, perverted, satanic.

Number Thirteen

Thirteen is not always the unlucky number it is superstitiously thought to be — although some hotels do not number the thirteenth floor and there are no seats numbered thirteen in Italian opera houses! The thirteenth Tarot card does nothing to allay this superstition because it represents 'Death'. Ancient Adepts, however, believed that 'he who understands the number thirteen hath the Keys of Power and Dominion'. Thirteen is widely used in the occult and is a fatalistic number of great power.

With the spread of the early Christian Church, it became widely known that thirteen people dined at the Last Supper and by implication it would be unlucky for thirteen to eat together as one of their number might die before the

Figure 18 The thirteenth card of the Tarot Major Arcana — Death.

year was out. However, in pre-Christian civilizations as far apart as India and Italy thirteen at table was already considered to be a bad omen. The dread of the number thirteen has a limited geographical range. In Japan Friday the thirteenth is considered to be an exceptionally lucky day but some British sailors still stubbornly refuse to put to sea on the thirteenth of any month.

There are thirteen Buddhas in the Indian Pantheon and thirteen mystical discs surmount Chinese and Indian pagodas. The hilt of the sacred sword in the Temple of Atsusa in Japan is formed of thirteen objects of mystery and thirteen is the sacred number of the Mexicans with their thirteen snake gods.

The Americans in particular seem to flaunt the superstitions surrounding this number or are, perhaps, oblivious to them. Thirteen states formed the original American Union and its motto *E Pluribus Unum* has thirteen letters. The American eagle has thirteen feathers in each wing and George Washington had a thirteen gun salute when he raised the Republican standard.

Key Words:
Positive — occult, fatalistic, flexible, sacred, beguiling
Negative — misunderstood, fearful, changeable.

Number Twenty-two

Universal meanings: Twenty-two is thought to be a sublime number for two reasons. Firstly, God is believed to have spoken in the Hebrew language — a language which comprises twenty-two letters — when He commanded the World to exist. Secondly, sacred numbers were never chosen haphazardly and the number twenty-two has a secret sense. It is the measure of the circumference of the circle when the diameter is seven (the magic number).

Figure 19 The Luminary.

This proportion, no longer a religious secret, is widely used today and is known as 'pi'. The real mathematical value of pi is the recurring number — $\frac{22}{7}$. The number of the prophet or the sorcerer.

Personal meanings: Twenty-two represents the luminary. These people are powerful and will undoubtedly achieve greatness during their lifetimes. They possess brilliant minds and are often regarded as having been born ahead of their time. They are courageous, forceful and hard-working. Twenty-twos are interested in anything and everything new or revolutionary, are quick witted and far-sighted. These people need little sleep and are often described as 'workaholics'. Some have very marked leanings towards the occult and mysticism.

Negative Twenty-twos may use their fine brains for criminal activities and may be the 'mastermind' behind daring crimes. They can be bigoted, malevolent and lured by the black arts.

In private life they may feel jealous but will never let it show. Twenty-twos are sincere and rather romantic people. They prefer to choose a partner who has the same intellectual ability as themselves, someone who they will find stimulating. They are kind, humorous and always ready to compromise.

Key Words:
Positive — creative, wise, successful, masterful, understanding, spiritual.
Negative — criminal, bigoted, malevolent, lured by the black arts.

Chapter 5

ASTROLOGICAL LINKS

Again the Almighty spake, 'Let there be lights
High in the expanse of heaven to divide
The day from night, and let them be for signs,
For seasons, and for days, and the circling years,
And let them be for lights as I ordain
Their office in the firmament of heav'n
To give light on earth', and it was so.

— *Paradise Lost* (Book 7), Milton

NUMBERS OF THE PLANETS

Numerology and astrology are undoubtedly closely linked although no one really knows quite when numbers were allotted to the planets which control our system. Certainly the Chaldeans, Hindus, Egyptians and Hebrews all used and adopted the idea of linking a planet with a number to represent its characteristics. There is evidence that ancient astrologers were aware of the existence of Uranus (discovered in 1781) and Neptune (discovered in 1846) because they included in their calculations the orbits for two planets which govern the mental, rather than the physical, aspects of life as well as the seven 'creative planets' which were known to them. Pluto (discovered in 1930 by Percival Lowell) was not included. The most generally used number/planetary correspondences are set out below although this does not preclude the existence of other variations.

Number 1 — The Sun
In astrology the Sun governs spirit, will, energy, vitality, wholeness, self-integration, rulership, organization and power. It also represents the will to live.

Figure 20 The Sun, Moon and Stars.

Number 2 — The Moon
The Moon governs the feminine essence, the Unconscious, feelings, emotions, rhythm, instinctual responses, reflection, passivity, the Soul, motherliness, the family and heredity. It also represents changeability.

Number 3 — Jupiter
Jupiter represents the ability to expand through growth and also by understanding.

Number 4 — Uranus
Uranus governs eccentricity, invention, independence, intuition, mobility, peculiarity, impulsiveness and drastic change.

Number 5 — Mercury
The planet Mercury is associated with the intellect, communication, mental

and nervous processes, dexterity, ambiguity, writing and diplomacy. Negatively it indicates untruthfulness, unreliability and weakness of mental processes.

Number 6 — Venus

Venus governs love, harmony, artistry, feminine sexuality, attraction, affection, physical beauty and art.

Number 7 — Neptune

Neptune is associated with psychic activity, mediumship, dreams, fantasies, illusion, extreme sensitivity, drugged states, alcoholism, refinement and the immaterial world.

Number 8 — Saturn

Saturn governs melancholy, reserve, limitation, seriousness, economy, authority and the ability to accept and work with the limitations of life.

Number 9 — Mars

Mythologically Mars has always been connected with war. It indicates the inability to accept and work with prevailing circumstances — and the desire for change produces conflict.

In the Book of the Wisdom of Solomon which is now included in the Apocrypha (Old Testament books not counted genuine by Jews and at the time of the Reformation excluded from the Canon, which is a list of Bible books accepted by the Church) Solomon says:

> For God himself gave me an unerring knowledge of the things that are, to know the constitution of the world, the beginning and the end and middle of times, the alterations of the solstices, the changes of seasons and the positions of the planets, the nature of living creatures and the thoughts of men, all things that are either secret or manifest I learned for He that is the artificer of all things taught me this wisdom.

In this passage Solomon declares a great knowledge of many things. The seven-pointed star within the hexagon, contains the nine numbers which are the foundation of all our calculations. If you read around the hexagon you will discover the (magical) order of the Seven Sacred Planets and if you read along the star you will be able to trace the planets which rule each day of the week in order (a discovery made by the late G.H. Frater D.D.C.F.).

The lines of the star tell the story of life, death and resurrection or, quite simply, the changing pattern of nature. As the story unfolds the star is drawn and this can be demonstrated by following the diagram with your finger or a pencil.

Life begins from the sun, a very positive, masculine planet, then proceeds on to the Moon when the feminine influence becomes felt. From the Moon the path travels on to Mars where the masculine and feminine influences may

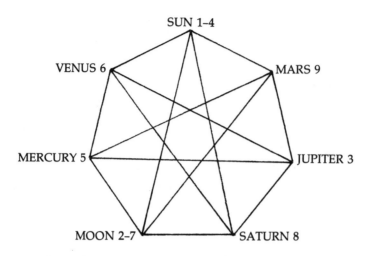

Figure 21 The 7-Pointed Star.

experience conflict. Mercury provides communication and the opportunity to live intelligently and harmoniously. The next planet in the story, Jupiter, brings growth through a greater understanding of life and by the time the path reaches Venus, love and affection become present. From Venus to Saturn is the journey through old age to death itself when the soul returns to the Sun to begin another cycle.

The Sun and Moon both share their place on the star with another planet — the Sun with Uranus and the Moon with Neptune. In the first combination the male quality of Creation represented by the Sun is balanced by the feminine qualities of Uranus on the mental or spiritual plane. The Moon, which is feminine and earthly, is balanced by Neptune which is a masculine and spiritual planet.

Each of the seven 'creative planets' has its own magic number square which is of interest to students of numerology, students of the occult and mathematicians alike. When engraved on the appropriate metal at a specific time these squares create powerful talismans which, among other things, will avert evil and bring good luck to their wearers. In ritual magic the consecration of a talisman must be done in accordance with the law of correspondences. The Order of the Golden Dawn treated these consecration ceremonies extremely seriously and went to great lengths to ensure their success. Magic number squares have to conform to the following rules:

1. each number, from one to the highest present, can appear only once, and —
2. the verticals, horizontals and two long diagonals must all add up to the same total.

The squares can also be given geometric expressions as shown in the diagram which gives an example for Mars.

Mathematicians of antiquity regarded magic number squares very highly and took them as paradigms (the inflexions of a word tabulated as an example) of universal laws. Ritual centres and temples were constructed according to one of the geometrical designs which exist in the essential framework of these squares — each of the Seven Wonders of the ancient world were constructed to such a pattern. These are the Wonders and the squares they are built upon according to Eliphas Levi:

Wonder	*Square*
The Colossus at Rhodes	The Sun
The Temple of Diana at Ephesus	The Moon
The Tomb of Mausolus	Venus
The Pyramids of Egypt	Mercury
The Towers and Gardens of Babylon	Mars
The Statue of Jupiter at Olympus	Jupiter
The Temple of Solomon	Saturn

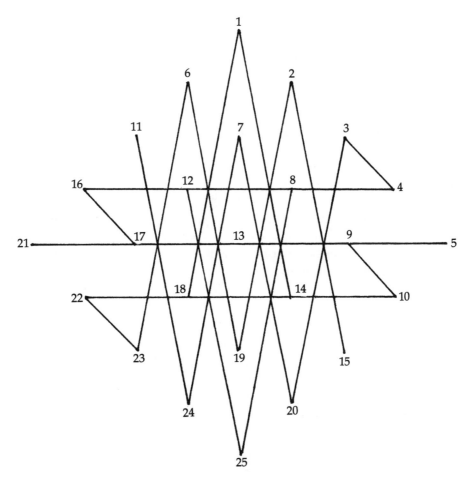

Figure 22 The geometric development of the Square of Mars. The numbers 1–25 are joined in the order in which they occur in the Magic Square.

Numbers when expressed in the plans of ancient sacred buildings referred to the dimensions and the musical tones of the building. The designs represented geometrical shapes and also the musical sounds which corresponded with the deity the temple was dedicated to.

THE MAGIC SQUARES

The Squares with their characteristic numbers (the sum of each line and the sum of the numbers contained in the square), talismanic virtues and associated metals:

Saturn

4	9	2
3	5	7
8	1	6

Sum of each line = 15
Sum of all the numbers from 1 to 9 = 45
Metal — pure lead.
Consecration day — Saturday, over fumes of alum, scammony and sulphur burned on a fire of cypress and ash.
Talisman to be carried in a blue silk pouch.
Protects against death by consumption, paralysis, apoplexy, cancer, being buried alive while in a coma, assassination, poison, ambush and death during childbirth. Useful in times of war because it prevents the enemy from entering any place in which it is hidden.

Jupiter

4	14	15	1
9	7	6	12
5	11	10	8
16	2	3	13

Sum of each line = 34
Sum of all the numbers from 1 to 16 = 136
Metal — pure tin.
Consecration day — Thursday, over fumes of frankincense, ambergris, balsam, cardamom and saffron on a fire of oak, poplar and fig.
Talisman to be carried in a sky-blue silk pouch.
The talisman protects against death by unforeseen accidents and diseases of the lungs or liver. It also draws sympathy and good will.

Mars

11	24	7	20	3
4	12	25	8	16
17	5	13	21	9
10	18	1	14	22
23	6	19	2	15

Sum of each line = 65
Sum of all the numbers from 1 to 25 = 325
Metal — pure iron.
Consecration day — Tuesday, over fumes of absinth and rue on a fire of the dried roots of black and white hellebore.
Talisman to be carried in a red silk pouch.
The talisman protects against death by enemies, epidemic or malignant ulcers. If hidden in a besieged city it ensures that no outside attack will succeed.

The Sun

6	32	3	34	35	1
7	11	27	28	8	30
19	14	16	15	23	24
18	20	22	21	17	13
25	29	10	9	26	12
36	5	33	4	2	31

Sum of each line = 111
Sum of all the numbers from 1 to 36 = 666
Metal — pure gold.
Consecration day — Sunday, over fumes of cinnamon, saffron and red sandalwood over a fire of laurel and dried heliotrope stalks.
Talisman to be carried in a yellow silk pouch.
The talisman protects against death by fire, heart disease and epidemic. It draws favour and good-will from people in high places.

Venus

22	47	16	41	10	35	4
5	23	48	17	42	11	29
30	6	24	49	18	36	12
13	31	7	25	43	19	37
38	14	32	1	26	44	20
21	39	8	33	2	27	45
46	15	40	9	34	3	28

Sum of each line = 175
Sum of all the numbers from 1 to 49 = 1225
Metal — pure copper.
Consecration day — Friday, over fumes of violet and rose on a fire of olive wood.
Talisman to be carried in a green silk pouch.
The talisman protects against death by cancer (women in particular), and poisoning. It brings harmony to marriage and will turn an enemy into a friend if dipped in his drink.

Mercury

Sum of each line = 260
Sum of all the numbers from 1 to 64 = 2080
Metal — an alloy of mercury, silver and tin.
Consecration day — Wednesday, over fumes of benzoin, mace and storax on a fire of dried stalks of lillies, narcissus and marjoram.
Talisman to be carried in a purple silk pouch.

8	58	59	5	4	62	63	1
49	15	14	52	53	11	10	56
41	23	22	44	45	19	18	48
32	34	35	29	28	38	39	25
40	26	27	37	36	30	31	33
17	47	46	20	21	43	42	24
9	55	54	12	13	51	50	16
64	2	3	61	60	6	7	57

The talisman protects against death by murder, poison, madness or epilepsy. If buried under business premises it ensures prosperity and if placed under the pillow during sleep brings prophetic dreams.

The Moon

37	78	29	70	21	62	13	54	5
6	38	79	30	71	22	63	14	46
47	7	39	80	31	72	23	55	15
16	48	8	40	81	32	64	24	56
57	17	49	9	41	73	33	65	25
26	58	18	50	1	42	74	34	66
67	27	59	10	51	2	43	75	35
36	68	19	60	11	52	3	44	76
77	28	69	20	61	12	53	4	45

Sum of each line = 369
Sum of all the numbers from 1 to 81 = 3321
Metal — pure silver.
Consecration day — Monday, over fumes of white sandalwood, camphor, aloes, amber and cucumber seeds on a fire of the dried stalks of artemisia, selenthrope and ranunculus.
Talisman to be carried in a white silk pouch.
The talisman protects against death by drowning, madness, dropsy and apoplexy. It also acts as a protection for travellers.

NUMBERS OF THE TWELVE SIGNS OF THE ZODIAC

In order to understand why each of the twelve signs of the zodiac is given its numerological number it is first necessary to know a little about astrology. The solar year, unlike the calendar year which commences on 1 January, begins between the 21st and the 23rd of March at the Vernal or Spring Equinox when the sun enters the sign of Aries and passes through each of the signs of the zodiac in turn — taking approximately 365 days to do so. The Earth revolves upon its own axis every twenty-four hours causing the signs of the zodiac in turn to pass over each portion of the Earth once during that period. The Moon revolves around the earth approximately once every 28 days — there being 13 lunar months in a year.

Seven days are allowed at the beginning and end of each sign — called the cusp. During this cusp period the number given to each sign and the qualities it represents are not so strongly felt because the sun is passing from one sign into another and sometimes the qualities of both signs are combined during this period.

It should also be remembered that planets have negative as well as positive qualities dependent upon which section of the zodiac they rule. The positive aspects are more forceful and physical than the negative ones which are mental and spiritual.

The zodiac signs with their numerological correspondences are as follows:

♈ **Aries, the Ram (21 March — 20 April)**
Ruled by Mars in its positive aspect.
Number = 9 (positive)
Element: Fire
Key words: I am
Brings out an objective attitude expressing urgency, together with an urge to project oneself energetically and actively into life.

♉ **Taurus, the Bull (21 April — 20 May)**
Ruled by Venus in its positive aspect.
Number = 6 (positive)

Element: Earth
Key words: I have
Brings out a productive attitude expressing endurance, together with an urge for organic relatedness, security and material sustenance.

Ⅱ Gemini, the Twins (21 May — 20 June)
Ruled by Mercury in its positive aspect.
Number = 5 (positive)
Element: Air
Key words: I think
Brings out an adaptive attitude expressing variableness, together with an urge to adjust oneself to environment, and communicate with others.

♋ Cancer, the Crab (21 June — 20 July)
Ruled by the Moon.
Number = 2
Element: Water
Key words: I feel
Brings out a defensive attitude expressing sensitiveness, together with an urge to protect and to nourish.

♌ Leo, the Lion (21 July — 20 August)
Ruled by the Sun.
Number = 1
Element: Fire
Key words: I will
Brings out a powerful attitude expressing impressiveness, together with an urge for authority.

♍ Virgo, the Virgin (21 August — 20 September)
Ruled by Mercury in its negative aspect.
Number = 5 (negative)
Element: Earth
Key words: I analyse
Brings out an analytical attitude expressing criticalness, together with an urge for efficiency and perfection.

♎ Libra, the Scales (21 September — 20 October)
Ruled by Venus in its negative aspect.
Number = 6 (negative)
Element: Air
Key words: I balance
Brings out an attitude of relatedness expressing harmony, together with an urge for unity with others.

♏ **Scorpio, the Scorpian (21 October — 20 November)**
Ruled by Mars in its negative aspect.
Number = 9 (negative)
Element: Water
Key words: I desire
Brings out a penetrating attitude expressing intenseness, together with an urge to identify oneself with one's source.

♐ **Sagittarius, the Archer (21 November — 20 December)**
Ruled by Jupiter in its positive aspect.
Number = 3 (positive)
Element: Fire
Key words: I see
Brings out an extensive attitude expressing freedom together with an urge to explore beyond one's known environment.

♑ **Capricorn, the Goat (21 December — 20 January)**
Ruled by Saturn in its positive aspect.
Number = 8 (positive)
Element: Earth
Key words: I use
Brings out a rational attitude expressing prudence together with an urge to conform to disciplined behaviour.

♒ **Aquarius, the Water-Carrier (21 January — 20 February)**
Ruled by Saturn in its negative aspect and Uranus.
Number = 8 (negative) and 4
Element: Air
Key words: I know
Brings out a detached attitude expressing unconventionality, together with an urge to identify oneself with the progressive aims of the community.

♓ **Pisces, the Fishes (21 February — 20 March)**
Ruled by Jupiter in its negative aspect and Neptune.
Number = 3 (negative) and 7
Element: Water
Key words: I believe
Brings out a nebulous attitude expressing impressionability, together with an urge to transcend the material.

NUMBERS FOR DAYS OF THE WEEK

A connection between the seven 'creative planets' and the seven days of the week can be found in many languages and cultures simply by studying the names given to each of the days and relating this to the planet they are ruled by. Monday, the day of the Moon, is named Lundi in French from 'lune', Lunes in Spanish and Montag in German whilst the planetary link, particularly in our language, for Sunday is very obvious indeed. The connection for Saturday, the last day of the week which is ruled by Saturn can be traced in a different way. On Saturdays many different peoples chose to rest, the Hebrews in particular, and Saturn in one sense means exactly that, the cessation of labour or the end of a phase. The numerical/weekday links together with the ruling planets are as follows:

Day	*Number*	*Planet*
Sunday — day of works of light	1–4	Sun and Uranus
Monday — day of works of divination and mystery	2–7	Moon and Neptune
Tuesday — day of works of wrath	9	Mars
Wednesday — day of works of science	5	Mercury
Thursday — day of works of politics or religion	3	Jupiter
Friday — day of works of love	6	Venus
Saturday — day of works of mourning	8	Saturn

As already explained, the Sun is linked with Uranus so Sunday bears the dual numbers 1 and 4 and the Moon, which is coupled with Neptune, gives Monday the numbers 2 and 7.

NUMBERS FOR HOURS OF THE DAY

It is possible, although somewhat complicated, to take the idea of assigning numbers to planets, zodiac signs and days of the week one step further and to assign a planet and number to each hour of the day right through the week from Sunday to Saturday. To do this students of numerology will need to refer to two charts. The first plots the times of sunrise (and sunset) Greenwich Mean Time throughout the year and its use is best explained by example. By referring to the chart overleaf it can be seen that sunrise on 15 April would be at approximately 5.10 am, 1 October at 6.00 am, 3 July at 3.30 am and so on. Dates towards the beginning of the month are calculated at the beginning of each month's section, dates between 12th – 20th of the month in the middle and from 21st – 30th/31st towards the end. This same process can also be applied to minutes in the hour.

Once the time of sunrise has been established it is necessary to refer to the Planetary Hours Chart which divides each day into twenty-four periods of one hour each commencing at sunrise. This system was commonly used by the Magi of Biblical days and Solomon himself is reputed to have used it for his magical workings. Still using the three examples if 15 April fell on a Tuesday and it was necessary to know the ruling planet/number for 7.00 am this would be calculated as follows on page 66.

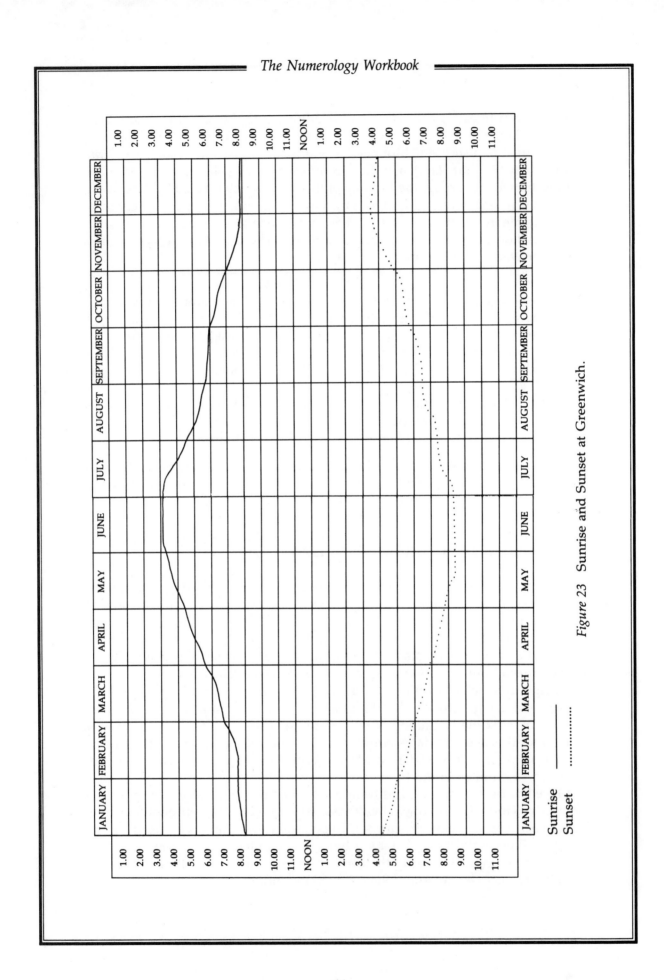

Figure 23 Sunrise and Sunset at Greenwich.

HOURS AFTER SUNRISE	SUNDAY	MONDAY	TUESDAY	WEDNESDAY	THURSDAY	FRIDAY	SATURDAY
1.	☉ 1+4	☽ 2+7	♂ 9	☿ 5	♃ 3	♀ 6	♄ 8
2.	♀ 6	♄ 8	☉ 1+4	☽ 2+7	♂ 9	☿ 5	♃ 3
3.	☿ 5	♃ 3	♀ 6	♄ 8	☉ 1+4	☽ 2+7	♂ 9
4.	☽ 2+7	♂ 9	☿ 5	♃ 3	♀ 6	♄ 8	☉ 1+4
5.	♄ 8	☉ 1+4	☽ 2+7	♂ 9	☿ 5	♃ 3	♀ 6
6.	♃ 3	♀ 6	♄ 8	☉ 1+4	☽ 2+7	♂ 9	☿ 5
7.	♂ 9	☿ 5	♃ 3	♀ 6	♄ 8	☉ 1+4	☽ 2+7
8.	☉ 1+4	☽ 2+7	♂ 9	☿ 5	♃ 3	♀ 6	♄ 8
9.	♀ 6	♄ 8	☉ 1+4	☽ 2+7	♂ 9	☿ 5	♃ 3
10.	☿ 5	♃ 3	♀ 6	♄ 8	☉ 1+4	☽ 2+7	♂ 9
11.	☽ 2+7	♂ 9	☿ 5	♃ 3	♀ 6	♄ 8	☉ 1+4
12.	♄ 8	☉ 1+4	☽ 2+7	♂ 9	☿ 5	♃ 3	♀ 6
13.	♃ 3	♀ 6	♄ 8	☉ 1+4	☽ 2+7	♂ 9	☿ 5
14.	♂ 9	☿ 5	♃ 3	♀ 6	♄ 8	☉ 1+4	☽ 2+7
15.	☉ 1+4	☽ 2+7	♂ 9	☿ 5	♃ 3	♀ 6	♄ 8
16.	♀ 6	♄ 8	☉ 1+4	☽ 2+7	♂ 9	☿ 5	♃ 3
17:	☿ 5	♃ 3	♀ 6	♄ 8	☉ 1+4	☽ 2+7	♂ 9
18.	☽ 2+7	♂ 9	☿ 5	♃ 3	♀ 6	♄ 8	☉ 1+4
19.	♄ 8	☉ 1+4	☽ 2+7	♂ 9	☿ 5	♃ 3	♀ 6
20.	♃ 3	♀ 6	♄ 8	☉ 1+4	☽ 2+7	♂ 9	☿ 5
21.	♂ 9	☿ 5	♃ 3	♀ 6	♄ 8	☉ 1+4	☽ 2+7
22.	☉ 1+4	☽ 2+7	♂ 9	☿ 5	♃ 3	♀ 6	♄ 8
23.	♀ 6	♄ 8	☉ 1+4	☽ 2+7	♂ 9	☿ 5	♃ 3
24.	☿ 5	♃ 3	♀ 6	♄ 8	☉ 1+4	☽ 2+7	♂ 9

Figure 24 Planetary/Hours Chart.

Date: 15th April sunrise 5.10 am
Day: Tuesday
Ruling planet/number required for: 7.00 am

7.00 am falls within hour 2 (6.10 am – 7.09 am), the second hour after sunrise at 5.10 am. By reading across line 2 and down the line for Tuesday it will be seen that   Mars is the ruling planet and that the ruling number is 9.

Other examples are:

Date: 1st October sunrise 6.00 am
Day: Friday
Ruling planet/number required for: 8.15 pm

8.15 pm falls within hour 15 (8.00 pm – 8.59 pm), the fifteenth hour after sunrise at 6.00 am. By reading across line 15 and down the line for Friday it will be seen that   Venus is the ruling planet and that the ruling number is 6.

Date: 3rd July sunrise 3.30 am
Date: Sunday
Ruling planet/number required for: 1.45 am

1.45 am falls within hour 23 of the previous day (1.30 am – 2.29 am) in the second hour before sunrise. By reading across line 23 and down the line for Saturday (the previous day) it will be seen that   Jupiter is the ruling planet and the ruling number is 3.

Although the charts may seem rather difficult to work with at first it is well worth persevering to find the ruling planets and numbers for specific times of day.

Personal Observations:
    Date: Sunrise:
    Day:
    Ruling planet/number required for:

...... falls within ..... (.....) the ..... hour before/after sunrise. By reading across line ..... and down the line for .... it will be seen that ...... is the ruling planet and the ruling number is ..... .

Chapter 6

THE DATE OF BIRTH

The date of birth is one number which cannot be altered. Probably the most often used method of analysing a birth date is by reduction. Here the date is written out in full (months are always expressed numerically) and the resulting numbers are added together.

eg.	27th		December		1963	
	2+7	+	1+2	+	1+9+6+3	= 31/4
	Date		Month		Year	
	....	+	....	+	....	= ....

Some American numerologists use a slightly different method. They would reduce the date of birth as follows:

December		27th		1963	
12	+	27	+	1963	
12	+	27	+	19 (1+9+6+3)	
12	+	27	+	19	= 58/4

The double digit number is different but the total, when reduced, is still the same.

The single number arrived at (11 and 22, the master numbers, being the only double-digited exceptions) represents the lessons which have to be learned during the lifetime under analysis and indicates the path which should be taken in order to reach that particular goal.

The birth date is also significant when it comes to choosing a career. Numerologists have referred to this number by many different names including 'the destiny number', 'life lesson/path number', 'birth number' or as one of the 'Fadic' numbers (Cheiro). In this chapter it will simply be referred to as the Date of Birth Number to avoid any possible confusion. The Date of Birth number is first reduced to a two-figured number and then further reduced to a single number (except in the case of 11 and 22 which are not reduced any further). In this chapter we are only concerned with the single digits 1 to 9, and the numbers 11 and 22. The meanings of two-figure numbers will be explained later.

Date of Birth Number — One
Lesson to be learned: to overcome obstacles by personal creativity.
Path to take: be original, independent, take charge and make your own decisions, concentrate, be perceptive, original, innovative, confident, don't be afraid to enter new fields of expression, keep driving forwards and don't look back, be efficient and well-organized, try to work alone when possible.
Negative traits: selfish, lazy, indecisive, also stubborn and dictatorial because you dislike restriction or to be directed by others.
Goal: to express your unique individuality through being creative; a pioneer or explorer who originates any enterprise.
Suggested career: creative work of all kinds, inventor, designer, engineer, explorer.

Date of Birth Number — Two
Lesson to be learned: to mix with others and understand the need to 'give and take' in life.
Path to take: be tactful, diplomatic when necessary, gregarious, show consideration for others, be friendly and patient, persuasive rather than forceful, be supportive of others (and you may benefit indirectly from their success), try to work in a group for a common cause.
Negative traits: moody and over-emotional, cannot keep a secret, tends to gossip.
Goal: to be co-operative and able to work as part of a team.
Suggested career: salesman, agent, clerk, politician, diplomat, teacher.

Date of Birth Number — Three
Lesson to be learned: to be able to express yourself freely.
Path to take: seize every opportunity for self-expression as and when it arises, don't waste your potential creativity — develop it, steer clear of business partnerships as these will be too restrictive, try to surround yourself with beautiful objects which give you pleasure.
Negative traits: critical, cynical, boastful, pessimistic. Routine work is not for you, don't become a Jack-of-all-trades — specialize.
Goal: to achieve success through the development of your creative talents and to find personal freedom through your work.
Suggested career: journalism, writing, artist, musician, entertainer.

Date of Birth Number — Four

Lesson to be learned: to be responsible for your actions.

Path to take: be prepared to work hard and to pay attention to detail, don't take unnecessary risks, be patient and persevering, learn from your mistakes, be efficient, don't give up when the going gets difficult, be able to face reality, be thrifty (savings represent security against possible losses).

Negative traits: lack of responsibility, a tendency to evade duties and obligations.

Goal: to lay down solid foundations on which to build your life, to be practical and a good organizer.

Suggested career: farmer, accountant, builder, executive, engineer, chemist.

Date of Birth Number — Five

Lesson to be learned: the right way to use freedom.

Path to take: be progressive, keep up with new ideas and tackle problems with ingenuity, shun monotony and don't get 'bogged down', learn through travel and personal experience, use money wisely, experience as much as possible of life, seek variety.

Negative traits: self-indulgent, careless with money.

Goal: to value freedom and realize that nothing in life is permanent.

Suggested career: communications, literary work, dealing with the public, linguist, anything connected with travel.

Date of Birth Number — Six

Lesson to be learned: responsibility for members of your family and the community.

Path to take: to be responsive to the social needs of others, to show compassion and understanding, to be loving and bring comfort, show sympathy when needed and try to equalize injustices through your own good judgement.

Negative traits: dominating others and trying to force your opinions and views upon them, making people emotionally dependent upon you.

Goal: to be of service to others and give help and support when it is called for.

Suggested career: any profession which provides a much needed service to others, nursing, welfare work, medicine, veterinary practice, the ministry, marriage counsellor, home-maker.

Date of Birth Number — Seven

Lesson to be learned: to develop your mind in order to gain wisdom and understanding.

Path to take: to study, learn, to search for truth, try to find the answers to life's problems, when you speak make sure you say something worth listening to, spend time on your own (this is essential for inner growth), study the past and the occult, read, think, meditate.

Negative traits: too hasty, unreasonable, unwilling to learn, a fear of failure and loneliness.

Goal: to be able to use your wisdom and knowledge to guide others.
Suggested career: research or library work, student, archaeologist, astrologer, philosopher.

Date of Birth Number — Eight

Lesson to be learned: to be materially successful and have authority.
Path to take: hard-work, organization, sound judgement, use your energy constructively and work towards a specific goal, be ambitious, learn poise, assurance and self-control.
Negative traits: being too aggressive, having no values in life other than purely material ones.
Goal: to demonstrate success and leadership by example.
Suggested career: business executive, financier, banker, broker, lawyer, supervisor, organizer.

Date of Birth Number — Nine

Lesson to be learned: to develop a broadminded attitude to life.
Path to take: be of service to others, show compassion and understanding, cultivate an understanding of world affairs, learn to live up to your ideals, be patient, don't give up half-way through projects, do-as-you-would-be-done-by.
Negative traits: petty minded, prejudiced.
Goal: to show others the right way to live through your breadth of thinking, and promote universal love and harmony.
Suggested career: teacher, lecturer, doctor, statesmen, diplomat, politician.

Date of Birth Number — Eleven

Lesson to be learned: to trust your intuition and to guide your mind into practical channels in order to gain wisdom.
Path to take: investigate the unusual and mystical, develop a philosophical attitude to life, let your feelings be your guide, seek balance, be original, creative, show courage and learn to deal with opposition, be altruistic and develop a regard for others as a principle of action.
Negative traits: critical, over-anxious, eccentric, impractical, you are inclined to let success go to your head.
Goal: to discover that the true mastership of life is to be found in service to others.
Suggested career: teacher, humanitarian, leader in public affairs, work in public service or in an advisory capacity.

Date of Birth Number — Twenty-two

Lesson to be learned: to find a way to challenge your capacity for achievement.
Path to take: by putting your skills and ideals into a broad and universal scheme, by spiritual healing, by founding new movements and watching them grow, by building and learning how to get round obstacles and problems.

Negative traits: easily side-tracked by minor details and liable to go off at a tangent.

Goal: to take charge of a large-scale operation and make it work both profitably and efficiently.

Suggested career: ambassador, government representative, mediator, business mogul, any work which is not only advisory but also in the public service.

Cheiro believed that the date of birth should be broken down into its three component parts and analysed as follows:

Day of birth = reveals individual/personal matters

Month of birth = reveals general matters

Year of birth = reveals the force of destiny and wider current events.

He also thought that if the year of birth was reduced and then added to the birth year this would indicate a particularly important year in a person's life.

Example	*Personal calculation*
1939 = 22	...... = ...
+ 22	+...
____	____
1961	

He did not regard the month and year of birth as being so 'intimate' as the actual day of birth and based a great deal of his work on the birthday alone which 'has its influence on the actions of our lives from the cradle to the grave'. However, the month and year of birth will be included in calculations later in this chapter. The key words for birthdays, both positive and negative, are given below.

Day *Keywords*

1st Positive - independent, determined, creative, innovative.
     Negative - overbearing, jealous.

2nd Positive - loves beauty, music and the company of others, easily
     influenced by surroundings.
     Negative - lacking in confidence, easily hurt.

3rd Positive - talented, good company, quick-witted.
     Negative - over-imaginative, easily bored.

4th Positive - well-organized, hardworking, faithful.
     Negative - intractable, tactless, undemonstrative.

5th   Positive - enthusiastic, quick-witted, many-sided
        Negative - over-confident, careless, headstrong.

6th   Positive - domesticated, loving, supportive.
        Negative - discontented, shy, timid.

7th   Positive - analytical, perfectionist, psychic, enigmatic.
        Negative - unfriendly, critical, self-aborbed.

8th   Positive - strong character, good money sense, sound judgement.
        Negative - easily discouraged, domineering, bossy.

9th   Positive - creative, intelligent, benevolent, enjoys travel.
        Negative - easily led, careless with possessions, keeps the wrong sort of company.

10th   Positive - self-assured, a loner, artistic, individual.
        Negative - lacking in confidence, dependent on others.

11th   Positive - intuitive, psychic, intellectual, humanitarian.
        Negative - over-emotional, easily hurt, highly strung.

12th   Positive - helpful, friendly, easy going, attractive.
        Negative - easily discouraged, reclusive, eccentric.

13th   Positive - enthusiastic, talented, ambitious, hard-working.
        Negative - misunderstood, unemotional, cold.

14th   Positive - versatile, many-sided, imaginative, industrious.
        Negative - incautious, unstable, thoughtless.

15th   Positive - willing, generous, co-operative, appreciative.
        Negative - disruptive, unhelpful, self-centred.

16th   Positive - spiritual, mystical, a thinker, a philosopher.
        Negative - fussy, irritable, never satisfied.

17th   Positive - traditionalist, home-loving, thoughtful, attracts money.
        Negative - moody, changeable, sensitive.

18th   Positive - capable, an organizer, a born leader, active.
        Negative - argumentative, hard to please, critical.

19th   Positive - resilient, resourceful, versatile, a survivor.
        Negative - depressive, pedantic, set in your ways.

20th   Positive - gregarious, meticulous, artistic, musical.
        Negative - insecure, emotional, introverted.

21st   Positive - expressive, diplomatic, charming, gracious.
        Negative - greedy, avaricious, envious.

22nd   Positive - balanced, realistic, caring, protective.
        Negative - egotistical, grasping, scatter-brained

23rd   Positive - versatile, trustworthy, responsible, proud.
        Negative - fault-finding, dull, withdrawn

24th   Positive - active, energetic, responsible, conscientious.
        Negative - jealous, fretful, dislikes routine.

25th   Positive - perfectionist, country lover, deep, thoughtful.
        Negative - erratic, moody, nervous.

26th   Positive - home-lover, parental, willing to make sacrifices for others
        especially members of the family.
        Negative - unenthusiastic, lacking in persistence, gives up too easily.

27th   Positive - ambitious, affectionate, good company, full of ideas.
        Negative - disagreeable, quarrelsome, disruptive.

28th   Positive - independent, unconventional, strong willed, spirited.
        Negative - day-dreamer, unmotivated, unrealistic.

29th   Positive - successful, creative, forceful character.
        Negative - difficult, changeable, moody.

30th   Positive - gifted, expressive, dramatic, good-tempered, loyal.
        Negative - obstinate, erratic, impatient, bad-tempered.

31st   Positive - a builder, constructive, never gives up, tireless.
        Negative - insecure, easily disappointed, unambitious.

The Birthchart

When drawing up a birthchart the full date of birth is entered on a grid like the one used in a game of noughts and crosses, in the following manner:

1. First make a note of the date of birth — the year should always be written in full. If we take 14 April 1926 for our example, this would be written 14.4.1926.

2. This information should then be transferred on to a blank chart by entering each number as it occurs in the date of birth in its appropriate position on the grid. Grid A shows the actual positions of the numbers from one to nine, while Grid B shows how our example would look when entered on a chart.

Grid A

3	6	9	top line
2	5	8	middle line
1	4	7	bottom line

Grid B
Date of Birth: 14.4.1926

	6	9
2		
11	44	

Any zeros which occur in a birthdate should be disregarded as they have no numerological value in this instance. All the other numbers from 1 to 9 should be entered in their appropriate sections regardless of the number of times they occur in a single date of birth. The numbers 3, 6 and 9 on the top line are concerned with the mind, awareness, imagination, thoughts, creative ideas — the mental processes. The numbers 2, 5 and 8 on the middle line are concerned with feelings such as love, hate, fear, desire, pain and so on — all matters involving the emotions. The numbers 1, 4 and 7 on the bottom line are concerned with 'doing' — actions, organization, learning — practical matters.

This method of analysis is attributed to Pythagoras who used a system of sixteen directional 'arrows' to interpret birthcharts. He believed that if a diagonal, vertical or horizontal line of the birthchart was complete (that is, all its numbers were present when the chart had been drawn up), this indicated a particular strength of character. However, if a line remained blank then this would point to a character deficiency. The 'Arrows of Pythagoras' and their interpretations are given below together with a blank grid for your own calculations.

Date of Birth: ....

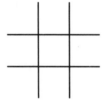

The Arrows of Pythagoras

No. 1 Fixed Intention: patience, endurance, persistence, determination, resolve, fixity of purpose, concentration, devotion.

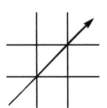

No. 2 Reluctance: unwillingness, disinclination, hesitation, indisposition, irresolution, indecision.

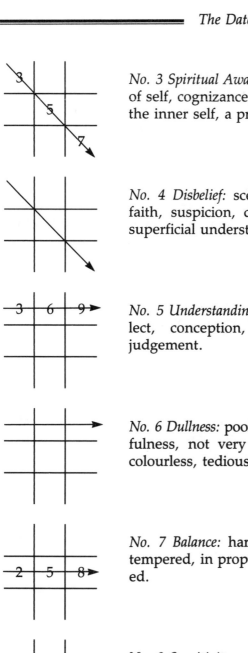

No. 3 Spiritual Awareness: understanding, consciousness of self, cognizance, perception of the mind, insight into the inner self, a practical philosophy of life.

No. 4 Disbelief: scepticism, doubt, uncertainty, loss of faith, suspicion, distrust of anything metaphysical, a superficial understanding of human nature.

No. 5 Understanding: reasoning power, the mind, intellect, conception, mental capacity, discrimination, judgement.

No. 6 Dullness: poor memory, absent mindedness, forgetfulness, not very active mental faculties, dreariness, colourless, tedious, unamusing.

No. 7 Balance: harmony of emotions, unbiased, even-tempered, in proportion, regularity, smooth, undistorted.

No. 8 Sensitivity: over-emotional, touchy, thin-skinned, excitable, easily hurt, shy, feelings of inferiority, unbalanced, inadequate.

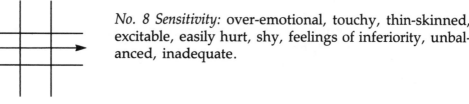

No. 9 Manual Dexterity: practical, clever with the hands, useful, capable, good at making things, action rather than theory or words.

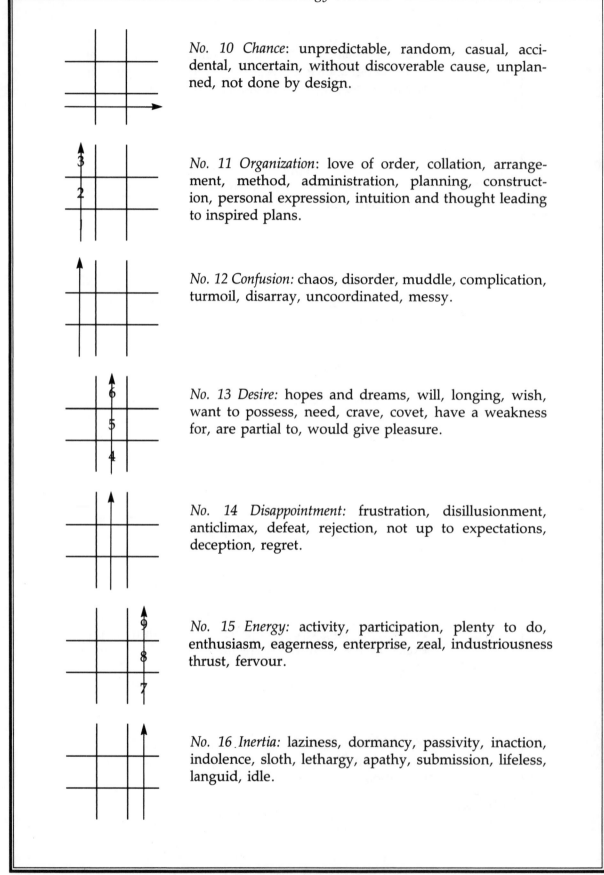

No. 10 Chance: unpredictable, random, casual, accidental, uncertain, without discoverable cause, unplanned, not done by design.

No. 11 Organization: love of order, collation, arrangement, method, administration, planning, construction, personal expression, intuition and thought leading to inspired plans.

No. 12 Confusion: chaos, disorder, muddle, complication, turmoil, disarray, uncoordinated, messy.

No. 13 Desire: hopes and dreams, will, longing, wish, want to possess, need, crave, covet, have a weakness for, are partial to, would give pleasure.

No. 14 Disappointment: frustration, disillusionment, anticlimax, defeat, rejection, not up to expectations, deception, regret.

No. 15 Energy: activity, participation, plenty to do, enthusiasm, eagerness, enterprise, zeal, industriousness thrust, fervour.

No. 16 Inertia: laziness, dormancy, passivity, inaction, indolence, sloth, lethargy, apathy, submission, lifeless, languid, idle.

THE BIRTHCHART — INTERPRETATIONS OF INDIVIDUAL AND RECURRING NUMBERS

One = personality and the way it is expressed.

One × 1. People with only one 1 on their birthchart sometimes find it difficult to show their feelings and because of this inability are often thought of as cold and uncaring.

Two × 1. Can express themselves easily and have a well-balanced outlook on life.

Three × 1. Sometimes have too much to say for themselves although they could never be described as 'boring'. They are interested and involved in a great many activities and make entertaining company.

Four × 1. Feel things very deeply but find it hard to communicate their feelings to others. They are easily hurt and often shy and retiring.

Five or more × 1 have such great difficulty in relating to other people that they sometimes become reclusive and shut themselves away from the world. Occasionally they find it so impossible to come to grips with life that they become mentally unbalanced.

Two = sensitivity, intuitive thoughts and feelings.

One × 2. People with only one 2 on their birthchart do not cope very well in a competitive environment. They are easily demoralized and take any form of criticism too much to heart.

Two × 2 are very perceptive and their assessment of others is generally reliable.

Three × 2 are numerical crabs. They build a protective shell around themselves because they find it difficult to get along with other people. Unfortunately this is often mistaken for insensitivity.

Four × 2 are inclined to over-react in emotive or difficult situations. They are difficult to live with because of their impatience, sarcasm and displays of bad temper.

Five × 2 is fortunately a rare occurrence on a birthchart. People with five 2s are bitter about the way life has treated them and their disappointment is often coupled with frustration and disillusionment.

Three = the 'mind' number concerned with intelligence, imagination and memory.

One × 3. People with one 3 on their birthchart have retentive memories and are usually bright and alert.

Two × 3 should channel their vivid imaginations into a creative pursuit, such as writing, or they run the risk of becoming day-dreamers.

Three × 3 often get so wrapped up in their thoughts and ideas that they lose contact with their family and friends. They tend to spend long periods of time on their own.

Four × 3 are too mentally active for their own good. Often their excessive imagination makes them confused and fearful.

Four = control, system and order.

One × 4. People with one 4 on their birthchart are naturally clever with their hands and are at their happiest when making or doing rather than thinking or theorizing.

Two × 4 should try not to become so involved with physical activities that they forget to make time to think occasionally. They could become very dull unless they learn to fantasize a little more.

Three × 4 are brutish human beings who are only capable of hard manual labour and seldom, if ever, think about anything. They live to work.

Four × 4. This is a combination which occurs only three times in a century. These people are mindless automatons who can damage their bodies with physical overwork.

Five = is situated in the centre of the birthchart and is concerned with the amount of effort required to turn thoughts into deeds.

One × 5. People with only one 5 on their birthchart are extremely self-controlled and possess great depth of character.

Two × 5. Although they may have trouble in coping with difficult or emotive situations these people are usually well-balanced and confident. On occasion they become dangerously over-confident and should guard against this.

Three × 5 can be tactless and hurtful because they don't bother to put their brains into gear before they open their mouths.

Four × 5 are life's 'stuntmen' who go from one potentially hazardous situation into another — often to their cost.

Six = decision, which can be either good or bad, when the five senses (smell, taste, touch, sight and hearing) are united with the ability to reason.

One × 6. People with one 6 on their birthchart are born home-makers. They are at their happiest when creating a harmonious atmosphere in which to live.

Two × 6 are also home-makers but carry their enthusiasm to extremes when they become fussy and over-anxious. They cannot feel at ease when away from their 'nest' and are always worried in case something should happen to it.

Three × 6 live in complete chaos and seem unable to put any order into their lives. They worry about the slightest thing and are over-protective of those they love.

Four × 6. This combination only occurs three times a century and when it does this indicates genius and all its attendant emotional problems.

Seven = understanding gained through sacrifice.

One × 7 on a birthchart indicates that wisdom and understanding will only be gained through personal suffering.

Two × 7 will not gain an understanding of life easily as many of their lessons will have to be learned the hard way. Sacrifices in love, money or health could be called for.

Three × 7 acquire their wisdom and maturity at great personal cost. They will have a high price to pay for their knowledge and understanding.

Four × 7 will need to develop great strength of character to survive the blows that life may deal them.

Eight = carries much the same meaning as the number four but is expressed on the emotional, rather than physical, plane. It calls for organization and control.

One × 8 on the birthchart indicates a neat, efficient person who pays great attention to detail. A positive attitude should prevent them from becoming mentally lazy.

Two × 8 are so good at assessing people and situations that others may find this somewhat unnerving at times. This could also cause emotional conflicts. They are extremely efficient at their work and know it. Over-confidence could be their downfall.

Three × 8 rarely find their true vocation in life when they are young. Only when they have tried everything that takes their fancy do they mature and settle down.

Four × 8 are emotional gypsies. Their restlessness and lack of concentration often causes them to miss opportunities.

Nine = ambition, high standards, concern for human welfare.

One × 9. People with one 9 on their birthchart must realize that life can never be 'perfect'. They should learn to accept their lot and enjoy what they already have.

Two × 9 set very high standards for themselves which sometimes makes them critical of others. They are serious, thoughtful pople with little or no sense of humour.

Three × 9 never know where to draw the line. Their continual struggle for perfection can, at times, make them bad-tempered and unpredictable.

Four × 9 are constantly at war with themselves and their surroundings. Nothing ever seems to come up to their expectations and this makes them withdrawn and unstable.

THE PYRAMIDS OF MATURITY

Maturity follows adolesence and is the period during which emotional control, responsibility and self-awareness are developed. The degree of success achieved during these years determines the quality of our later life. The years of maturity have a twenty-seven year span and commence at different ages for different people depending on their Date of Birth Number, ranging from 27-35 years of age. Your age of commencement is found by subtracting your Date of Birth Number from thirty-six.

36 – ...... = ... (commencement age).

The number thirty-six was of great esoteric significance to the Egyptians in their construction of the pyramids. It is interesting to note that 36 reduces to 9 and that when the total of the numbers of each line (260) of the Square of Mercury (on whose geometric pattern the pyramids were built — see Chapter Five) is added to the sum of all its numbers from 1-64 (2080) the grand total also reduces to 9 (2340/9).

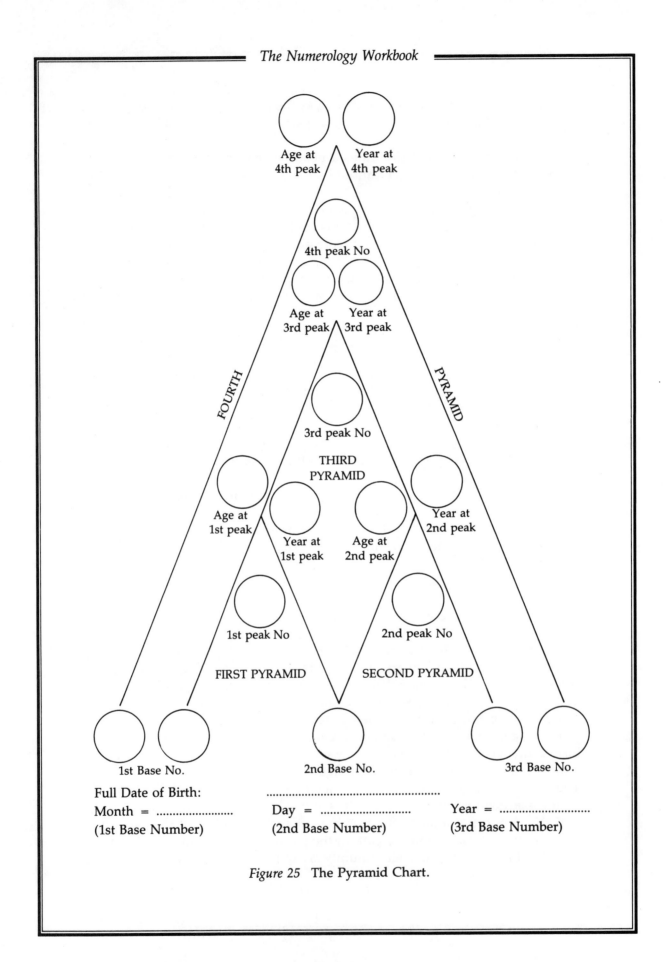

Figure 25 The Pyramid Chart.

CONSTRUCTION

The Pyramids are constructed as follows:

1. Reduce each of the numbers of your date of birth to three single figures in the following order - the month, the day, the year. Enter these in the space provided on the chart (Figure 25). These three numbers form the foundation of your pyramid and it is imperative to use them in the correct order.

2. Enter your reduced month and day number (the first and second base numbers) where indicated on the first pyramid. Your first peak number will be found by adding the two base numbers together and reducing the total if necessary. This number should always be entered inside the peak where indicated.

3. The second pyramid is built on your reduced day and year numbers (the second and third base numbers). Your second peak number will be found by adding the second and third base numbers together and reducing the total if necessary. Again this number should be written inside the peak. Enter this information where indicated on the second pyramid.

4. The third pyramid is constructed on the first two, as can be seen from the diagram. Your third peak number is found by adding together the first two peak numbers and reducing the total if necessary. At this stage of the pyramids the numbers 10 or 11 are the only exceptions to this rule of reduction. Should your total come to 10 or 11 this number should be entered as it is and never reduced.

5. The last pyramid is built outside the other three and the first and third base numbers are totalled and reduced if necessary (with the exception of 10 or 11) to find your fourth and final peak number.

6. The age at which your first peak is reached (the age at which maturity commences) is found by substracting your Date of Birth Number from 36. Enter this age (and the year when it is reached) where indicated on the first peak.

7. Your second, third and fourth peaks follow at nine-year intervals. The accompanying chart will be of assistance to those who do not wish to make their own calculations. Enter the ages (and years when they are reached) where indicated on the remaining peaks.

Age at	Date of Birth Number								
	1	2	3	4	5	6	7	8	9
1st Peak	35	34	33	32	31	30	29	28	27
2nd Peak	44	43	42	41	40	39	38	37	36
3rd Peak	53	52	51	50	49	48	47	46	45
4th Peak	62	61	60	59	58	57	56	55	54

PEAK NUMBERS

Peak numbers begin to make their influence felt towards the end of the year before a peak. Their greatest strength is experienced during the peak year itself and then gradually fades away over the course of the following year. Their purpose is to supply extra strength and drive at important nine-year intervals throughout the course of maturity.

Peak Number One

The number one only ever occurs on the first and second pyramids. It indicates a time when great personal effort will be required after much soul-searching. For some it could mean breaking away from past commitments, which have become restrictive and emotionally fraught, by a change of job, finding new friends or ending a marriage. Others may decide to work harder and try to improve existing circumstances. Whichever approach is taken the result will be the same — voluntary change, with eventual improvement.

Peak Number Two

This is not a time for rapid material advancement and people with a two as their peak number will find progress slow and laborious. Attempts to hurry matters along will only result in arguments or frustration. During this peak year you should try to express your feelings more, get your emotions properly under control and learn to use your instincts to their best advantage. Co-operation and diplomacy are the keywords.

Peak Number Three

A year for learning and development. Travel is indicated when a peak number three occurs and you should take every opportunity to do so. The experience will enable you to gain valuable insight into other cultures, lifestyles and philosophies. If, however, travel is not possible every attempt should be made to study, broaden your outlook or develop literary, creative or social abilities.

Peak Number Four

If your motives are honourable then this is a time for advancement. Material success is within the reach of those prepared to work hard to achieve it. Greedy, avaricious, mercenary types could find that the reverse is true and may sustain heavy financial losses during this year. A practical period.

Peak Number Five

A peak year ruled by a five brings greater personal freedom. You will have learned in the past how negative emotions such as jealousy or envy can be and once you can put these feelings behind you there is much to be gained. Understanding will lead to spiritual growth. A lively, interesting period of experience.

Peak Number Six

Marriage, home-making and parenthood are all possibilities during this period. It is a time to put down roots and become involved in domestic matters. It can also be a very creative year when ideas begin to take shape, plans are put into action and you can see some results after much preparation.

Peak Number Seven

Change is the keyword of a peak number seven but it is experienced in a most unlikely way — not in a manner which can be planned for. In the midst of change will come the opportunity to help others by passing on a skill which you have already acquired. You should also benefit indirectly from this charitable act.

Peak Number Eight

Now is the time to stand on your own two feet. You must become more independent and stop relying on other people so much. If your Date of Birth Number is even you could benefit financially during this peak year but if it is odd your rewards could be academic. This year is not to be wasted.

Peak Number Nine

When the number nine occurs at a peak you should be prepared for almost anything to happen. This is a period of opportunity. Travel is likely and so is a change of job and/or home. You could also be required to give up some of your time to help others less fortunate than yourself.

The last two peak numbers can only occur at the third and fourth peaks of the pyramids when maturity is reaching its height.

Peak Number Ten

Your developing inner strength could be called upon during this period when the needs of other people are more important than your own. Do not be afraid to take on the extra responsibility of guiding them through a difficult period in their lives.

Peak Number Eleven

Eleven is a very powerful peak number to live up to. During this period you will need to demonstrate that you have acquired a high level of maturity to cope with its demands. However the demands made upon you will never exceed your capacity to give. A time to develop visionary ideas.

Chapter 7

WORKING WITH THE NAME

What's in a name? that which we call a rose
By any other name would smell as sweet.
–Romeo and Juliet — Shakespeare

What's really in a name? Numerologists believe that it contains the essence of a person's being and that all the qualities and characteristics, which together form the identity, are hidden within its letters. Naming is a symbol of becoming conscious of the exact nature of whatever is named — a belief which is illustrated in the fairy story of Rumpelstiltskin.

In ancient times important names, particularly those of gods, were always kept secret. The Egyptians chose names which were virtually unpronounceable in an attempt to prevent their enemies from using them for nefarious purposes. In other cultures gods were simply referred to as 'he whose name is unknown' or 'he whose name is never spoken'.

It was once widely believed that a secret name existed which contained the power to control the Universe. The Jews thought this word was the Tetragrammaton (or word of four letters) — the unspoken name of God. The letters are Y H V H and are generally pronounced today as Yahweh or Jehovah although the correct pronunciation is unknown because there are no printed vowels in Hebrew. Although the Tetragrammaton was the secret name of God there is an even longer and more powerful word which is His 'supreme name', the Shemhamphorash or 'name of seventy-two syllables'. The source of this can be found in the Old Testament (Exodus XIV, 19–21). Each verse contains seventy-two Hebrew letters which are written from right to left in verse 19, left to right in verse 20, and right to left again in verse 21. So if you begin at the top right-hand corner and work downwards seventy-two three-

Figure 26 The Tetragrammaton.

lettered syllables can be read. The first syllable is composed of the first letter of verse 19, the last letter of verse 20, and the first letter of verse 21 and so on until the name is complete.

Moses was believed to have used the Shemhamphorash to part the Red Sea when the Israelites were fleeing from the Egyptians. The Zohar states that God's name is hidden in the Ten Sepiroth of the Tree of Life because He created the Universe by expanding His own character, while the Sepher Yetzerah says that God created the Universe by engraving His name. In *The Book of the Magi*, Francis Barret writes: 'God Himself, though He be only one essence, yet hath divers names which expound not His divers essences or deities; but certain properties flowing from Him; by which names He pours down upon us, and all His creatures, many benefits.'

John Reuchlin, the Renaissance Qabalist, linked the Shemhamphorash and the Tetragrammaton by means of gematria. Using the letter/number correspondences Y = 10, H = 5, V = 6, H = 5 for the letters of the Tetragrammaton, he built up the following table which totals seventy-two—the number of syllables in the Shemhamphorash.

Y	= 10
YH	= 15
YHV	= 21
YHVH	= 26
	72

Throughout history powerful words have been used as talismans. An example is the word Abracadabra which is thought to originate from the name of Abraxas, a fat-bellied demon. It was usually inscribed on a parchment or metal plaque and worn at the neck like a scapular. The triangular shape which the letters formed was believed to add to its efficacy.

```
A  B  R  A  C  A  D  A  B  R  A

   B  R  A  C  A  D  A  B  R

      R  A  C  A  D  A  B

         A  C  A  D  A

            C  A  D

               A
```

Palindromes — especially powerful words because they retain their identity whichever way they are read — are also used as talismans. They are often arranged in a square shape to reinforce their strength. The most frequently used palindromic talisman, and some believe the most potent, is the Sator square — an anagram of *Pater Noster*. The letters A and O are repeated twice so that it also contains the first two words of the Lord's Prayer.

S A T O R

A R E P O

T E N E T

O P E R A

R O T A S

Adepts in many ancient civilizations attached great importance to names and, even today, some people still believe that the names we are given at birth are not merely the results of random choice. There are two theories concerning the reason for the apparently subconscious selection of a particular name. The first is that outside forces which influence a child's personality and destiny are also capable of influencing the subconscious minds of the parents who are responsible for naming the child. The second is that when a soul enters the body of a new-born child it selects a name which is in harmony with the mission to be accomplished in that particular life-time. One question which students of numerology frequently ask is, 'How should I go about analysing a name?' There are no hard and fast rules to follow although the name we usually work with is the one by which a person is most commonly known — this could, on occasion, be a nickname or alias.

The name given to a person at birth represents his basic character and potential while the surname, when analysed separately, provides genetic information. Any change of name in life is considered to be significant. When a woman marries she usually changes her surname. The maiden name indicates character and destiny before marriage while the number of her married name reveals what effect marriage will have on her. Any name which is acquired or adopted at some stage in life, other than the birth name, yields what is known as the 'Number of Development' when reduced. Some people deliberately change either the spelling of, or in some cases their entire name in order to live under a more favourable numerological influence.

THE VOWEL NUMBER

In the Hebrew language there are no written vowels and so in numerology they signify the 'hidden self' or 'soul'. The Vowel Number has been referred to by many different names such as the 'Soul Number' or 'the Secret-Self

Number'. In this chapter it will simply be called the Vowel Number in order to avoid any possible confusion. The Vowel Number represents the inner you, that side of your personality which is usually hidden from all but a few close friends and loved ones. It is the 'real' you, as you secretly like to picture yourself, and all that you desire to be.

To numerologists who believe in reincarnation, this number also indicates the character which was developed in previous lives and the amount of wisdom and learning acquired and retained during that time. The past revealed through the Vowel Number can strongly influence actions in this present life.

To find the Vowel Number enter the name to be analysed in the space below and place the corresponding numbers above each vowel that occurs in the name. Vowels are the letters A, E, I, O and U. An example has been included for your guidance together with the number/letter correspondence.

1 2 3 4 5 6 7 8 9

A B C D E F G H I

J K L M N O P Q R

S T U V W X Y Z

Vowels: 6   +6   +1   +6   +5   +6 =30/3
Name: J O N O T H A N R O B E R T S O N

Vowels: = /
Name: ....

Add the resultant numbers together one by one, working from left to right. The Vowel Number is first written as a double-digit number and then further reduced to a single number (the master numbers eleven and twenty-two are not reduced any further). Two-figure numbers will be explained in detail in a later chapter.

Vowel Number One

In past lives you probably fought hard to gain leadership and control over others. This strong character trait has carried on into this lifetime but now you seem to be fighting to gain higher consciousness rather than power over others. Freedom of thought is what you hope to achieve but you should not let this desire totally overshadow any material goals you may also wish to attain. People whose Vowel Number is one do not like taking orders or working in a subordinate capacity — they like to be the ones in charge.

From a negative viewpoint, you could develop such a powerful, larger-than-life character that you try to dominate others and so run the risk of becoming labelled 'bossy' or even 'tyrannical'. However, one thing which you can always rely on is your great inner strength to pull you through when times are hard — loved ones may also draw inspiration from you during difficult periods in their lives.

Vowel Number Two

Ones are the leaders but Twos would sooner follow any day. Not for you the cut and thrust lifestyle necessary to rise to the top — twos need peace and harmony in every corner of their lives. Your role in life is to maintain balance and peace between rival factions for which your past lives have equipped you with depth of understanding and the tact necessary to fulfil this mission. This does not mean that you should become a doormat for everyone else to trample over; there are times when it is necessary to hurt the feelings of other people in order to retain your own identity. You must be prepared to take what is deservedly yours without hesitating because there are others who won't think twice about grasping your missed opportunities.

Vowel Number Three

An innate sense of duty is what you carry with you from past lives and you should be only too aware that by helping others you will also be helping yourself. There is a great deal of truth for a number Three in the saying: 'Laugh and the world laughs with you'. In order to fulfil your mission in life you must be prepared to devote a great deal of your time to making other people happy and your imagination can be put to best use in the service of others. If you are a negative Three you could become so involved in pleasing others that you forget about such small matters as earning a living, paying the bills and so on.

Vowel Number Four

People with a Vowel Number Four are solid and practical through and through, their lifestyle is neat, tidy, well-ordered and programmed to run at maximum efficiency.

You are so well-organized that you set the standards for those around you to depend upon and look up to. People know just where they stand with you which is a comfort in this fast-moving, changeable world we live in. Your key-words are dependability and orderliness. You should succeed at anything you set your heart on because you will go about achieving it in a methodical, well-planned, orderly way. If you are a negative Four, you may be inclined to take life too seriously and not allow enough time to relax and enjoy yourself. You could also be so totally obsessed with method and order that you eventually become slightly unbalanced by it all.

Vowel Number Five

Freedom, change and travel are the three ingredients in life for which your soul yearns but freedom is the most important — without this your other desires are impossible.

There is no one more unhappy and miserable than a number Five who feels trapped because he is unable to explore new situations and formulate new ideas which are so vital for his personal well-being. Fives need constant mental stimulation and travel, with its constantly changing scenery and ways of life, provides them with the variety they seek. Fives cannot tolerate people with narrow outlooks and believe that life should be lived and experienced to the full. Negative Fives are dull and listless. They need major changes in their lifestyles to shake them out of their tedium.

Vowel Number Six

The three most important words to remember in connection with this Vowel Number are beauty, harmony and, above all, peace. Sixes are here to pass on the understanding they have learned in previous existences through sympathy, and a show of loyalty and affection. These people are heavily committed to the well-being and happiness of their families and homes.

Negative Sixes are inclined to be over-protective to their loved ones and don't allow their children enough space for emotional growth or the expression of desires which do not fall into line with their own. They can be completely smothering and oppressive — their negative type of kindness can emotionally kill.

Vowel Number Seven

Sevens are emotional hermits who rarely show their feelings. Many remain unmarried throughout their lives and prefer their own thoughts and company to that of other people.

People with the Vowel Number Seven may, in fact, have been hermits or priests living in a closed order in former lives because even in this present life they still need peace and quiet so that they can meditate. They are thinkers, they are sensitive and some are psychic with powers of clairvoyance and extra-sensory perception.

Sevens are here to develop even greater depth of character which they should use for the benefit of others through philosophy. Negative Sevens run the risk of getting so involved with their thoughts and secret beliefs that they become totally divorced from reality and lose touch with life, as most people experience it, on the material plane.

Vowel Number Eight

This is not an easy Vowel Number to live up to because in this lifetime you will be called upon to handle problems, and organize events, on a very large scale. However, if you have accumulated sufficient ambition from previous existences and are capable of a sustained effort there is no reason why you should not succeed. You can not only make it to the top — but you can stay there too.

One lesson you will have to learn during this lifetime is how to understand the needs and emotions of other people. Once you have mastered this important step you will be able to bring out the best in them and channel it to your mutual advantage.

Negative Eights may find that they are called upon to give more than they are prepared to give and, because their approach to life is not wholehearted, the rewards and honours they could have achieved will always elude them.

Vowel Number Nine

Those of you whose Vowel Number reduces to a nine could quite possibly have been a master or adept during a previous existence. This is a powerful number and those who fall within its influence are intuitive, sensitive and in possession of vivid imaginations.

Although Nines may appear rather distant and self-absorbed at times they are, deep down, very warm-hearted people who need to love and be loved in return. Nines must remember to keep both feet on the ground and resist the temptation to exist only in their minds rather than on this earthly plane. Provided that they can maintain a working balance between the spiritual and the material sides of life, humanity has much to learn from the care and concern they show for others less fortunate than themselves.

Vowel Number Eleven

People whose Vowel Number is eleven have definitely been here before, and not just once but several times, to have developed such an understanding of life and all its attendant mysteries. They are wise beyond their years, understanding and magnetic. There is little that life could throw at an Eleven which they could not cope with or even turn to their positive advantage. Elevens are super-sensitive, spiritual people many of whom are clairvoyant or possess ESP abilities.

Negative Elevens are occasionally too courageous for their own good and because they consider they know all the answers they often take risks which other people would blanch at. Some are also inclined to be dictatorial and too wrapped up in their own importance that they are oblivious to the needs of those around them.

Vowel Number Twenty-Two

Twenty-twos have an important mission in life to fulfil which is endorsed by experience gained in past lives. In order to fulfil themselves they must build something tangible which will benefit humanity but which will also live on after them as a memorial to their achievement.

Twenty-twos have a difficult target to reach in life but are well equipped, both mentally and physically, to reach it. They must keep their sights firmly set on their goal and never allow themselves a moment's deviation from their intended course.

Negative Twenty-twos are always full of magnificent ideas for earth-shattering reforms but they never seem to see them through to fruition.

THE CONSONANT NUMBER

The Consonant Number, which is sometimes referred to by numerologists as the 'External Image' or 'Outer Personality Number', is found by adding together the numerical values of all the consonants in a name. To calculate your Consonant Number follow the example given below. Remember to place the value of each consonant below the name so that they are not confused with the vowels. Reduce the total first to a double-digit and then a single number as you do when calculating the Vowel Number and enter these two numbers in the space provided. The values of the consonants can be found on page 87.

Name: J O N O T H A N R O B E R T S O N

Consonants: 1 +5 +2 +8 +5 +9 +2 +9 +2 +1 +5

= 49/4

Name: ....

Consonants:.. = ../..

Consonants represent the Outer Personality and analysis of the Consonant Number will reveal the face you show to the world. In other words, you will be able to see yourself as others do — although this may not necessarily give a true reflection of who or what you really are. Analysis of the Consonant Number will also enable you to understand what is expected of you because of the outward image you project.

Consonant Number One

Ones appear cool, calm, collected and somehow different from everyone else. They look capable and as if they should be able to handle any situation with poise and the utmost efficiency. Ones are stylish individuals who often project the stereotyped executive image of the smart suit, which is beautifully tailored and soberly coloured. Occasionally they seem so impeccably dressed and aloof that others are unnerved by the sheer perfection of their appearance and become nervous of approaching them. They love to wear designer clothes but prefer to create their own fashion rather than to slavishly follow the current trend. Negative Ones have a tendency to carry their fashion sense to extremes and can appear eccentric, loud or 'overdressed'.

Ones are expected to be leaders — efficient, capable, individual and full of novel ideas.

Consonant Number Two

Twos are mouselike creatures. They are always careful to keep in the background and are hardly ever noticed and seldom heard. They are clean and neatly dressed sometimes to the point of fussiness with never a hair out of place. They prefer classic styles of clothes which won't stand out in a crowd.

Twos, however, are seldom at a loss for company of the opposite sex because they look as if they are good listeners and how could anyone who looks so quiet and amiable have strong opinions or ever argue? They also look as if they need the protection of someone more aggressive and worldy-wise than themselves. Negative Twos are just that — so negative and dull-looking that no one can be bothered to find out what they are really like.

Twos are expected to be quiet — inconspicuous, even-tempered, co-operative, neat and willing to serve.

Consonant Number Three

People whose Consonant Number reduces to a three look as if they should be good fun. They have magnetic personalities and friendly, animated faces. They are the 'life and soul of the party' types and always sure to be the centre of attraction at any social gathering. Threes have a way of their own with clothes and are especially gifted at choosing just the right accessories to enhance an otherwise ordinary outfit.

These people are great talkers and usually have something interesting to say unless they are negative Threes, in which case they probably rely on gossip and exaggeration to add a little spice to their conversation. Negative Threes are superficial, rather conceited people who are jealous of the success and popularity achieved by other people. Threes are expected to be interesting — entertaining, fun, charming, sociable, extrovert, attractive and full of suggestions for interesting things to do.

Consonant Number Four

Fours look like country-loving outdoor types but rather dull and boring with it. There's no hint of fun to be seen on their faces or daredevil sparkle in their eyes. They look like solid, honest, sober citizens who do everything to the letter of the law and never take short cuts for fear of somehow spoiling the end result.

They tend to dress in serviceable, well-cut clothes which are chosen to give years of wear rather than a fashionable appearance. In fact, their conduct is as conservative as their dress.

Negative Fours are mean and penny-pinching with rather unpleasant tempers when roused. Some are lazy and extremely careless about their appearance while others become workaholics who never take any time off to enjoy themselves. Fours are expected to be hard-working — industrious, practical, conservative, dull, honest, reliable, conventional people who are interested in the environment and its conservation.

Consonant Number Five

Fives are sparkling, witty and often sexually attractive people. They are life's salesmen who would sell anything to anyone given half a chance. They know exactly how to promote and advertise ideas and products too. Fives are not the sort of people who like to remain in one place or situation for too long and are continually searching for change and variety. They need to be free to do whatever they want and to go wherever they choose.

Fives dress fashionably and well. They have the personality to get away with bright colours without appearing loud or flashy.

Negative Fives are rather unpleasant people — restless, shifty and totally unreliable. They talk too much and often indulge themselves in excessive eating, drinking, drug abuse and frequent casual sexual encounters.

Fives are expected to be sensual — well-travelled, unattached, curious, sparkling, witty, dynamic salespeople who know what they want and how to get it.

Consonant Number Six

Sixes are motherly/fatherly looking people who give the appearance of being both responsible and protective. People are instinctively drawn to seek help and advice from them. They are homely people with an artistic flair and an eye for colour. They prefer to dress in comfortable clothes which are pleasant to look at — they never wear clothes which are bright or clash with each other.

Negative Sixes can be rather slovenly in their appearance and live in untidy, badly-run homes. Their desire to help others sometimes becomes out of control and they become interfering or over-protective.

Sixes are expected to be responsible — helpful, parental, homely, domesticated, artistic and appreciative of beauty.

Consonant Number Seven

People with a Consonant Number Seven often have an air of mystery and secrecy about them. They seem solitary and totally absorbed in thought — almost as though they are not really conscious of their immediate surroundings. They appear sharp, perceptive, intelligent and dignified.

They dress quietly and with taste unless in a negative, indifferent frame of mind when this is reflected in their general appearance. Negative Sevens look gloomy, disappointed and withdrawn as well as unkempt.

Sevens are expected to be philosophical — mysterious, secretive, thoughtful, observant, dignified and refined.

Consonant Number Eight

Eights emanate strength and power. They often appear larger than life and resemble the cartoon concept of the successful big businessman or tycoon — even down to the big cigar! Their appearance conjures up thoughts of commerce, authority and material success. Eights carry their successful, material image into their clothing and always wear expensive and exclusive clothes and accessories.

Negative Eights tend to go over the top with their desire to impress — they succeed in looking loud, flashy and vulgar.

Eights are used to command but when in a negative mood can abuse this privilege. They can also be spiteful and malicious if their plans are thwarted. Eights are expected to be big businessmen or women — strong, powerful, wealthy, successful and respected.

Consonant Number Nine

Nines look friendly and sympathetic. They have broad shoulders to cry on and plenty of ideas for solving problems. Beneath their calm, kind exteriors they are big 'softies' at heart — as emotional and romantic as everyone else. People are attracted to Nines. They are greatly loved and respected by all who come into contact with them.

Their clothes are striking and often very figure-hugging. There is usually something rather dramatic about their appearance and like Dorian Gray many remain young looking well into middle age.

Negative Nines sometimes do not have the emotional strength of character required to cope with the problems presented by other people. They get too involved in other people's lives and could become unbalanced by the emotional strain placed on them.

Nines are expected to be understanding — kind, compassionate, forgiving, tolerant and artistic.

Consonant Number Eleven

Number Elevens are seen as visionaries because of their constant struggle to establish a system of equal opportunity for all, regardless of sex, race, creed or colour. They are an inspiration to others and often possess a streak of genius. They seem to live on a higher, more spiritual level than everyone else around them. Their dress is artistic, inventive and always original.

Negative Elevens sometimes use their undoubtedly brilliant minds for the wrong purposes and occasionally their nefarious deeds attract notoriety.

Elevens are expected to be brilliant — humanitarian, artistic, spiritual, individual and a source of inspiration.

Consonant Number Twenty-Two

People whose Consonant Number reduces to twenty-two look as if they could control the world and right all its wrongs with the greatest of ease. They appear masterly, diplomatic and very efficient. Twenty-twos dress conservatively and often wear tailor-made clothes.

When in a negative frame of mind they are capable of misusing the trust placed in them to amass private fortunes and achieve personal ambitions which are not within the scope of their working brief.

Twenty-twos are expected to be super-human — masterful, efficient, tactful, honest and totally devoted to the well-being of mankind.

THE WHOLE NAME NUMBER

The Whole Name Number is found by adding together the unreduced Vowel and Consonant Numbers and is sometimes referred to as the 'Destiny' or 'Life Mission Number'. Analysis of this number will reveal what we must achieve in this lifetime and how it should be done. In other words, it makes us aware of the path we will have to take through life and the sort of person we must become to fulfil our mission successfully.

6   +6   +1   +6   +5   +6   = 30/3 Vowel
Number

J O N O T H A N R O B E R T S O N   = Name

1   +5   +2 +8   +5 +9   +2   +9 +2 +1   +5   = 49/4
Consonant
Number

Vowel Number 30/3 + Consonant Number 49/4 = Whole Name Number 16/7 (When added together the total came to 79 and because we only go up to 78 with our double-digit numbers it was necessry to reduce the 79 to 16/7).

.... = ../.. Vowel Number
.... = Name
.... = ../.. Consonant Number
Vowel Number .../... + Consonant Number .../... = Whole Name Number
..../... .

Whole Name Number One
Mission: to become a leader and develop 'the self'.
You must learn: to use your resources to the full; to employ the first person singular whenever possible; to accept your destiny; to use your initiative in all situations; to be self-reliant and believe in yourself.
Pitfalls: there is a danger of becoming totally self-absorbed and selfish. You will need to show determination in difficult situations and resist the temptation to give up at the first hint of trouble or opposition.
Key Word: Leadership.

Whole Name Number Two
Mission: to create a better world in which to live.
You must learn: to be diplomatic and tactful; to develop your innate creativity; to listen and sympathize; to maintain peace whenever possible; to expand your awareness.
Pitfalls: You could find yourself cast in the role of mediator in some tricky situations which require handling with kid gloves.
Key Word: Peacemaker.

Whole Name Number Three
Mission: to uplift and inspire others.

You must learn: how to communicate on all levels; to improve your knowledge of the world around you; to use your time wisely; to concentrate on one thing at a time; to understand the meaning of real friendship.

Pitfalls: Lack of personal organization leading to much wasted time; putting too great a strain on your energy source because you have too many irons in the fire at one time.

Key Words: Cheerful optimism.

Whole Name Number Four

Mission: to build something which is tangible and worthwhile.

You must learn: to be organized and work at maximum efficiency; to give proof of your reliability and instil confidence in others; to handle money wisely; to know when and how to keep a secret.

Pitfalls: Your impatience to get things done quickly might tempt you to cut corners with disastrous results; your desire for perfection may not always be humanly possible.

Key Word: Building.

Whole Name Number Five

Mission: to make progress through the ability to adapt and alter.

You must learn: to be adaptable; to try new ideas and to understand new theories and concepts; to present your ideas in an acceptable form; to make changes work for you; to try everything and to gain something positive from each new experience.

Pitfalls: If you become too revolutionary in your way of thinking you could quite possibly be dismissed as a crank or an eccentric. Be prepared to let go of the past as it will only hold back your progress and blinker your views.

Key Word: Change.

Whole Name Number Six

Mission: to share your good taste and appreciation of beauty with others.

You must learn: to take care of, and be proud of, your family; to make your home a comfortable, pleasant place in which to live; to mix with other people; to be a good host/hostess and put your guests at ease; to pass on your artistic appreciation through your own example.

Pitfalls: You must always be honest and never try to acquire beautiful possessions by doubtful means. Remember too that it is quite permissible to be proud of what you have acheived but you should resist the temptation to boast, brag or show off, even when sorely tempted.

Key Word: Domesticity.

Whole Name Number Seven

Mission: to develop your mental powers for the benefit of others.

You must learn: to distinguish the true from the false; to seek out the hidden mysteries of life; to think, observe and try to understand; to enjoy solitude and silence; to teach others your moral philosophies so that they may benefit from your wisdom.

Pitfalls: You must remember to keep your feet firmly on the ground. Your danger lies in becoming so involved in spiritual matters that you lose touch with reality.

Key Words: Mind Power.

Whole Name Number Eight

Mission: to attain mastery of self before embarking upon your life's work.

You must learn: to achieve success through your own efforts; to accept your destiny with humility; to work hard, persevere and never give up when things become difficult.

Pitfalls: Always resist the temptation to accept something which is second best or mediocre — go for best, the top. Unless you learn to be disciplined you will never be sufficiently well organized to make the grade.

Key Words: Material Success.

Whole Name Number Nine

Mission: to lead an ideal life and to inspire others to follow your example.

You must learn: charity, forgiveness and temperance; to face up to life and be prepared to tackle anything it may throw at you; to move in wide circles and broaden your horizons and viewpoints as often as possible.

Pitfalls: Impatience could be your downfall and you must learn to accept that some things take time and cannot be accomplished immediately.

Key Word: Perfection.

Whole Name Number Eleven

Mission: to give selfless service to humanity.

You must learn: to live up to, and accept, your destiny; to take the lead in public/civic affairs; to promote better standards of living for the less fortunate in the community; to use your creativity and psychic powers to enhance your work.

Pitfalls: You must not allow personal recognition for your services to humanity go to your head. Always be modest and unassuming.

Key Words: Public Service.

Whole Name Number Twenty-Two

Mission: to be responsible for important, tangible projects which will ultimately benefit mankind.

You must learn: to have confidence in your decisions; to accept great responsibility; to be involved in community projects such as the construction of new roads, health centres and public libraries; to serve the community with love and honesty.

Pitfalls: You will be involved in many great, and financially costly schemes during your lifetime — never be tempted to act dishonestly or in an underhand

manner. You are in a position of trust.
Key Words: Power and Responsibility.

THE NAMECHART

Names are analysed on a Namechart in an attempt to reveal further evidence of their influence on the development of a person's character. Analysis of the name pattern is of great assistance in the evaluation of the personality. The namechart is a grid, exactly like the birthchart, and the numerical value of each letter is entered in its appropriate section. Two examples are given for your guidance and two blank grids for your own calculations.

Sample layout

3	6	9	Mental
2	5	8	Emotional
1	4	7	Physical

```
      1           5                      3       1
C   H   A   R   L   E   S          S   U   S   A   N
3   8       9   3       1          1   1       1   5
```

33		9
	5	8
11		

Namechart

3		
	5	
111		

Birthchart

When you have completed your namechart transfer the details from your birthchart (which we discussed in the previous chapter, page 73) onto the other blank grid. Now you can compare both charts. There are two points you should be looking for:

1.   Are there any strengths on the namechart which will balance weak areas on the birthchart?

2.   Are any strengths, already apparent on the birthchart, further endorsed by the information contained in the namechart? An 'overbalance' in one particular area is undesirable because it will mean weaknesses in other areas. This vulnerability will require balancing. Pythagoras' system of 'Arrows', which we discussed in Chapter 6, page 74, will also be of great help when analysing your namechart.

MISSING NUMBERS

It is important to identify your 'Missing', or 'Karmic' numbers as they are sometimes called, because they represent the characteristics which you must try to develop during this lifetime. Your Middle Life Number represents the talents you should have developed, and the skills you should have learned, by the time you reach middle life — the years between thirty and fifty. To find this number add your unreduced Date of Birth Number to your unreduced Full Name Number and reduce the total in the usual manner. To find your Missing Numbers enter the following details where indicated:

```
Date of Birth Number        =   /
Vowel Number                =   /
Consonant Number            =   /
Full Name Number            =   /
Middle Life Number          =   /

1   2   3   4   5   6   7   8   9
```

Once you have these numbers before you, both reduced and double digit, look at them carefully and check off each number in turn by putting a tick against it on the 1 to 9 list given above, each time it occurs. When you have completed this exercise, any numbers which do not have a tick against them are your missing numbers.

Missing Number One
You must learn to take control and show others the way. Assert yourself more and make others listen to what you have to say. Try to excel at something. Become more adventurous and dare to live your life more dynamically.

Missing Number Two
You must learn that it is sometimes wise to be seen and not heard — like a Victorian child. Try to co-operate with others and learn to work as a member of a team rather than an individual. Try to be more understanding and sympathetic.

Missing Number Three

You must learn to communicate with others and to be able to express your feelings clearly and concisely so that people can understand you. Try to adopt a more cheerful, positive approach to life — a miserable face turns people away. Pay attention to your appearance because first impressions often count.

Missing Number Four

You really must take yourself in hand and gain control of your life. Once you have some firm and orderly foundations to build on the rest should be relatively simple. You will need to handle money wisely, learn discipline and be prepared to work hard if you wish to earn any material rewards in this lifetime.

Missing Number Five

People with a missing number five will have to get out of their rut and see more of life and the world around them. They need to travel and experience change to keep their minds working and their bodies healthy. They must learn to adapt and fit in with any routine or situation any time and anywhere they happen to be. Change is stability.

Missing Number Six

You must become more aware of the needs of others and less concerned with yourself. Family responsibilities should be taken more seriously and you should try to show more love and affection to those closest to you. Be more demonstrative.

Missing Number Seven

You need to spend more time alone in quiet, peaceful surroundings which are so necessary when developing the mind. You must learn to think, ponder and imagine. You should turn your back slightly on the material world and allow other aspects of your personality time to develop. Serious study could also broaden your outlook.

Missing Number Eight

You must acquire some business sense if you are ever going to get on in the world. A positive effort, hard work, determination and will-power could get you to the top of your chosen profession but without them you will just be mediocre. Financial rewards could be yours if only you would persevere in spite of obstacles.

Missing Number Nine

You should try not to live such a narrow, blinkered life — see things on a much grander scale than you do now. Think big, the world is your oyster! Care more about people and try to become an inspiration and a source of hope to others because of the example you set them.

Chapter 8

CHOOSING A NAME

Choosing a name is something most of us have to do at some time in our lives — whether for a child, a pet, a new business venture or maybe even as an alias or a pen-name. The ancients believed that the name mystically encoded the essential character of a person or object as well as information about its destiny, and that there should be nothing random or haphazard about its choice. This process of selection evolved into a form of numerology known as Onomancy, or Onomomancy, which stems from the word 'onomastic' meaning 'relating to name'. Each letter of the name was given a numerical value, as in numerology, and portents were drawn from the total. The ancients even went so far as to jumble the letters of a name to form smaller words which were also scrutinized for omens, and this became known as Anagramatic Onomancy.

In this chapter we will see how to make such a choice with special emphasis on the selection of a suitable name for a new-born child. (It will be necessary to refer closely to Chapter Five on Astrological Links.) You will need to know the full date of birth, day and time of birth. Most mothers will have this information but don't worry if you don't have a record of the time — it is still possible to make calculations without it. This method can always be applied to your own name should there be no new-born child handy to practice on. Enter your findings on the following chart.

Step One
Date of Birth ....
Date of Birth Number .... Planet ....

Step Two
Date and Month of Birth .... Zodiac Sign ....
Number .... Positive/Negative

Step Three
Birthdate .... Birthdate reduced ....
Day of Birth .... Number .... Planet ....

Step Four
Time of Birth .. am/pm   Planet ....   Number ....

Step One — Enter the full date of birth on the chart. Calculate the Date of Birth Number by reducing the full date of birth to a single digit and enter this information. Look up the ruling planet and enter this on the chart.
Step Two — Enter the date and month of birth on the chart and also the sign of the Zodiac which rules this period of the year. Enter the number associated with the particular zodiac sign and delete positive/negative as appropriate.
Step Three — Enter the actual birthdate, and reduce it where necessary. You will also need to make a note of the day — Sunday, Monday, and so on — and the number and planet connected with it.
Step Four—(Only complete this section if you have the necessary information.) Enter the actual time of birth and the ruling planet/number which can be found on the planetary/hours chart (page 65).

Once the four stages of the chart have been completed intuition and numerological judgement will be required for its interpretation. This analysis is, necessarily, very much a matter of personal opinion. However, the following guidelines should help you to form your own conclusions.

1.   Does any one number occur more frequently than others on the chart, and if so what are your feelings about this number — is it strong, weak, masculine, feminine, materialistic, spiritual?
2.   Does any one planet occur more frequently than others? Analyse this in the same way as a recurring number.
3.   Is the balance of numbers good (odds/evens) and if not what seems to be missing?
4.   What are the characteristics of the ruling Zodiac sign? Are they in harmony with your findings so far?
5.   When deciding finally upon the Name Number be sure that it is:
a)   either the same as the most frequently recurring number on the chart if you wish to carry its characteristics through into the name, or
b)   is strong enough to balance negative qualities which show up on the chart, or
c)   brings more sprirituality to a material chart and therefore balance, or vice versa, or
d)   if the numbers on the chart and characteristics seem very mixed, that it supplies an important quality which is missing.

Once you have decided upon a Name Number the list given below provides a varied selection of names to choose from together with their esoteric meanings and Name Numbers. The calculations were based on the following number/letter correspondences:

```
1  2  3  4  5  6  7  8  9
```

```
A  B  C  D  E  F  G  H  I

J  K  L  M  N  O  P  Q  R

S  T  U  V  W  X  Y  Z
```

Alternative spellings, and variations of names, have also been included to assist you in choosing an appropriately numbered name.

When it comes to naming a new company, a pet or an inanimate object such as a house or a boat, this procedure is not relevant but care should still be taken to select a name which reduces to a number in keeping with the character of the thing to be named.

ALEXANDRA 8 (Greek) The helper of mankind and protector of men. (Alex 6, Lexie 1, Sandy 9, Sandra 3, Zandra 1).

AMANDA 7 (Latin) Worthy of being loved; lovable (Mandy 5, Mandie 1).

ANGELA 22/4 (Greek) Heavenly messenger; the bringer of good tidings (Angeline 4, Angel 3, Angie 9).

ANNE 7 (Hebrew) Full of grace (Ann 11/2, Anna 3, Annette 7, Annie 7, Anita 9, Nan 11/2, Nancy 3, Hanna 2).

ADAM 1 (Hebrew) Of the red earth; the first man.

ALAN 1 (Gaelic) Cheerful harmony (Alain 1, Allan 4, Allen 8, Allyn 1).

ANDREW 11/2 (Greek) Strong and manly (André 6, Anders 7, Andie 6, Andy 8, Drew 5).

ANTHONY 7 (Latin) Praiseworthy; of inestimable worth; a man without peer (Antony 8, Antoine 6, Anton 1, Antonio 7, Tony 2).

BARBARA 7 (Latin) Beautiful stranger; the lovely unknown visitor (Bab 5, Barbie 1, Barbra 6).

BETH 8 (Hebrew) House of God (Bethel 7).

BRIDGET 11/2 (Irish/Celtic) Strong and mighty; strength (Brigid 4, Biddie 6, Brydie 9).

BARRY 1 (Celtic) Spearlike; one whose intellect is sharp (Barrie 8,).

BENJAMIN 5 (Hebrew) Son of my right hand; the beloved youngest son (Ben 3, Bennie 4, Benjy 2, Benny 6).

BRIAN 8 (Celtic) Powerful strength with virtue and honour; strong (Briant 1, Bryan 6, Bryon 11/2).

BRUCE 22/4 (French) From the thicket; a man from the brushwood.

CAROLINE 5 (Teutonic) Little woman born to command; noble (Carol 22/4, Charleen 3, Sharleen 1, Caro 1, Lina 9).

CHRISTINE 6 (French) Christian one; the anointed (Christina 11/2, Crystal 8, Chris 3, Crissie 5).

CLARE 3 (Latin) Bright, shining girl; illustrious; one of outstanding beauty (Clara 8, Claire 3, Klara 7, Clarette 3).

CHARLES 3 (Teutonic) The strong man; the personification of all that is masculine (Carl 7, Carol 22/4, Charlie 11/2, Chas 4, Cary 2, Karl 6).

CHRISTIAN 11/2 (Latin) Believer in Christ; a Christian (Chris 3, Christy 3, Kit 4).

CHRISTOPHER 4 (Greek) The Christ carrier; bearer of Christ (Chris 3, Kris 3, Crissie 5).

COLIN 8 (Gaelic) Strong and virile; or, the young child; or, victorious army (Collin 11/2, Colan 9, Nicholas 9).

DAWN 6 (Anglo-Saxon) The break of day; one who brightens the darkness.

DENISE 11/2 (French) Wine goddess (Denice 4, Denys 22/4).

DIANA 2 (Latin) Divine Moon goddess (Deanna 7, Diane 6, Dyane 22/4, Di 4, Dee 5).

DULCIE 9 (Latin) Sweet and charming; one who believes that love is the sweetest thing (Dulcea 1, Dulcine 5).

DAVID 22/4 (Hebrew) The beloved one; beloved of God (Dave 5, Davie 5, Davis 1).

DENNIS 11/2 (Greek) Wine lover (Denis 6, Denys 22/4, Denzil 7, Dion 6, Den 5, Denny 8).

DOMINIC 4 (Latin) Belonging to the Lord; born on the Lord's day (Dominy 8, Nick 8, Nicky 8).

DYLAN 2 (Welsh) Man from the sea.

ELIZABETH 7 (Hebrew) Consecrated of God; God's promise (Elisabeth 9, Elsa 1, Elspeth 4, Bess 9, Beth 8, Betty 9, Liza 3, Libby 5).

EMILY 1 (Teutonic) Industrious (Amelia 5).

EMMA 5 (Teutonic) One who leads the Universe; a woman of command.

EVE 5 (Hebrew) Life giver; mother of mankind (Eva 1, Eveline 9, Evita 3, Evonne 3).

EDWARD 1 (Anglo-Saxon) Prosperous guardian; rich and happy protector (Eddie 9, Ned 5, Teddy 6).

ELVIS 22/4 (Norse) all wise; the prince of wisdom.

EVAN 6 (Gaelic) Well-born young warrior (Welsh form of John 2, Ewan 7, Owen 3).

FAITH 8 (Teutonic) Trust in God; one who is loyal and true; free (Fay 5, Faye 1).

FELICITY 8 (Latin) Joyous one; happiness (Felis 6, Felicie 4).

FIONA 9 (Gaelic) Fair one (Fionn 4).

FERGUS 4 (Gaelic) The best choice (Fergie 5).

FRANCIS 7 (Latin) Free man (Frank 5, Franz 11/2, Frankie 1, Fran 3).

FREDERICK 7 (Teutonic) Peaceful ruler; one who uses diplomacy not war (Frederic 9, Fritz 7, Fred 6, Freddy 8).

GENEVIEVE 4 (French) Pure white wave (Genevra 9).

GRACE 7 (Latin) The graceful one (Grazia 8, Gracie 7, Girosal 9).
GEOFFREY 6 (Teutonic) God's divine peace; joyful (Godrey 8, Jeffery 3, Geoff 3).
GEORGE 3 (Greek) Land holder; the farmer (Georgie 3, Geordie 9, Jorge 1, Joris 8, Jurgen 3).

HAZEL 7 (English) The hazel tree (Aveline 5).
HELEN 8 (Greek) Light (Eleanor 7, Elaine 1, Ella 3, Isleen 1, Lora 1, Norah 11/2, Nell 7, Lena 5).
HOPE 8 (Anglo-Saxon) A virtue name; cheerful optimism.
HENRY 7 (Teutonic) Ruler of the Estate; Lord of the Manor; head of the house (Hamlin 3, Heinrick 5, Henri 9, Harry 7, Hal 3, Hank 7).
HUGH 8 (Teutonic) Brilliant, shining mind; thoughtful (Hubert 9, Bert 9, Hugo 6, Hughes 5).

INGRID 7 (Norse) Hero's daughter; child of a warrior (Inga 22/4, Ingeborg 5).
IRENE 6 (Greek) Peace; the goddess of peace (Eirene 11/2, Irena 11/2, Renata 5, Rene 6, Rennie 11/2.
IAN 6 (Celtic) God is gracious; God has favoured (Iain 6, Iaian 7).
IVOR 1 (Norse) Battle archer; the warrior with the long bow (Iva 5, Ivon 6, Ives 1).

JANE 3 (Hebrew) God's gift of grace (Janet 5, Jayne 1, Jean 3, Joan 4, Sheena 7, Sean 3).
JUDITH 9 (Hebrew) Admired; praised (Jodie 7, Judy 6).
JULIA 8 (Greek) Youthful; young in heart and mind (Julie 3, Juliana 5, Juliet 5, Jill 7).
JAMES 3 (Hebrew) The supplanter (Jacob 4, Jacques 22/4, Jimmy 7, Seamus 6, Jock 3).
JEREMY 4 (Hebrew) Holy name; exalted by the Lord (Jeremiah 6, Jerry 4).
JOHN 2 (Hebrew) God's gracious gift; Jehovah has favoured (Jean 3, Jon 3, Johnny 5, Sean 3, Shane 2, Ivan 1, Ian 6).

KATHERINE 1 (Greek) Pure maiden (Kathryn 7, Catherine 11/2, Kathleen 4, Kitty 22/4, Kay 1, Kara 4, Karen 22/4).
KIRSTY 3 (Norse) The anointed one (Kirstin 1, Kirstina 11/2, Kirstie 1).
KEITH 8 (Celtic) A place; or, from the forest; or, windy.
KEVIN 7 (Gaelic) Gentle; kind and lovable (Keven 3, Kev 11/2).

LINDA 22/4 (Spanish) Pretty one (Belinda 11/2, Rosalinda 3, Lindy 1, Lynda 2).
LOUISE 9 (Teutonic) Famous battle maid; one who leads victorious armies (Louisa 5, Lois 1, Loyce 6, Eloisa 7, Allison 1).
LUCY 7 (Latin) Light; one who brings the lamp of learning to the ignorant.
LAWRENCE 9 (Latin) Crowned with laurels; he who wears the victor's crown (Laurence 7, Larry 11/2, Laurie 3, Lori 9).
LUKE 4 (Latin) Light (Lucas 11/2, Luck 11/2, Lucian 6).

MARGARET 11/2 (Latin) A pearl; a woman without equal (Margarita 7, Margery 6, Margo 9, Marge 8, Meg 7, Maisie 11/2, Peggy 6, Rita 3, Daisy 22/4).

MARY 3 (Hebrew) Bitterness (Maria 6, Marie 1, Marylin 11/2, Miriam 9, Muriel 6, Moira 11/2, Maureen 5, Molly 5, May 3, Polly 8).

MARK 7 (Latin) Follower of Mars; the warrior (Marcus 3, Marco 5, Marc 8).

MATTHEW 9 (Hebrew) Gift of God; one of the twelve Apostles (Mathias 8, Matt 9, Matty 7).

MICHAEL 6 (Hebrew) Like unto the Lord (Mitchel 7, Mitch 8, Mike 2, Micky 7).

NICOLE 4 (Greek) The people's victory (Nicola 9, Nicol 8, Nickie 6).

NEIL 22/4 (Gaelic) The champion (Neal 5, Niels 5).

NEVILLE 7 (Latin) From the new town (Nevil 8, Nev 5).

NICHOLAS 9 (Greek) Victorious people's army; the leader of the people (Nicholas 1, Nicol 8, Nik 7, Nikki 9, Klaus 1, Colin 8).

NIGEL 11/2 (Latin) Black-haired one.

ODETTE 6 (French) Home-lover; one who makes a house a home.

OLIVE 9 (Latin) Symbol of peace (Olivia 5, Olga 8, Livia 8, Nola 6).

OMAR 2 (Arabic) The first son; most high follower of the prophet.

OSCAR 2 (Anglo-Saxon) Divine spearman; a fighter for God (Oskar 1, Os 7, Ossie 22/4).

PATRICIA 5 (Latin) Well-born maiden; a girl born to the noblest of families (Pat 1, Patsy 9).

PAULA 6 (Latin) Little (feminine of Paul 5, Paulette 1, Pauline 6).

PENELOPE 7 (Greek) The weaver (Penny 11/2).

PETER 1 (Latin) The stone; the rock (Pearce 3, Pierre 8, Pete 1).

PHILIP 9 (Greek) Lover of horses (Phillip 1, Phil 9).

RACHEL 11/2 (Hebrew) Innocent as a lamb; one who suffers in silence (Raquel 11/2, Ray 8, Shelley 5).

REBECCA 1 (Hebrew) The captivator (Rebekah 5, Beckie 8, Bekky 9).

ROSEMARY 6 (Latin) Dew of the sea (Rose 3, Rosalie 7, Rhoda 1, Rosy 5).

RALPH 1 (Anglo-Saxon) Swift wolf (Randolph 7, Ralf 1, Rolph 6).

RICHARD 7 (Teutonic) Wealthy, powerful one (Rick 5, Ricky 3, Ritchie 7, Dick 9, Diccon 3).

ROSS 8 (Celtic) From the peninsula; or (Teutonic) horse.

SARAH 2 (Hebrew) Princess; one of royal status (Sara 3, Sadie 6, Sally 6, Zara 1).

SHEILA 9 (Celtic) Musical (Cecilia 6, Sheela 5).

SUSAN 11/2 (Hebrew) Graceful lily (Susanna 3, Sue 9, Susie 1).

SAMUEL 8 (Hebrew) His name is God (Sam 6, Sammy 8).

STEPHEN 6 (Greek) The crowned one; a man who wears the victor's laurel wreath (Steven 4, Stefan 2, Steve 8).

STUART 9 (Anglo-Saxon) The steward (Stewart 7, Stew 4).

TERESA 5 (Greek) The harvester (Therese 8, Terri 7, Tessa 1).

TRACY 22/4 (Gaelic) Battler (Tracey 9).

THOMAS 22/4 (Hebrew) The twin; the devoted brother (Tomas 5, Tom 3, Tommy 5, Massey 1).

TREVOR 11/2 (Gaelic) Prudent, wise and discreet; one who can be trusted with secrets. (Trev 2).

VICTORIA 7 (Latin) The victorious one (Vicki 9, Vicky 7).

VICTOR 6 (Latin) The conqueror (Vincent 6, Vic 7).

WANDA 7 (Teutonic) The wanderer; the restless roamer (Wendy 8, Wenda 2, Gwendoline 9).

WILLIAM 7 (Teutonic) Determined protector; the strong guardian (Willis 3, Will 2, Bill 8, Billy 6).

YVONNE 5 (French) Archer with the yew bow (Yvette 7, Vonnie 7).

ZOE 1 (Greek) Life; the mother of all living (Eve 5, Zoa 6).

Chapter 9

COMPATIBILITY

Compatability can be determined by comparing Date of Birth Numbers. This comparison enables you to discover why you get along better with some people than others and can be applied to anyone — family, friends, colleagues, loved ones. The following list details all the possible number combinations. Ratings are as follows:

A = Excellent
B = Good
C = Average
D = Poor

1:1 This is a powerful combination provided you work together towards a common goal. Should an element of rivalry creep into your relationship then it would be a different story altogether. You are both born leaders, with a tendency towards aggression, and would need to learn how to co-operate with each other to maintain a peaceful co-existence.
Business Rating — B
Personal Rating — B

1:2 This is an excellent combination because what one lacks the other can provide. You complement each other perfectly. The 2 partner has the talents and ability required to carry out the plans and ideas of the 1 partner.
Business Rating — A
Personal Rating — A

1:3 Together you can accomplish almost anything provided that the 1 partner does nothing rash and the 3 partner learns to keep his/her mind on the matter in hand. The 1 will always be the leader and will instigate all the ideas which the 3 will eagerly expand upon. This combination could be rewarding materially as well as emotionally.
Business Rating — C
Personal Rating — B

1:4 This would make a good combination from a business point of view, but, on a more personal level, a 1 and a 4 could find each other exasperating. A 1 person often acts impulsively — this is something a 4 never does and cannot understand. 4s are extremely cautious and careful about everything they do and never make a move without careful consideration. Both partners would need to make an effort for this combination to succeed.
Business Rating — B
Personal Rating — D

1:5 Versatility, which both of you possess, could be the saving grace in an emotional combination of 1:5 because you are also both changeable and would need to be able to adapt quickly and readily to cope with each other's demands. However in a business partnership you could do very well and have a lot to offer each other.
Business Rating — B
Personal Rating — C

1:6 A joint business venture, provided there was sufficient scope for the 6 to be creative, should be successful because the 1 person is quite willing to manage almost anything. On a personal level, a 1 with a 6 should make a good combination — as long as the 1 doesn't become too domineering. 6s like luxury and a busy social life which a 1 can provide.
Business Rating — B
Personal Rating — B

1:7 You are strong characters who need to express yourselves in different ways — 1 is the doer and 7 the thinker. The 7 in particular needs to spend some time alone. If you are both prepared to make allowances for each other's needs then this can be a rewarding partnership. When working together, in a professional capacity, the 7 curbs the tendency of the 1 to act without reflection and generates ideas which the 1 is better equipped to promote.
Business Rating — C
Personal Rating — C

1:8 This combination can be either very good or very bad — there are no shades of grey. Unless you are both prepared to control your forceful natures, you might as well call it a day right now. But from a business point of view you possess all the right ingredients between you for success — courage, determination and the will to succeed.
Business Rating — A
Personal Rating — A/D

1:9 There can be no doubt at all that this partnership will prosper, from an emotional or a business point of view. Together you possess a touch of genius. The 9's integrity tempers the creative flair of the 1 and his/her wisdom acts as a sounding-board for the often brilliant ideas of the 1.
Business Rating — A
Personal Rating — A

2:2 You were meant for each other — no one can understand a 2 better than another 2. Should you decide to go into business, however, you will both need to make a few adjustments. Because you are so alike, you will have to guard against working for each other (that is, to please each other) and try to work as a team instead. Be decisive and know when to act.
Business Rating — C
Personal Rating — A

2:3 *How to Make Friends and Influence People* aptly describes a 2:3 partnership. A 2 makes friends easily and a 3 is only too ready to turn this to his/her advantage. A good combination which works well on all levels provided that the 2 is prepared to play second fiddle most of the time.
Business Rating — C
Personal Rating — B

2:4 The keyword is harmony. You would do well together in business because the 4 knows how to build things up and the 2 instinctively knows what is required of him/her to keep things running smoothly. In a personal relationship you complement each other and the possibility of disagreements is remote.
Business Rating — B
Personal Rating — B

2:5 This combination will require a great deal of hard work, from both parties, to keep it going. Fives can survive very well on their own and will need to tone down their natural inclination to 'take over'. Twos on the other hand, like a quiet life and, because they prefer to stay in the background, may not have sufficient vitality to hold a 5's interest for very long. Not good business prospects.
Business Rating — D
Personal Rating — D

2:6 Not a particularly dynamic combination of numbers which lacks the drive and ambition necessary for business success. But one which should work well on a personal level because 2s are home-lovers who like comfort and beautiful surroundings and 6s are artistic, co-operative and refined.
Business Rating — D
Personal Rating — B

2:7 Business life is too demanding for a combination like this unless they decide to open a transcendental meditation centre. This combination of numbers is so peaceful and harmonious that a little injection of friction occasionally could be a good thing. A 2 and 7 when together are very spiritual and seem to be in complete agreement on this plane.
Business Rating — D
Personal Rating — B

2:8 These people can live and work together in harmony. They seem to attract money because they are honest, industrious and, above all, reliable. These people often strike up lasting friendships although the 8 can outshine the 2 at times with his/her dynamic personality.
Business Rating — B
Personal Rating — B

2:9 A 2 with a 9 makes a winning team. They both have much to offer and when working together for a common cause they seldom fail. The 2 contributes understanding and stability while the 9 has imagination, vision and insight. These two could put the world to rights.
Business Rating — A
Personal Rating — A

3:3 Any venture for two 3s will be a risk. You are both reckless, headstrong people who trust too much to luck. This is a combination of gamblers and the odds on your survival together are not in your favour. Unless you both become more responsible and reflective your relationship won't stand a chance.
Business Rating — D
Personal Rating — D

3:4 A combination of numbers which will require a compromise for it to work successfully. The 3, who is by nature incautious, must make allowances for the 4's caution. The 4, who always seems to be 'too busy' must make time to listen to the ideas of the 3. Once these differences of personality have been conquered a stable business/personal relationship can develop.
Business Rating — C
Personal Rating — C

3:5 These two numbers, when combined, produce many viable ideas which the 5 knows how to market once the 3 has 'packaged' them attractively. They are bound to succeed. The only danger, in a partnership like this, lies in overhastiness.
Business Rating — B
Personal Rating — C

3:6 You should get on very well together because you have similar personalities. When you finally decide to put down roots, this will be a partnership which can withstand almost anything that life chooses to throw at it. In the world of business, people with this combination of numbers often form partnerships for life.
Business Rating — B
Personal Rating — B

3:7 If you allow each other room to breathe within this partnership then you won't go far wrong. The 3 gives energy and receives understanding in return. The 7 gives wisdom and gains inspiration. All in all a very complementary couple on any level.
Business Rating — B
Personal Rating — B

3:8 This combination makes a better business than personal relationship because you both have such big ideas combined with the ability to convert them into reality — 3s are communicators and 8s are entrepreneurs. If you are aiming for the same goal there is little that can stop you.
Business Rating — A
Personal Rating — C

3:9 An extremely compatible combination provided that neither of you has to work for a living. With private means you could spend your days socializing or trying to discover the meaning of life. However, as most people have to earn their livings, you must become more realistic, down to earth and practical if you ever want to get on in life.
Business Rating — D
Personal Rating — A

4:4 A combination like this can sometimes represent the 'Jones' that everyone is proverbially trying to 'keep up with'. You are compatible, financially successful, materially secure and lucky too. Any business you enter will expand as you are both 4s — builders. Watch out that you don't become so materially minded that other aspects of life pass you by unnoticed and untried.
Business Rating — A
Personal Rating — B

4:5 Opposites sometimes attract and this is just the case here. With a little effort on both sides this combination can be made to work. Fours are practical and 5s are adjustable. Once these opposites gain balance they can work well together.
Business Rating — C
Personal Rating — C

4:6 4 and 6 together work hard and play hard too so both of you feel happy and fulfilled. This combination, when found in the business world, is often connected with the leisure industry, entertainment or advertising. A sound business and personal partnership.
Business Rating — B
Personal Rating — B

4:7 This is a combination which points to great success because it is balanced by the best characteristics of both worlds. The 4 provides solid foundations for the brilliant ideas of the 7 to stand upon and grow.
Business Rating — A
Personal Rating — A

4:8 When a 4 and an 8 combine forces they achieve perfect balance in both personal and business life. An 8 sees everything on a very large scale and the 4 provides the balance because he/she sees things on a much smaller scale and can put minor errors right before they cause any great damage to the overall scheme.
Business Rating — A
Personal Rating — B

4:9 A 4 and a 9 have much to teach each other but as the process of teaching/learning is rather slow this combination works better in private than during business hours. Nines are wise and have much knowledge to impart to a 4, who in turn can pass on many practical skills that the 9 would otherwise not have acquired.
Business Rating — C
Personal Rating — B

5:5 This is a dangerous combination whichever angle you may choose to view it from. Fives are restless, changeable, highly excitable and rebel against any form of restraint. Put two 5s together and you create a potentially explosive environment which should be avoided if at all possible.
Business Rating — D
Personal Rating — D

5:6 When a temperamental, excitable 5 is coupled with a quiet, homeloving 6 they undergo a very marked change of personality. The calming 6 influence enables 5s to put their thoughts in order and the resultant partnership proves stimulating for both of them.
Business Rating — C
Personal Rating — B

5:7 This combination of numbers seldom works for long as invariably the excitable 5 becomes too much for a 7 to cope with. Sevens need peace and quiet so that they can think and a 5 is the least likely sort of person to provide them with that.
Business Rating — D
Personal Rating — D

5:8 Watch out when these two dynamic personalities get together. An 8 can convert ideas into reality almost as fast as a 5 can dream them up. This is a winning business/personal partnership while it lasts but does tend to burn itself out fairly quickly if someone doesn't apply the brakes.
Business Rating — A
Personal Rating — A

5:9 This combination can prove very successful when it occurs. A 5 knows just how a 9 should pass on his/her wisdom and knowledge in the most profitable way because 5s are salesmen and have good contacts. Conversely a 9 seems to know just how to get the best out of a 5 without appearing to have done anything.
Business Rating — B
Personal Rating — B

6:6 Domestic bliss, great beauty and comfort are all created when two 6s join forces but as they rarely have any interests outside their homes this combination seldom leaves its mark on the business world with the possible

exception of interior design.
Business Rating — D
Personal Rating — A

6:7 Lack of common ground for communication is very often the downfall of a 6:7 relationship. Sevens are always too busy thinking to notice what a 6 has been up to. Similarly a 6 spends so much time creating visual impressions that he/she never has a penny for 7's thoughts. Only a superhuman effort can make this combination work.
Business Rating — D
Personal Rating — D

6:8 This combination of numbers has great potential because the roles of each partner are clearly defined. An 8 knows how to take the lead and which direction to take while the 6 is happy to give support, offer ideas and provide a comfortable home to relax in.
Business Rating — B
Personal Rating — A

6:9 This numerical combination is always rather special becaue it combines beauty (6) with truth (9). Sixes and 9s instinctively know how to give and take, on all levels of consciousness, and a partnership like this rarely breaks up.
Business Rating — A
Personal Rating — A

7:7 When two 7s are together they make a perfect couple who seldom argue because they are completely in tune with each other's needs. However, they do tend to live in a world of their own — a world of ideas — which is totally divorced from reality. This combination must develop a more materialistic approach to life, if they are to survive.
Business Rating — D
Personal Rating — A

7:8 A 7 and an 8 work well together in business because the 7 provides just enough stability to keep the 8's restless energy in check and channelled in a constructive direction. Sevens also possess a visionary quality which is invaluable in forward planning. This is also an excellent combination in private life as long as the 8 doesn't become too domineering.
Business Rating — A
Personal Rating — B

7:9 Peace, harmony and understanding are all qualities to be found in a 7:9 relationship. Their two minds think as one. The danger lies in becoming too spiritual and losing touch with reality. A 7 and a 9 together do not make a good business team unless involved with the organization of humanitarian projects at which they excel.
Business Rating — C
Personal Rating — A

8:8 Unless two 8s handle their combined strength and organizational abilities with considerable care and respect there could be disastrous results — they could destroy each other completely. When, however, they decide to co-operate the result is a well-organized, dynamic team which is completely unstoppable!
Business Rating — A/D
Personal Rating — A/D

8:9 This combination of numbers often results in an excellent research team. The 8 is practical and has stability while the 9 draws his/her creativity from an entirely different plane of thought than most people. In private life too they seem to bring out the best in each other.
Business Rating — C
Personal Rating — B

9:9 Wisdom, knowledge and imagination are just three of the qualities to be found in this combination. Two 9s together could do much to benefit humanity by sharing their own deep understanding of life with others. These two are so well matched that they often remain together for life.
Business Rating — B
Personal Rating — A

QUICK-GLANCE COMPATABILITY CHARTS

Business

	1	2	3	4	5	6	7	8	9	
1	B	A	C	B	B	B	C	A	A	1
2	A	C	C	B	D	D	D	B	A	2
3	C	C	D	C	B	B	B	A	D	3
4	B	B	C	A	C	B	A	A	C	4
5	B	D	B	C	D	C	D	A	B	5
6	B	D	B	B	C	D	D	B	A	6
7	C	D	B	A	D	D	D	A	C	7
8	A	B	A	A	A	B	A	A/D	C	8
9	A	A	D	C	B	A	C	C	B	9
	1	2	3	4	5	6	7	8	9	

Personal

	1	2	3	4	5	6	7	8	9	
1	B	A	B	D	C	B	C	A/D	A	1
2	A	A	B	B	D	B	B	B	A	2
3	B	B	D	C	C	B	B	C	A	3
4	D	B	C	B	C	B	A	B	B	4
5	C	D	C	C	D	B	D	A	B	5
6	B	B	B	B	B	A	D	A	A	6
7	C	B	B	A	D	D	A	B	A	7
8	A/D	B	C	B	A	A	B	A/D	B	8
9	A	A	A	B	B	A	A	B	A	9
	1	2	3	4	5	6	7	8	9	

There is an alternative way to determine compatability, which is favoured by some numerologists, and there are three main points to look out for when using this method (detailed below). The results achieved sometimes differ from the compatability analysis already given and it is up to the student to decide which method he/she prefers to use. Points to look for:

1. Analogous Numbers: These occur when the two numbers under analysis are either both odd or both even. Such a combination indicates harmonious co-existence, because each partner will have special qualities to contribute which the other lacks, and together they bring out the best in each other.

2. Conflicting Numbers: These are found when the two numbers under analysis oppose each other — one odd, one even. When this combination occurs there are often very marked differences of opinion and frequent clashes of personality. Two people with conflicting numbers can be physically attracted but their difficulties lie in understanding each other's thoughts and motives. A great deal of mutual give and take is required to make such a partnership work.

3. Group Numbers: These occur when the two numbers under analysis both come from the same numerical group. Such a combination indicates people of similar ability and temperament. The groups and their numbers are:

a) Mind Numbers 1, 5 and 7: People with these Date of Birth Numbers are often intellectual, well-educated, intuitive and great thinkers.

b) Expression Numbers 3, 6 and 9: People with these Date of Birth Numbers are often emotional, creative and, at times, inspired. Writers and artists fall into this category.

c) Business Numbers 2, 4 and 8: People with these Date of Birth Numbers are good organizers, stable, efficient and business-minded. They often become merchants, bankers and executives.

One final point to remember when looking for compatability is that odd numbers are generally masculine, active, creative and extrovert while even numbers are generally feminine, passive, receptive and introvert. And that all numbers, whether odd or even, have negative as well as positive characteristics of their own.

Chapter 10

THE ALPHABET

Numerologists usually analyse a name by converting the letters into numbers using the appropriate correspondence table. However, names can be viewed from a slightly different angle by evaluating each letter separately, and in sequence, to discover its strengths or weaknesses. Letters and vowels which appear more than once in a name should be noted as these are 'letters of emphasis' and the first letter/vowel in a name is also important.

The ancients believed that the soul entered the body upon the vibration of the first vowel and for this reason they were regarded as the most important aspects of the alphabet. The number/letter correspondences used in this chapter are as follows:

1	2	3	4	5	6	7	8	9
A	B	C	D	E	F	G	H	I
J	K	L	M	N	O	P	Q	R
S	T	U	V	W	X	Y	Z	

Another way of showing the correspondences is as follows:

A = 1	G = 7
B = 2	H = 8
C = 3	I = 9
D = 4	J = 10/1
E = 5	K = 11/2
F = 6	L = 12/3

M = 13/4	T = 20/2
N = 14/5	U = 21/3
O = 15/6	V = 22/4
P = 16/7	W = 23/5
Q = 17/8	X = 24/6
R = 18/9	Y = 25/7
S = 19/1	Z = 26/8

A = 1 A is the first letter of the alphabet and also the first vowel. It represents 'the head'.

Characteristics:

Determination — exertion, will-power, resolution, intent, purpose.

Enterprise — initiative, spirit, drive, energy.

Courage — boldness, audacity, daring, self-reliance.

When A is the first vowel in a name this points to a great interest in life in general and an independent nature. When another A also appears in the name there is level-headedness and a capacity to think problems over, but three As or more in a name tips the balance and points to selfishness.

A negative A can be a very critical person who is sceptical about everything and sneers at the efforts of others.

B = 2 B is the second letter of the alphabet and represents 'emotions'. It is not a particularly strong letter and is easily influenced by others around it.

Characteristics:

Amicable — sympathetic, friendly, hospitable.

Homeliness — a love of domesticity, peace and quiet. A female B has a very motherly nature while her male counterpart has a great love of Nature and the country life. They both feel a strong need for marriage or partnership and dislike being on their own.

Over-sensitive — excitable, emotional, nervous, highly-strung.

Fixed views — unchanging sentiments, firm beliefs, inflexible opinions.

A negative B can be a very selfish person, totally absorbed in himself and out for all he can get. Also very greedy and possessive.

C = 3 The third letter of the alphabet representing 'energy'.

Characteristics:

Good-humoured — cheerful, willing, genial, light-hearted, carefree.

Extravagant — lavish, liberal, unthrifty, improvident, spendthrift.

Dexterous — skilful, proficient, handy, versatile, an all-rounder.

Orator — eloquent, outspoken, a speech-maker, a talker.

An Organizer — planner, promotor, engineer, inventor.

Impulsive — spontaneous, impatient, spur of the moment actions.

A negative C can be shameless, negligent, inattentive, immoral, unscrupulous, careless and unprincipled.

D = 4 The fourth letter of the alphabet representing 'balance'.

Characteristics:
Will-power — determination, resolution, intent, purpose.
Business acumen — perception, understanding, judg. ment, shrewdness.
Perseverance — patience, endurance, concentration, application.
Authority — power, leadership, influence, sway, command.
An organizer — planner, builder, designer, promoter.

A negative D can be stubborn, unyielding, obstinate, pig-headed and uncompromising.

E = 5   The fifth letter of the alphabet and the second vowel. A particularly strong letter which represents 'communication'.

Characteristics:
Amusing — entertaining, interesting, diverting, delightful.
Independent — needs freedom and liberty, room to move, dislikes restraint.
Skilful — versatile, dextrous, proficient.
Intellectual — intelligent, thoughtful, perceptive, aware.
Imaginative — idealistic, creative, original, inventive.
Instinctive — intuitive, impulsive, inspirational, clairvoyant.

When E is the first vowel in a name this points to an exciting and eventful life. However, a person with three or more Es in their name could be nervous and temperamental especially when E is the first vowel.

A negative E can be irresponsible, unreliable, unstable, flirtatious and fickle.

F = 6   F is the sixth letter of the alphabet representing 'love'.
Characteristics:
Domesticated — home-loving, paternal/maternal.

Friendly — amicable, hospitable, sympathetic, cheerful.
Planner — organizer, promotor, builder, designer.
Helpful — kind, warm-hearted, loving, unselfish.
Comforting — compassionate, humane, gentle, tender, considerate.
Loyal — responsible, honourable, moral, conscientous, dutiful.

A negative F can be melancholy, unhappy, sad, miserable, wretched, depressed, anxious and uneasy.

G = 7 G is the seventh letter of the alphabet representing 'mysticism and religion'.

Characteristics:
Purposeful — determined, strong-willed, intent, resolute.
Inventive — imaginative, idealistic, creative, original.
Instinctive — intuitive, impulsive, inspirational, clairvoyant.
Orderly — methodical, disciplined, systematic, tidy.

Negative Gs like to do things their own way and dislike advice which they see as interference, they can also be very doubting and difficult to convince.

H = 8 H is the eighth letter of the alphabet representing 'creativity and power'.

Characteristics:
Self-contained — independent, complete, a loner.
Nature-lover — ecologist, concerned with the earth and its flora and fauna.
Victorious — successful, profitable, unbeatable, a winner.
Money-maker — solvent, well-off, attract money, have the Midas touch.

Negative Hs can be greedy, possessive, self-absorbed, and selfish.

I = 9 I is the ninth letter of the alphabet, and the third vowel, representing 'law'.

Characteristics:

Elegant — stylish, tasteful, sensitive, artistic.
Warm-hearted — helpful, kind, loving, unselfish.
Impulsive — instinctive, intuitive, inspirational.
Gentle — compassionate, humane, tender, considerate.

When I is the first vowel in a name this suggests a person who is interested in the arts, drama or science. When I occurs three or more times in a name this indicates a person who is sensitive and shy and who can sometimes become over-emotional.

A negative I can be nervous, lack confidence, be timid, hesitant and fearful or quick to anger, bad-tempered, impatient and easily offended.

J = 1 J is the tenth letter of the alphabet representing 'aspiration'.

Characteristics:

Truthful — fair, honest, correct, genuine, reliable, loyal.
Creative — original, inventive, imaginative.
Helpful — kind, well-meaning, benevolent, warm-hearted.
Clever — bright, intelligent, talented, brilliant, shrewd.

A negative J can be lazy, listless, dull and lifeless probably because he lacks a goal in life.

K = 2 K is the eleventh letter of the alphabet representing 'extremes'.
Characteristics:
Vigorous — strong, potent, forceful, lusty, powerful.
Unyielding — enduring, lasting, unceasing, steady.
Versatile — many-sided, diverse, an all-rounder.
Sensitive — emotional, responsive, feeling, passionate.
Creative — original, imaginative, inventive, idealistic.
Authority — leadership, influence, command, sway.

   A negative K may be timid, hesitant, fearful and nervous or dejected, miserable and dissatisfied.

L = 3 L is the twelfth letter of the alphabet representing 'action'.
Characteristics:
Benevolent — generous, charitable, giving, good-natured.
Management — control, command, leadership, executive ability.
Loyal — truthful, fair, honest, correct, genuine, reliable, moral.
Talented — clever, bright, intelligent, shrewd, intellectual.
Balanced — even, in harmony, well-adjusted, unbiased.
Travel — successive change of place, progress, movement, journeys.

   A negative L may be rather accident-prone especially where falls are concerned.

M = 4   M is the thirteenth letter of the alphabet and represents 'spirituality'.
Characteristics:
Industrious — hard-working, active, tireless, diligent, efficient, indefatigable.
Courageous — brave, bold, daring, audacious, self-reliant.
Patient — tolerant, uncomplaining, enduring, resigned, long-suffering.
Domesticated — a home-lover, a strong need for material security.
Psychic powers — perceptive, cognitive, clairvoyant.
   A negative M may be rather hasty and behave rashly or impatiently, be bad-tempered and quick to anger.

N = 5   N is the fourteenth letter of the alphabet and represents 'imagination'.
Characteristics:
Certain — sure, positive, unshakable, confident, self-opinionated.
A writer — scribe, diarist, reporter, record-keeper.
Spokesman — messenger, publicizer, ambassador, go-between.
Imaginative — creative, inventive, inspirational, intuitive.
Pleasure — enjoyment, sensuality, contentment, well-being.
   A negative N can be envious, covetous and jealous which could cause divorce if carried to extremes.

O = 6 O is the fifteenth letter of the alphabet and the fourth vowel. It represents 'patience'.

Characteristics:

Scholarly — studious, bookish, well-read, learned, erudite.

Intellectual — knowledgeable, well-informed, aware, enlightened.

Virtuous — pious, religious, solemn, God-fearing, moral.

When O is the first vowel in a name this points to a frank and methodical person who has a great respect for law and order in all things. When there are three or more Os in a name, especially when O is also the first vowel an obstinate, monotonous, slow type of person is indicated.

A negative O should learn to control his emotions, not to wear his heart upon his sleeve and should guard against jealousy which is a particularly negative, destructive feeling.

P = 7 P is the sixteenth letter of the alphabet and represents 'power'.

Characteristics:

Talented — bright, clever, shrewd, intelligent.

Enlightened — knowledgeable, aware, well-informed, intellectual.

Wise — thoughtful, level-headed, realistic, objective.

Expressive — emphatic, intelligible, straightforward, makes sense.

Influential — dominating, commanding, powerful, impressive.

Impetuous — hasty, impatient, in a hurry, urgent.

A negative P may be possessive, self-absorbed and totally selfish with neither time nor sympathy to spare for other people and their problems.

Q = 8   Q is the seventeenth letter of the alphabet and represents 'originality'.
Characteristics:
Command — authority, leadership, influence, sway.
Resolute — determined, strong, intent, will-power.
Shrewd — intelligent, talented, clever, bright.
An orator — talker, speech-maker, outspoken, eloquent.
Ardent — intense, vehement, violent, capable of great effort.
Enigmatic — puzzling, deep, mysterious, hard to analyse, unknowable.
  Negative Qs can become extremely boring especially when over-talkative and are also inclined to become totally self-absorbed.

R = 9   R is the eighteenth leter of the alphabet and represents 'possibilities'.
Characteristics:
Warm-hearted — helpful, kind, loving, unselfish.
Compassionate — gentle, tender, considerate, humane.
Patient — tolerant, even-tempered, placid, stable, composed.
Enthusiastic — eager, active, lively, zealous, hard-working.
  A negative R is rather apt to mislay or lose possessions entirely and can be rather irritable, niggly and touchy. He is also easily aggravated and short-tempered at times.

S = 1 S is the nineteenth letter of the alphabet and represents 'beginnings'.
Characteristics:
Strong feelings — vehement, ardent, intense, capable of great effort, violent.
Attraction — charm, glamour, influence, fascination, enchantment.
Love — warmth, tenderness, desire, attachment, devotion.
Money — wealth, means, capital, financially sound.
Commencements — beginnings, fresh starts, openings, inaugurations.

A negative S may experience many upheavals and failures during his or her life and may also be inclined to act impulsively and without reflection.

T = 2 T is the twentieth letter of the alphabet and represents 'growth'.
Characteristics:
Action — movement, bustle, activity, restlessness, unquiet.
Authority — leadership, control, influence, command, sway.
Creativity — style, make, mould, form, fashion, produce.
Development — growth, building, increase, enhance, broaden.
Religious — pious, spiritual, solemn, virtuous, moral.

Negative Ts are over-emotional and very easily influenced by the opinions of others. They need to learn self-control both in thought and deed.

U = 3 U is not only the twenty-first letter of the alphabet but also the fifth and last of the 'true' vowels. It represents 'accumulation'.

Characteristics:

Clever — talented, bright, intelligent, shrewd.

Fascination — attraction, charm, glamour, influence.

Acquisitive — a collector, gatherer, possessive, avaricious.

Fortunate — lucky, blessed, good breaks, happy accidents.

Retentive memory — learned, well-informed, remembers, never forgets.

When U is the first vowel in a name this points to a person with a mind which is capable of grasping and understanding a great deal; it also indicates the capacity for formulating ideas and carrying them through. When there are three or more Us in a name, especially when U is the first vowel this shows not only greed and selfishness but also possible loss caused by avarice.

Negative Us can be selfish, greedy, indecisive or a combination of all three undesirable qualities.

V = 4 V is the twenty-second letter of the alphabet and represents 'construction'.

Characteristics:

Honest — truthful, fair, genuine, reliable, moral, loyal.

Industrious — hard-working, diligent, active, tireless, efficient.

Practical — handy, useful, produce results.

Firm beliefs — fixed views, unchanging sentiments, inflexible opinions.

Gregarious — sociable, a good mixer, affable, cordial, fond of company.

Sensitive — emotional, responsive, passionate, feeling.

Jealous — possessive, envious, anxious, over-imaginative.

A negative V can be not only impractical but also totally unpredictable.

W = 5 W is the twenty-third letter of the alphabet and represents 'self-expression'.

Characteristics:

Resolute — determined, persistent, intent, purposeful.

Imaginative — original, creative, intuitive, thoughtful.

Attractive — magnetic, charming, fascinating, mysterious.

Affable — sociable, fond of company, a good mixer.

A negative W can be selfish and greedy but also too fond of taking risks and cutting corners for his own good.

X = 6 X is the twenty-fourth letter of the alphabet and represents 'sexuality'.

Characteristics:

Hedonistic — a pleasure-lover, craves luxury, self-indulgent, comfort seeker.

Easily-led — a willing pupil, receptive, eager to learn.

Intemperance — unrestraint, excess, addiction, dissipation.

Sensual — thrill-seeker, earthiness, high living, sexual excess.

A negative X can be an extremely promiscuous person who is not only unfaithful in his promises but in his affections too.

Y = 7 Y is the penultimate letter of the alphabet which, in certain circumstances, is used as a vowel. It represents 'freedom'.

Characteristics:

Enterprising — go-ahead, progressive, ambitious, pioneering, daring.

Independence — freedom, liberty, privilege, self-expression.

Dislikes restraint — hates restriction, limitation, control, condition.

Aesthetic — appreciates beauty, good taste, refinement, good manners.

Y is only treated as a vowel when it takes on the sound of either E or I in a name depending upon the pronounciation and is given the significance of the sound it produces — such as E in the name Yvonne and I in the name Lynda.

Negative Ys can be indecisive especially when faced with a choice. This hesitancy can also cause them to miss some good chances in life.

Z = 8 Z is the last letter of the alphabet and represents 'hope'.

Characteristics:

Trust — confidence, hope, expectations, beliefs.

Considerate — gentle, compassionate, understanding, humane, tender.

Common-sense — capable, quick-thinking, able, practical, down-to-earth.

Diplomatic — a mediator, peacemaker, discreet, wise, level-headed.

A negative Z can be a very impatient, headstrong person who should learn to think before he acts.

When analysing a name by this method — whether it be a Christian name, surname or 'whole name' — there are four main points to watch out for which may seem rather obvious but can, nevertheless, be overlooked if working in a hurry.

1. Is the name spelt correctly?
2. Are there any 'letters of emphasis'? (These are consonants or vowels which appear more than once. The more often a letter appears the stronger the meaning of that particular letter. Should it feature three or more times in a name this can cause an overbalance of a particular charcteristic in a personality). Make a note of these letters and the number of times they occur.
3. What is/are the initial letter(s) of the name(s) being analysed?
4. What is the first vowel to occur in the name?

The name can then be viewed as a whole to see if the personality is balanced or lacking in any particular attributes. If there were four Bs in the name, indicating a bland, mouse-like character, this lack of drive may be compensated for elsewhere by stronger letters such as D, P and A. Likewise too many Xs would need to be toned down by letters such as L, T or several Os.

Personal observations

Name: ....

Letters of Emphasis

No.	*Vowel*	*No.*	*Consonant*
.... x		.... x	
.... x		.... x	
.... x		.... x	

Initial letter(s)   ....
First vowel   ....
Remarks:

Chapter 11

GOOD OR BAD

Numerology can be used to calculate many things, such as a person's lucky and unlucky days, the most propitious day for marriage, or the most appropriate place for someone to live. It is also possible to discover what a specific year has in store, as well as any four-month period in that year, or even what a specific month has to offer. In this chapter we will see how these calculations can be made with the application of some basic numerology.

There are two ways to discover a person's good or bad days. When using the first method you must add together the Date of Birth Number and the Full Name Number (which will give you the Middle Life Number) and also the number of the day on which the enquiry is being made. Reduce the total to a number below ten, if necessary. The 1 to 9 correspondences are as follows:

1-day Do not waste a moment because this is a day of opportunity and you may not be given a second chance. Be positive, do something active and face up to any problems which have been worrying you recently. Action is your keyword.

2-day A time for thoughts and plans rather than for actions. Stay at home — think over your problems and how best to solve them. Do not enter into any form of agreement today, whether a verbal promise or a signed contract, the outcome will not be favourable.

3-day A particularly lucky day when you should get out and about and generally have a good time. There's plenty to be done but you should have more than enough energy to cope with anything today and still find time for fun.

4-day There will be no excitement for you today. A 4-day is always rather dull and routine, and sometimes even boring. Be practical, get all your chores done now then you will have more time to enjoy yourself later in the week.

5-day A day to expect the unexpected because anything can happen and probably will. Today will be full of excitement and adventure — you can even afford to take a chance and get away with it.

6-day If you are in someone's bad books, or perhaps have argued with your partner recently, then now is the time to bury the hatchet and say you're sorry. Any conflicts can be reconciled today. Also a favourable day for social gatherings, meetings or just visiting friends.

7-day This is a day when you should seek peace and quiet far away from people and distractions. You need some time on your own to meditate or just think things over. Also a good day for those of you involved in study or research.

8-day A day for big business and anything concerning finance or large-scale plans. You should make a constructive effort to produce something tangible today.

9-day This is a particularly favourable day when you could achieve a great deal. A day of personal satisfaction coupled with fulfilled ambitions.

For the second method of determining lucky and unlucky days you will need to have a calendar or almanac handy which gives details of the moon's phases. You must first discover the day of the full moon during the month of enquiry. Now count the number of days from the full moon until the end of the month and multiply this by the number of days in the month in question to find your answer. If the full moon fell on 7 September there would be twenty-three days until the end of the month. There are thirty days in September and $23 \times 30 = 690$ so the lucky days would be the 6th and the 9th. To calculate unlucky days count the number of days in the month before the full moon and multiply this by the number of days in the month. In our example the full moon fell on the 7th of the month so $6 \times 30 = 180$ — the unlucky day would fall on the 18th of the month in question.

You will still require the use of a diary or almanac to decide the most promising day for marriage. Once again find the day of the full moon but this time in the month that the wedding will hopefully take place. Count up the number of days from the full moon until the end of the month, deduct this amount for the number of days in the month and multiply the remainder by the age of the groom/bride-to-be. (If he/she should happen to be 22 years and 5 months old for instance his/her age would be calculated as 23 as he/she is in her twenty-third year.) The figure you arrive at will indicate the most propitious day/days for the marriage to take place.

THE NINE-YEAR CYCLE OF CHANGE

It is believed our lives are made up of a series of nine-year cycles during which gradual changes take place in our way of thinking and in our emotional and material needs — a pattern which is repeated time and again for as long as we live. To find your present position in this cycle of change, your 'Personal Year', simply add the month and day of your birth to the year of your last birthday (reduced to a double digit). The year of birth is *not* used in these calculations. Personal years always run from birthday to birthday, not from January to December like a calendar year. This procedure can be applied to any year of your life whether past, present or future provided that the appropriate 'year of last birthday' has been correctly calculated. Enter your own details below:

Day of Birth   + Month of Birth + Year of Last Birthday = Personal Year
.... + ... + ... = ... / ....

Each of the nine Personal Years in the cycle of change can be analysed as follows:

Personal Year One

A very powerful year and one when adjustments will be necessary for the start of a new cycle. Now is the time to make a clean break from dead or dying relationships, which are a constant drain on your emotional energy, and to give up bad habits which you have fallen into over the past nine-year cycle. Off with the old and on with the new in a Personal Year One.

You must try to develop more self-confidence and learn how to assert yourself — don't be a 'yes' man or woman any longer. If you feel that things are not quite right then say something; you must not suffer in silence. This could be an exciting year of personal development if you are prepared to make an effort.

Circumstances should also improve financially and a great deal of buying and selling is indicated with the emphasis placed firmly on property transactions.

Personal Year Two

Not a year for planning any major changes or for making great material advances. Spiritual development is the key phrase for a ruling Year Two. You should try to visualize yourself as others see you in order to evaluate strengths and weaknesses in your character.

Emotional upsets can be expected during this year and you must learn to be more self-controlled in order to hide your feelings of insecurity from others. By the end of the year you should be able to recognize the difference between actions and reactions.

Personal Year Three

Still not a time for major change. A peak Year Three is concerned with the intellect and is a year when our mental capacity reaches its peak. During this period you must stretch yourself to the full and really use your brains. Look, listen, and, above all, learn. You can amass knowledge in a variety of ways — join a study course, make the effort to travel more this year or become involved in a humanitarian scheme through which you will gain an insight into other aspects of life.

Personal Year Four

A year to relax and take things easy after all the changes made during year one, the soul-searching so necessary in year two and the sudden thirst for knowledge experienced in year three. A Personal Year Four is when you should safeguard your health — mental as well as physical.

Try not to make any major alterations such as changing your job or moving house as these sort of endeavours are rarely a great success when made under the influence of a Year Four. Give yourself time to adjust this year and allow your energy batteries time to recharge themselves. Look after yourself!

Personal Year Five

Still not a particularly dynamic year when no great changes or material progress can be expected. Brush up on all you have learned so far during this cycle. Keep your emotions firmly under control, conserve your energy, continue with your spiritual development and should you have any time left over it should be spent in re-awakening the artistic side of your nature.

The only change you could contemplate, with any hope of success, is a move from town to country.

Personal Year Six

This will be a particularly favourable year for relationships of all kinds. Business partnerships formed under the influence of a number six should prove profitable and personal involvements, of a romantic nature, could lead to marriage later in the year.

Those of you who are already married and in a Personal Year Six will find that the emphasis falls on your home and family during this period. On a personal level, you should endeavour to develop your artistic abilities — this is a year for beauty and creative achievement.

Personal Year Seven

Very similar in nature to a Personal Year Four — a time for consolidation and adjustment when no major changes, or progress, should be looked for. Try to establish some order and routine in your daily life, get your priorities right and try not to let your personal problems get out of proportion with reality.

Personal Year Eight

After the previous four years of gradual preparation, you are approaching the peak of this cycle. You should, by now, have learned how to use the freedom and independence which this year will bring in a responsible manner — especially where money is concerned. Full cyclic maturity is not reached until a Personal Year Nine.

Personal Year Nine

You have now reached the end of this nine year cycle of change which should finish on the crest of a wave. During this period you should demonstrate the tolerance and understanding you have learned, try to forget past injustices and settle old scores. Changes which you put into effect this year may not show results until well into Year One as the transition period between cycles frequently overlaps. This is a time to make new friends, visit new places and set your sights on the future.

A personal year can be sub-divided into three periods each of four-months' duration. This enables us to analyse the year in greater depth because we can establish which number influences each four-month period. These numbers are calculated in the following way:

1.   Re-enter the calculations used to find your personal year in the space provided.

2.   Enter the month of birth and the fourth month after it. (If the month of birth was December then April would be the fourth month, and so on.)

3.   Next enter the second four-month period where indicated. (If December to April was the first, April to August would be the second period).

4.   Enter the final four-month period in the same way. (Following our example this would be from August to December). The year has now been divided into three four-month periods commencing from the birth month.

5.   To find the number which influences the first period add your age (attained at the year of enquiry) to the year of enquiry, then reduce your total, first to a two-figure number and then to a single digit, in the usual manner.

6.   To find the number which influences the second period, add the unreduced (double digit) Date of Birth Number to the year under analysis and reduce the total.

7.   The influential number for the final four-month period is found by adding the unreduced Vowel Number to the year of enquiry and reducing the total to a single digit.

A hypothetical example has been included for your guidance (see page 138). It would be an interesting exercise for a student of numerology to analyse a past personal year in order to evaluate the accuracy of this system.

A Personal Year can be further sub-divided to discover the underlying trends for a particular month. Personal month analysis helps to pin-point when important events are likely to occur during a specific personal year.

It is quite simple to find the numerical influence for a particular month by adding the number of the month in question (January would be 1, February 2, March 3 and so on up to December which would be 12), to the unreduced (double digit) personal year number. Still working with the example given, if we needed to know the number influencing the month of April 1978 for Jonothan Robertson we would add 4 (for April) to 40 (the unreduced Personal

Example: JONOTHAN ROBERTSON born 3 DECEMBER 1956 (27/9)
             Year under analysis = 1978

Personal Year	*December to April*	*April to August*	*August to December*
	(Add age to year of enquiry)	(Add Date of Birth Number to year of enquiry)	(Add Vowel Number to year of enquiry)
$3+12+1978$	1978	1978	1978
$3+12+25=40/4$	22+	27+	30+
	(_____)	(_____)	(_____)
	2000 = 2	2005 = 7	2008 = 10/1

Year under analysis:

Personal	.... to	.... to	.... to
Year	....	....	....
	(Add age to year of enquiry)	(Add Date of Birth Number to year of enquiry)	(Add Vowel Number to year of enquiry)

Year Number) giving us a total of 44/8. Eight would therefore be the personal month number for April 1978.

The following list of keywords can be applied to Personal Months and Four-month periods:

1. new beginnings, decisions, exertion of energy, creativity.

2. co-operation, peace, agreement, balance.

3. freedom of movement and expression, diversity, enjoyment.

4. constructive effort, organization, capability, labour.

5. voluntary/involuntary change, travel, new horizons, personal freedom, intellectual development.

6. love, beauty, harmony, domesticity, family ties, artistic expression.

7. success, attainment of object, self-analysis, health worries.

8. money, commerce, strength, power, control, responsibility.

9. public service, humanitarian schemes, endings.

Some very elementary numerology is used to calculate whether a particular location is in/out of harmony with a person's numerical vibrations. This method can be applied to very large areas (such as countries and shires), towns, villages, streets and even house names, with equal effect.

To discover the ruling number of a particular place simply transpose all its letters into their numerical equivalents and reduce the total to a single digit. Once you have discovered the 'Place Number' intuition and numerological understanding will be required when comparing this with your four Personal Numbers (Date of Birth Number, Vowel Number, Consonant Number and Full Name Number). The following points should always be borne in mind:

1. Analogous numbers occur when the numbers under analysis are all odd or, conversely, all even. Such number combinations indicate harmony and a peaceful existence — therefore a place number which is in tune with your personal numbers would bring out your best qualities.

2. Conflicting numbers occur when some of the numbers being analysed are odd and others are even. A location whose number clashes with your personal numbers would not be the most suitable place for you to put down roots.

3. Group numbers are found when the numbers under consideration all come from the same numerical grouping.

Group 1 and numbers 1, 5 and 7. If all your personal numbers and the Place-Number, fall within Group One this indicates a location where you could develop your intellect, gain knowledge or continue your education. A place where you can really use your intuition because 1, 5 and 7 are all 'mind' numbers.

Group 2 numbers, 3, 6 and 9. If all your personal numbers, and the Place Number, fall within this group it indicates a location to pursue artistic talents such as painting or writing, a place where you will be creative and inspired. Emotionally you could be stretched to the full here because 3, 6 and 9 are 'expression' numbers.

Group 3 numbers 2, 4 and 8. If all your personal numbers, and the Place Number, fall within this group it indicates a location where business ventures will flourish and money problems could be solved. The numbers 2, 4 and 8 are all 'business' numbers.

4. Finally, always remember that when making any numerical comparisons odd numbers are generally masculine, active, creative and extrovert while even numbers are generally feminine, passive, receptive and introvert.

Some examples of the various categories of location are given below as well as space for your own calculations.

Countries:

America = 32/5
Australia = 30/3
Canada = 15/6
France = 29/11/2
Germany = 38/11/2

Holland = 30/3
Italy = 22/4
Russia = 24/6
South Africa = 49/4
United Kingdom = 65/11/2

Counties:

Kent = 14/5
Cumbria = 31/4
Norfolk = 37/1
Lancashire = 45/9

Yorkshire = 59/5
Cornwall = 35/8
Devon = 24/6
Avon = 16/7

Towns/Cities:

Birmingham = 58/4
London = 29/11/2
Manchester = 43/7
Bristol = 32/5

Liverpool = 52/7
Leeds = 18/9
Norwich = 45/9
Winchester = 52/7

Streets:

Station Road = 46/1
Royal Parade = 53/8
Regency Crescent = 74/11/2

Acacia Avenue = 41/5
School Lane = 41/5
High Street = 56/11/2

House Names:

Dunromin = 45/9
Laurel Cottage = 50/5

The Gables = 34/7
Holly Lodge = 52/7

....

....

POLITICAL ASTROLOGY

Political astrology is a system of correspondences whereby each country and city in the world is correlated with an astrological sign. Continents also have their own rulers. The whole concept is based upon the following four considerations:

1. the geophysical nature of each country

2. its climate

3. its inhabitants, and

4. its geographical location in relation to other countries/continents.

Quite simply, this means that as the planets pass through, or aspect, a particular sign there should be a reaction to their passage in the countries and cities with which the sign corresponds.

   If we take political astrology one logical step further and, using the number/planetary links already detailed in Chapter 5 number each house of the zodiac, we find ourselves an alternative method of ascertaining 'Place Numbers'. As with so many correspondence lists there are often discrepancies between one school of thought and another. Those given below are widely used but this does not preclude the existence of other, slightly different, lists. The student will have to decide which of the two methods of determining 'Place Numbers' he prefers to use as the two systems outlined do not interrelate.

Aries
Planet — Mars (positive)
Ruling Number — 9 (positive)
Regions — England, Denmark, Germany, Lesser Poland, Burgundy, Palestine, Syria, Japan.
Cities/Towns — Birmingham, Oldham, Leicester, Blackburn, Florence, Naples, Verona, Padua, Marseilles, Cracow, Saragossa, Utrecht, Capua, Brunswick.

Taurus
Planet — Venus (positive)
Ruling Number — 6 (positive)
Regions — Ireland, Poland, Asia Minor, Georgia, Caucasus, Grecian Archipelago, Cyprus, White Russia.
Cities/Towns — Dublin, Leipzig, Mantua, Parma, Palermo, Rhodes, St. Louis, Ashton-under-Lyne.

Gemini
Planet — Mercury (positive)
Ruling Number — 5 (positive)
Regions — United States of America, Belgium, Brabant, Lombardy, Lower Egypt, Sardinia, West of England, Armenia, Tripoli, Flanders, Wales.
Cities/Towns — London, Plymouth, Melbourne, Bruges, Cordova, Metz, Nuremberg, Versailles, Louvaine, San Francisco, Wolverhampton, Wednesbury.

Cancer
Planet — Moon
Ruling Number — 2
Regions — Scotland, Holland, Zeeland, North and West Africa, Isle of

Mauritius, Paraguay, Tunis, Algiers.
Cities/Towns — Amsterdam, St. Andrews, York, Venice, Berne, Lübeck, Magdeburg, Milan, Cadiz, New York, Manchester, Stockholm, Genoa, Constantinople, Deptford, Rochdale.

Leo
Planet — Sun
Ruling Number — 1
Regions — France, Italy, Bohemia, Sicily, Chaldea to Bassorah, North of Romania, Apulia, The Alps, and parts near Sidon and Tyre.
Cities/Towns — Rome, Bath, Bristol, Portsmouth, Philadelphia, Prague, Taunton, Damascus, Chicago, Bombay, Blackpool.

Virgo
Planet — Mercury (negative)
Ruling Number — 5 (negative)
Regions — Turkey, Switzerland, West Indies, Assyria, Mesopotamia from the Tigris to the Euphrates (Iraq), Crete, Croatia, Silesia, Babylonia, the Morea, Thessaly, Kurdestan, Greece, Virginia, Brazil.
Cities/Towns — Jerusalem, Corinth, Paris, Lyons, Tolouse, Cheltenham, Reading, Heidelberg, Norwich, Boston USA, Los Angeles, Maidstone, Strasburg, Brindisi, Bury.

Libra
Planet —Venus (negative)
Ruling Number — 6 (negative)
Regions — Algeria, Barbary, Bavaria, China, Judea, Jutland, Morocco, Norway, North Syria, Transvall, Catalonia, Queensland.
Cities/Towns — Fez, Valencia, Frankfurt on Oder, Dover, Liverpool, Messina, Worthing, East Grinstead, New Orleans, Washington DC., Baltimore, Cincinnati, Hull, Milwaukee, St. John's Newfoundland, Halifax, Stockport, Newcastle, Glossop.

Scorpio
Planet — Mars (negative)
Ruling Number — 9 (negative)
Regions — Austria, Indo-China, Tibet, Borders of Caspian, Upper Egypt, Savoy, North China, Burma, Argentina.
Cities/Towns Antwerp, Charleston, Frankfurt, Fribourg, Vienna, Lisbon, Johannesburg, Copenhagen, Middleton, Leeds, Nottingham.

Sagittarius
Planet — Jupiter (positive)
Ruling Number — 3 (positive)
Regions — Arabia, Australia, Cape Finisterre, Dalmatia, Hungary, Moravia,

Sclavonia, Spain, Tuscany, Provence in France, Madagascar.
Cities/Towns — Avignon, Buda, Cologne, Narbonne, Rottenburg, Nottingham, Sheffield, Stuttgart, Sunderland, Toledo, West Bromwich, Bradford.

Capricorn
Planet — Saturn (positive)
Ruling Number — 8 (positive)
Regions — India, Punjab, Afghanistan, Thrace, Macedonia, Illyria, Albania, Bosnia, Bulgaria, South-west Saxony, Mexico, Lithuania, Orkney Islands.
Cities/Towns — Oxford, Port Said, Prato in Tuscany, Brandenburg, Constanz, Brussels.

Aquarius
Planet — Saturn (negative) and Uranus
Ruling Number — 8 (negative) and 4.
Regions — Arabia, Prussia, Red Russia, USSR, Poland, Sweden, Tartary, Westphalia, Abyssinia.
Cities/Towns — Brighton, Ingolstadt, Salzburg, Trent, Hamburg, Salisbury.

Pisces
Planet — Jupiter (negative) and Neptune
Ruling Number — 3 (negative) and 7.
Regions — Portugal, Calabria, Galicia, Normandy, Nubia, Sahara Desert.
Cities/Towns — Alexandria, Seville, Compostella, Bournemouth, Farnham, Tiverton, Christchurch, Cowes, Grimsby, Southport, Lancaster, King's Lynn, Preston.

Chapter 12

COLOURS AND MUSIC

NUMBERS AND COLOURS

Have you ever wondered why you have a favourite colour, or the reason you feel uncomfortable in clothes of some other hue? One theory is that you are either in or out of tune with a specific colour. The numbers one to nine all have positive and negative colours associated with them and by applying simple numerology it's possible to determine which colours are right for you. Once you have discovered your 'right' colours, and if you use them correctly, you will be on the road to a more harmonious existence — more in tune with yourself.

Clothes and surroundings play an important part in our lives so, whenever possible, we should try to choose colour schemes which suit our personalities. There are several ways to determine your 'Colour Number' and the first, favoured by Cheiro, uses only the day of birth — where double numbers are reduced, and single numbers retained as follows:

Number Ones — all those people born on the 1st, 10th, 19th or 28th of the month.
Number Twos — all those people born on the 2nd, 11th, 20th or 29th of the month.
Number Threes — all those people born on the 3rd, 12th, 21st, or 30th of the month.
Number Fours — all those people born on the 4th, 13th, 22nd or 31st of the month.
Number Fives — all those people born on the 5th, 14th or 23rd of the month.
Number Sixes — all those people born on the 6th, 15th or 24th of the month.
Number Sevens — all those people born on the 7th, 16th or 25th of the month.
Number Eights — all those people born on the 8th, 17th or 26th of the month.
Number Nines — all those people born on the 9th, 18th or 27th of the month.

Some numerologists use the Date of Birth Number when determining the best colour combinations for a particular individual while others prefer to work with the Full Name Number.

Another slightly more complicated way to determine the Colour Number, calls for a full analysis of both the name and date of birth. One number will often seem to dominate the calculations and this should be selected as your Colour Number. However, if one number does not clearly stand out from the rest don't attempt to select your Colour Number by this process.

No two numerologists work alike, although their methods may be similar, and its up to the individual student to decide for himself which of the above methods of selection he prefers to use when establishing the Colour Number. It should also be noted that colour correspondences often differ, quite dramatically, between various schools of numerological thought. The number/colour correspondences detailed below are those used by Cheiro. He taught that certain gem stones could also be linked with each of the numbers from one to nine and believed they were most beneficial when worn next to the skin. These correspondences are also given below.

Number One
Principal/Foundation Colours — all shades of yellow and bronze right through to golden brown with the inclusion of orange and gold.
Subsidiary Colours — cream and white, purples, blues and deep pinks.
Colours to Avoid — green, black, and grey.
Gem Stones — any stone of a yellowish colour such as citrine, topaz, amber and yellow diamond.

Number Two
Principal/Foundation Colours — all shades of green, cream and white.
Subsidiary Colours — pale pink and pale blue.
Colours to Avoid — maroon, deep red, purple and black.
Gem Stones — jade, pearls, cat's eyes and moonstones.

Number Three
Principal/Foundation Colours — all shades of mauve and violet through to the palest purples and lilacs.
Subsidiary Colours — blue, rose pink and yellow.
Colours to Avoid — greens, black and grey, also dark browns.
Gem Stones — amethyst and garnets.

Number Four
Principal/Foundation Colours — half-tones and 'electric' colours such as blues and greys.
Subsidiary Colours — fawn, pale green and pale yellow.
Colours to Avoid — all bright, strong colours of any sort.
Gem Stones — sapphires of any shade.

Number Five
Principal/Foundation Colours — very light shades of any colour, particularly grey.

Subsidiary Colours — white or anything which is shiny or sparkles.
Colours to Avoid — any very dark or very bright colours.
Gem Stones — any pale stones especially if they sparkle, diamonds, silver and platinum.

Number Six
Principal/Foundation Colours — all shades of blue except the 'electric' or 'petrol' hues.
Subsidiary Colours — all shades of pink and rosy reds.
Colours to Avoid — black and dark purple.
Gem Stones — turquoise and emeralds.

Number Seven
Principal/Foundation Colours — all shades of green and yellow, also gold.
Subsidiary Colours — all shades of very pale or pastel colours.
Colours to Avoid — any really deep or dark colours.
Gem Stones — any white stones, moonstones, cat's eyes, pearls, moss agate.

Number Eight
Principal/Foundation Colours — dark grey, dark blue, purple and black.
Subsidiary Colours — all brown and russet shades.
Colours to Avoid — all pale colours, bright reds, greens or yellows.
Gem Stones — all dark stones, dull rubies, carbuncles, amethyst, black pearl, black diamond, but best of all a deep-toned sapphire.

Number Nine
Principal/Foundation Colours — pink, rose, crimson, red and reddish-purple — the darker and richer the shade the better.
Subsidiary Colours — all shades of blue.
Colours to Avoid — green, yellows, browns and black.
Gem Stones — rubies, garnets and bloodstones.

NUMBERS AND MUSIC

Numbers and music show very marked affinities and the discovery of a relationship between the two is generally credited to Pythagoras. Each of the single digit numbers can be linked with a particular style of music as follows:

One Bright, cheerful-sounding music, usually with a fairly pronounced beat, is associated with the number One. This can range from the arrangements of James Last, Bert Kampfaert and Herb Alpert, through most of today's popular repertoire to standards, the big band sound and even some classical rondos.

Two String and wind instruments, such as the cello, violin, harp, pipes, flute and so on, are generally linked with the number Two. The music these instruments can produce embraces most of the classical repertoire with particular emphasis on the symphonic works of the great composers.

Threes The number Three is also generally associated with the 'middle of the road' style of music already described under the heading of the number One but with the emphasis, in this instance, on 'popular' music rather than 'pop music'.

Four Organ and choral music is linked with the number Four, especially when it is plaintive, melancholy or religious — and preferably all three at once! This could include the works of J.S. Bach, Corelli and many of the pre-Renaissance composers such as John Dowland and William Byrd.

Five The types of music associated with the number Five are either original compositions, or pieces which are written in a very unusual, out of the ordinary style. While jazz and the blues have clearly defined origins the music itself depends upon immediate improvisation and could therefore be regarded as 'original'. Also included are some of the approaches which do not conform to conventional music form and construction. Here some synthesizer or electronic compositions can be included along with avant-garde and *musique concrète*.

Six The number Six is numerologically associated with sweet, romantic music of all kinds especially when it also has a lilting rhythm. This includes a great deal of todays 'standards' which have a romantic content. George Gershwin, Cole Porter and other romantic composers — even stretching as far back as Gaetano Donizetti (1797–1848) — can be included.

Seven The number Seven shares the same musical affinities as the number Two (see above).

Eight The number Eight shares the same musical affinities as the number Four (see above for details).

Nine The number Nine is particularly associated with martial music and stirring, patriotic anthems. This could include the works of such composers as Souza, who wrote a great many marches, and Elgar, composer of *Pomp and Circumstance*. Even Wagner could be considered in this vein.

It is interesting to note the accuracy with which the number/musical correspondences tie in with other aspects of numerology, particularly when specific countries and their planetary rulers are used for comparison.

The number Nine is astrologically coupled with Mars, the planet associated with war and destruction. It even represents the metal iron from which the weapons of warfare are manufactured. Germany and England both come under the planetary rulership of Mars (=9) and if we look under the Number Nine in the musical correspondences we will see that martial, patriotic music fits in very well with the national image of both countries. Shakespeare was probably hinting at this symbolism when he wrote 'England, thou seat of Mars'.

Ireland is a country governed by Venus (=6), the planet of love and beauty, and these sentiments are expressed in the lilting, sweetly-romantic music so often associated with the Emerald Isle.

Scotland is ruled by two planets — the Moon (=2) and Saturn (=8) and when the numbers associated with these planets are combined in a numerical context we arrive at plaintive, melancholy (8) pipe (2) music — a perfect description of the Scottish musical image.

Another country under dual planetary rulership is Wales — Uranus (=4) and Mercury (=5) being the two planets in question. Wales is primarily associated with choral/choir music (4) although it does have another, lesser known, side to it musically and some original and extremely unusual (5) compositions are produced in its valleys.

The United States of America come under the rulership of Mercury and the number Five. America is a vast country which has received contributions from many diverse lifestyles during its cultural development. Under the influence of the number Five, the American people seem to possess an innate appreciation of original music, especially when it is strikingly different, which makes it the natural birthplace for syncopated music and jazz.

Chapter 13

HEALTH AND HERBS

Numerologists readily accept that numbers have an extraordinary influence upon the lives and destinies of every man, woman and child on this earth and that the date of birth is probably the most important number of all because it cannot be changed in any way — unlike a name which can be spelt differently, shortened or even, in some cases, altered completely.

Students of the occult have discovered that certain herbs, fruit and plants are related to individual planets which, in their turn, make their presence felt at different times of the year. Therefore, when both beliefs are combined, it should be possible to devise a blueprint for a healthier existence simply by reducing the date of birth to a single number, being aware of the health problems connected with that particular number and of the herbs and plants which are most beneficial to people whose birthdate reduces to that number. Cheiro felt that it was only necessary to reduce the actual day of birth and some numerologists prefer to follow his method. It would be a useful exercise to try both and compare the results.

Full date of birth reduced   =
Day of birth reduced   =

The Order of the Golden Dawn gave a great deal of time and thought to drawing up their list of correspondences and Aleister Crowley in *The Book of Thoth* also discusses the subject at some length. The correspondences detailed here are attributed to Cheiro, however, as so often occurs, there are discrepancies to be found between the different versions and space has been provided to enter any observations of your own after each number.

NUMBER ONE - THE SUN

The heart and circulatory system are associated with the Sun and number Ones could be troubled with irregular circulation, high blood-pressure, palpitations or heart disease at some time in their lives. Bright sunlight can also damage the eyes and people who come under this number should particularly guard against this.

Beneficial Herbs, Fruit and Plants for Number Ones
Borage *(Borrago officinalis)* — believed to stem from Latin, *borrago,* being a corruption of the words *cor ago* 'I stimulate the heart'. The stem and leaves, as a decoction, are used to treat fevers, influenza and contagious diseases such as measles, scarlet fever and chicken-pox.
Chamomile *(Matricaria chamomilla)* — and be drunk as a herb tea or bathed on the eyelids to combat inflammation and conjuctivitis.
Eyebright *(Euphrasia officinalis)* — a mild decoction can be taken internally for coughs and colds or bathed on the eyelids for eye conditions.
Lavender *(Lavandula spica* or *Lavandula vera)* — is a useful disinfectant, vulnerary, sedative, stimulant, tonic and carminative.
St. John's Wort *(Hypericum perforatum)* — used as a treatment for gout, rheumatism, burns and dressing wounds. Can be used both internally and externally for curing 'minor ailments'.
Sorrel *(Rumex acetosa)* — useful as a laxative, for the treatment of acne and eczema, and as a poultice for boils and abscesses. (Will, incidentally, also clean silver, bamboo, and remove ink stains!)

Figure 27   Bay — *Laurus nobilis.*

Thyme *(Thymus vulgaris)* — a powerful antiseptic. Taken as an infusion for poor digestion, cardiac weakness, angina, fits of coughing, insomnia and menstrual disorders or as a gargle for sore throats.

Also: raisins, saffron, cloves, nutmeg, gentian root, bay leaves, oranges, lemons, dates, ginger, barley and honey. Years for important changes in health (good or bad) — 19th, 28th, 37th and 55th. (It should be noted that these years all reduce to the number one). Months when ill health or strain from overwork are most likely — October, December and January.

Personal observations:

NUMBER TWO — THE MOON

The digestive system, lymphatic system, synovial fluids, stomach, breasts, ovaries and sympathetic nervous system are associated with the Moon, and Number Twos could have a tendency to disorders or disease of these parts.

Beneficial Herbs, Fruit and Plants for Number Twos

Cabbage *(Brassica oleracea)* — as a poultice for varicose ulcers, burns, migraines and lumbago. Cabbage can also be used as a decoction for whooping-cough, bronchial infections and hoarseness.

Chicory *(Cichorium intybus)* — taken for the treatment of anaemia, it also stimulates the stomach and bowels, aids digestion and relieves liver disorders.

Lettuce *(Lactuca sativa)* — since ancient times it has been known for its narcotic properties which facilitate sleep and sedate the sexual drive. Also useful for gastric spasms, palpitations and congestion of the liver when taken as a decoction.

Plantain *(Plantago major)* — used as a poultice for stings and bites, varicose ulcers and wounds. Also as a decoction for bronchitis, whooping-cough, enteritis and dysentery.

Also: turnips, cucumber, melon, rapeseed, colewort, moonwort and willow ash. Years for important changes in health (good or bad) — 20th, 29th, 47th and 65th. Months when ill health or strain from overwork are most likely — January, February and July.

Personal observations:

NUMBER THREE — JUPITER

The liver and disposition of fats are associated with Jupiter. People whose birthdate or date of birth reduces to a three should guard against excess strain on the nervous system caused by overwork. They could also be susceptible to attacks of neuritis, sciatica and skin troubles.

Beneficial Herbs, Fruits and Plants for Number Threes
Apple *(Malus communis)* — prescribed for constipation, intestinal infections, gout, mental overstrain, anaemia, excess cholesterol in the blood. They promote sound sleep if eaten last thing at night.

Figure 28   Apple — *Malus communis.*

Barberry *(Berberis vulgaris)* — good for the treatment of rheumatism, gout or lumbar pains.
Bilberry *(Vaccinium myrtillus)* — as a decoction for cystitis and skin diseases such as pruritus and eczema. The berries are used in the treatment of diarrhoea, enteritis and dysentery and in a compress form for the relief of haemorrhoids.
Cherry *(Prunus cerasus)* — the berries are rich in vitamins and when crushed and applied to the skin help tone up tired tissues. If applied to the forehead they relieve migraine.
Dandelion *(Taraxacum officinale)* — infusions of the leaves and root are tonic, depurative and also mildly laxative. Dandelion is beneficial for hepatic congestion, jaundice, sluggish digestion, diabetes and gout.
Lungwort *(Pulmonaria officinalis)* — for chest complaints, bronchial inflammation and tuberculosis, it soothes coughs and acts as an expectorant.
Mint *(Mentha)* — is the great remedy for digestive disorders and also tones up the nervous system.
Strawberry *(Fragaria vesca)* — has a high iron content and is rich in salicylic acid which aids the liver, kidneys and joints. The berries when applied externally are extremely good for the complexion and help to combat wrinkles.

Also: beetroot, asparagus, endive, mulberries, peaches, olives, rhubarb, gooseberries, pomegranates, pineapple, figs and wheat. Years for important changes in health (good or bad) — 12th, 21st, 39th, 48th and 57th. Months when ill health or strain from overwork are most likely — December, February, June and September.

Personal observations:

NUMBER FOUR — URANUS

Uranus is associated with mental disorders, sudden nervous breakdowns, hysteria and all forms of spasms, cramps and palpitations. Number Fours could be subject to mysterious ailments which are particularly difficult to diagnose, at some time in their lives. They are also rather prone to melancholia, anaemia and pains in the back of the head and neck.

Beneficial Herbs, Fruit and Plants for Number Fours

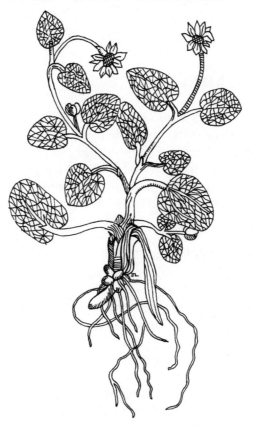

Figure 29 Lesser Celandine — *Ranunculus ficaria.*

Celandine, Lesser *(Ranunculus ficaria)* — belongs to the buttercup family. The

roots consist of small whitish bulbs and the plant is a remedy for haemorrhoids.

Sage *(Salvia officinalis)* — the 'sacred herb' of the Romans which aids the digestion and acts as a tonic. Sage leaves dried and smoked like tobacco bring relief to asthma sufferers.

Wild Spinach *(Beta vulgaris)* — rich in iron and various trace elements; vital for a healthy body.

Also: wintergreen, medlars, Icelandmoss and Solomon's seal. Number Fours can derive great benefit from mental suggestion, hypnotism and electric treatment of all kinds. They should try to avoid red meat and highly seasoned dishes such as curries and Chilli Con Carne if at all possible. Years for important changes in health (good or bad) — 13th, 22nd, 31st, 40th, 49th and 58th. Months when ill health or strain from overwork are most likely — January, February, July, August and September.
Personal observations:

NUMBER FIVE — MERCURY

Physiologically Mercury is associated with the central nervous system, the brain generally, the respiratory system, the thyroid and all sense, perception and sensory organs. Number Fives should not put undue strain on their nervous system although they are naturally inclined to live too much on their nerves and to attempt too much mentally. Insomnia could be one of their main problems and periods of self-imposed rest and quiet during each day would be beneficial.

Beneficial Herbs, Fruit and Plants for Number Fives
Hazel *(Corylus avellana)* — the nuts are a major source of protein amongst wild plants.

Marjoram, Sweet *(Origanum majorana)* — is considered to be an antispasmodic, expectorant, antiseptic, stomachic and vulnerary and as such is prescribed for nervous disorders of the stomach, migraine and insomnia.

Oats *(Avena sativa)* — are a treatment for insomnia, loss of appetite and exhaustion. They also assist convalescence. Oats may also be used as a poultice for sharp stabbing pains (stitches) and lumbago.

Parsley *(Apium petroselinum)* — is rich in iron, calcium, vitamins and various trace-elements indispensable to the body. Crushed fresh leaves will relieve irritation from insect stings and can be used as an emergency dressing for wounds.

Also: parsnips, sea-kale, mushrooms, caraway seeds and nuts of all kinds. Years for important changes in health (good or bad) — 14th, 23rd, 41st and 50th. Months when ill health or strain from overwork are most likely — June, September and December.
Personal observations:

NUMBER SIX — VENUS

Venus is associated with the lumbar region, venous circulation, parathyroids and, indirectly, the throat and kidneys. Number Sixes could have a tendency to disorders or disease through these parts. However, they generally have a strong constitution especially if they work in the open or exercise regularly. Women of this number have a tendency to suffer with their breasts and in later life members of both sexes could experience some trouble with their circulation.

Beneficial Herbs, Fruit and Plants for Number Sixes

Dog Rose *(Rosa canina)* — the hips (seeds) possess numerous properties and are an old remedy for gravel, kidney stones and renal colic.

Vervain *(Verbena officinalis)* — sometimes called Juno's tears. The plant is used as a decoction for the treatment of general debility, jaundice, feverish complaints and irregular menstruation especially when this is accompanied by migraine.

Violet *(Viola odorata)* — the flowers, in syrup form, are beneficial for colds, bronchitis and whooping cough while the leaves make a fine poultice for benign tumours and cracked nipples.

Walnut *(Juglans regia)* — a decoction of the leaves is helpful for anaemia, disorders of the digestive tract, disorders of the female reproductive organs and also excessive perspiration.

Also: all kinds of beans, melons, apricots, almonds, juice of the maidenhair-fern, daffodils and musk. Years for important changes in health (good or bad) — 15th, 24th, 42nd, 51st and 60th. Months when ill health or strain from overwork are most likely — May, October and November.
Personal observations:

NUMBER SEVEN — NEPTUNE

Neptune seems particularly associated with the thalamus (the part of the brain from which optic and hearing nerves spring), the spinal canal and the nervous and mental processes generally. Number Sevens are easily worried or annoyed by either circumstances or people. They are also rather inclined to magnify their problems and tend to become despondent and depressed at the slightest little thing. As a rule they are usually stronger mentally than physically and often overtax their strength to the point of exhaustion. Sevens are also inclined to have some peculiar delicacy of the skin which usually manifests itself as being extremely sensitive to friction or excessively sweaty.

Beneficial Herbs, Fruit and Plants for Number Sevens
Blackberry *(Rubus fruticosus)* — the fresh, crushed leaves will check bleeding and the berries have astringent, tonic and restorative properties.
Elder *(Sambucus nigra)* — the leaves are both diuretic and depurative; the flowers, as a decoction, are beneficial as any eyewash for conjunctivitis, to soothe chilblains, and the berries are used as purgative.
Hop *(Humulus lupulus)* — regenerates and purifies tired blood. A pillow filled with hops is considered helpful for combatting sleeplessness and nervous irritation.
Juniper *(Juniperus communis)* — juniper berries are used for the treatment of general debility, sluggishness of the nervous system and skin complaints because they contain a depurative.

Also: linseed, mushrooms, grapes and fruit juice of all kinds.
Years for important changes in health (good or bad) — 7th, 16th, 25th, 34th 43rd, 52nd and 61st.
Months when ill health or strain from overwork are most likely — January, February, July and August.
Personal observations:

NUMBER EIGHT — SATURN

The planet Saturn is usually associated with the skeletal system, skin, teeth, the gall bladder and spleen. People whose birthday or date of birth reduce to the number eight could have trouble with their liver, bile or intestines at some stage in their lives and are generally prone to suffer with headaches and rheumatism.

Beneficial Herbs, Fruit and Plants for Number Eights
Angelica *(Angelica archangelica)* — Renaissance doctors called its root the 'root of the Holy Ghost' because of its 'great and divine properties' against very serious illness. It was thought, like ginseng, to be the elixir of long life and was widely used as a medicine during the great outbreaks of plague in the sixteenth century.
Marsh Mallow *(Althaea officinalis)* — used internally to soothe irritation, bronchitis, colds, laryngitis, enteritis, cystitis, sore throats and dental abscesses.
Shepherd's Purse *(Thlaspi bursa pastoris)* — the plant should preferably be used fresh. It acts on circulatory disturbances, inflammation of the mucosae and high temperatures. It is also beneficial, as a decoction, for haemorrhages, excessive menstrual discharge and spitting of blood.

Also: ragwort, pilewort, gravel root, mandrake root and celery. Number Eights would benefit from a vegetarian diet of fruit, herbs and vegetables and should avoid animal food if at all possible. Years for important changes in health (good or bad) — 17th, 26th, 35th, 44th, 53rd and 62nd. Months when ill health or strain from overwork are most likely — December, January, February and July.
Personal observations:

NUMBER NINE — MARS

Mars is physiologically associated with the muscular system, uro-genital system and gonads (sex glands), red corpuscles of the blood and the kidneys. Number Nines are highly susceptible to contagious diseases of all kinds such as measles, chicken-pox, scarlatina, and so on.

Beneficial Herbs, Fruit and Plants for Number Nines
Broom *(Sarothamnus Scorparius)* — was once used for making the broomsticks ridden by medieval witches and today is still helpful as a diuretic when employed in the treatment of disorders of the urinary tract, oedema, nephritis and rheumatism.
Garlic *(Allium sativum)* — never go a day without garlic because it is one of the most remarkable 'food remedies' known to man.
Nettle *(Urtica dioica)* — nettle juice can be taken medicinally for internal and uterine haemorrhages, frequent nose bleeds, haemorrhoids and enteritis. Nettle soup is also a very nutritious dish although the plant should not be picked for eating after the beginning of June when it becomes coarse and rather bitter in taste.
Onion *(Allium cepa)* — raw onion is particularly beneficial in the treatment of

exhaustion, genito-urinary infections, arthritis, rheumatism, diabetes and retention of urine. As a poultice it provides relief for chilblains, rheumatic pains and burns.

Wormwood *(Artemisia absinthium)* — when taken in large amounts, and in a highly concentrated form, it is a poison that is rightly illegal. However, it is still a valuable plant when used with care. In carefully measured doses wormwood is a powerful tonic, a preventative against seasickness and also promotes menstrual discharge.

Also: leeks, horse-radish, mustard-seed, pepper, rape and white hellebore. Number Nines should be particularly careful about the amount of alcoholic drinks or wines they consume and should also avoid over-rich food of all types. Years for important changes in health (good or bad) — 9th, 18th, 26th, 36th, 45th and 63rd. Months when ill health or strain from overwork are most likely — April, May, October and November.

Personal observations:

Chapter 14

ARITHOMANCY

Arithomancy, or numeromancy as it is sometimes known, is an ancient offshoot of numerology seldom heard of today. It evolved for use in divination rather than the character analysis with which modern day numerology is primarily concerned. However, obsolete it may have become, but it is still worth a closer study as an important stage in the development of numerology as we now know it.

Pythagoras is thought to be responsible for the following number/letter correspondences although this is open to conjecture for many reasons.

A = 1	B = 2	C = 3	D = 4
E = 5	F = 6	G = 7	H = 8
I = 9	K = 10	L = 20	M = 30
N = 40	O = 50	P = 60	Q = 70
R = 80	S = 90	T = 100	U = 200
X = 300	Y = 400	Z = 500	J = 600
V = 700	Hi = 800	Hv = 900	W = 1400 (double V)

When employing this method the numerical equivalent of a name is found in the usual manner — that is by changing each letter into a number. However, the total, should it exceed 1390, is reduced by deleting the first numeral. Therefore, if the total should come to 3710 the number 3 would be omitted and the number to work with would be 710.

Some numerologists when applying arithomancy feel that the sound of the name is more important that its actual spelling and calculate their totals phonetically. It would be a useful exercise to try both ways and compare the outcome.

Name (normal spelling)   =
Name (phonetic spelling)   =

Once the name total has been calculated it is very easy to interpret from the list of meanings, as the following three examples show.

Example 1

Total 490   Meaning: 490 = spiritual advancement

Example 2

Total 707   Meaning: 700 = authority, power
                                      7 = happiness

Example 3

Total 2833   Meaning: 800 = victory
Reduced = 833   33 = good fortune

Number Meanings

1. ambition, passion, purpose
2. ruin, fatality
3. the recognition of God, the soul, destiny
4. wisdom, strength, power
5. marriage, happiness
6. perfected labour
7. happiness
8. justice, protection
9. worry, fallibility
10. success, future happiness
11. discord, evasion, lack of integrity
12. city, town, name
13. injustice
14. sacrifice, generosity
15. kindness, integrity
16. love, happiness, integrity
17. carelessness
18. selfishness, callousness
19. foolishness
20. wisdom, asceticism
21. occult wisdom
22. retribution
23. prejudice
24. travel
25. intelligence, productivity
26. humanitarianism

27. resoluteness, bravery
28. love
29. news, information
30. marriage, recognition, fame
31. desire for acclaim
32. marriage
33. good fortune
34. actions in one life determine one's condition in lives to follow
35. kindness, gentleness, serenity, charm
36. genius, an advanced consciousness of being
37. faithfulness
38. spite, avarice
39. distinction, respect
40. celebrations, a wedding
41. shame, dishonour
42. anxiety, possible ill health
43. spiritual awareness
44. happiness and prosperity
45. descendants
46. abundance
47. a long and happy life
48. good taste and judgement
49. greed
50. a great improvement in circumstances
60. a temporary separation from a loved one
70. knowledge, wisdom, intuition
75. material pleasures
77. repentance, forgiveness
80. restoration to health
81. great knowledge and wisdom
90. temporary problems and set-backs
100. divine favour
120. commendation, honour
200. fear, uncertainty, indecision
215. misfortune
300. love of wisdom
318. God's messenger
350. hope, justice
360. home, fellowship

365. astrology, astronomy
400. long journeys
490. spiritual advancement
500. spiritual awareness
600. spiritual and material perfection
666. malevolence, conspiracy, vindictiveness
700. authority, power
800. victory
900. quarrels, war
1000. compassion
1095. caution, restraint
1260. anxiety
1390. dejection

The answers arrived at with this method of divination are a little cryptic, to say the least, in comparison with the amount of effort required to reach them and it is most probably the limited scope of the answers that has caused arithomancy to have fallen from popularity in modern times.

Chapter 15

THE QABALAH AND TAROT

Tarot and mystic numerology have been linked by many students of the occult, among them Eliphas Levi, the Order of the Golden Dawn and Aleister Crowley as well as the palmist/numerologist Cheiro. In this chapter we will be taking a look at the Qabalah to discover why each Tarot card is linked with either a sephiroth or path of the Tree of Life to enable you to understand how this information is translated into numerological terms. Each of the Tarot cards will be given a number, a fixed meaning from both a positive and a negative point of view (for numbers in life which seldom alter), and a temporary vibration for use when looking into the future or plotting a particular course in life with numerology.

We are only concerned with the numbers 1-78. Seventy-eight was not chosen at random or simply because it happens to be the number of cards in the Tarot deck — it represents the total and complete experience. The 1 to 9 cycle of learning plus the numbers 10 and 11 (which are added to allow time for personal development, and to put into practice the experience gained during the 1 to 9 period), plus the number twelve (which represents the twelve months of the year), brings us to the number seventy-eight — a complete cycle $(1+2+3+4+5+6+7+8+9+10+11+12=78)$.

The year, representing as it does an important period upon which to base calculations, can be found by a second method of calculation. Once the numbers 1 to 9 have been passed, what is known as the 'greater symbolism of numbers' begins. This continues until we reach number 45, or 5×9. When the mystical number 7, is added to 45 we arrive at 52 (the number of weeks in a year and also the number of cards in a deck of ordinary playing cards). Finally when 52 is multiplied this time by the mystical number 7 it gives us the answer 364 — the number of days in a year (in ancient times).

There is another interesting story concerning the number of days in a year. Early astronomers believed that the Sun took 360 days to go round the zodiac. They wished to keep this discovery a secret and so hid this number in the divine name Mithras $(M40+I10+Th9+R100+A1+S200=360)$. Later they discovered that 365 days was a more accurate calculation and they hid this knowledge in the word Abraxas (A1 + B2 + R100 + A1 + X60 + A1 + S200 = 365). When the name Mithras was altered in spelling to Meithras (365) it could still contain their secret.

THE QABALAH

Qabalah is a Hebrew word meaning knowledge or tradition. The story goes that the secret wisdom, which came direct from God, was whispered to Moses on Mount Sinai, who passed it on to the seventy elders, who in turn handed it down to their successors, and so on. For centuries its doctrines remained essentially oral. Now the word Qabalah has come to be used as a term which describes a vast mass of arcane wisdom amassed over many centuries, the two most important literary contributions to its philosophy being the *Sefer Yetzirah* (Book of Creation) and the *Zohar* (Book of Splendour). The first comes from Palestine/Babylon between the third and sixth centuries AD and the *Zohar* is believed to have been written by Moses de Léon in Spain during the late thirteenth century. Although predominantly Jewish in concept, the Qabalah has been a rewarding source of study and contemplation for occultists, philosophers, psychologists, humanists and numerologists throughout the world since Renaissance times. It made such a deep impression upon the seeker after truth that it evolved into Platonic, Gnostic (Neo-Platonic), Muslim and Christian variations of the central theme.

The Qabalah teaches that the way to reach God is through knowledge acquired along the path to wisdom. Qabalists believe that something of God can be found in all things and that all things which exist within the universe are interconnecting parts of an organized whole — although no apparent connection need necessarily be visible between them. Their God — En Sof, Infinite Radiance — is completely unknowable and unapproachable. He was not responsible for creating the universe but rather it flowed from him. 'A single ray of light burst out from the closed confines of En Sof, and from this light came nine further lights' is the creation story according to the Book of Splendour.

The Ten lights are the sephiroth (numbers) which are regarded as the forces behind man and the universe. Twenty-two paths connect the ten sephiroth to each other. Each sephiroth is named and numbered (Qabalists were greatly influenced by Pythagorean number theory) and each path corresponds with a letter from the Hebrew alphabet. Together they form the Tree of Life—a map of the universe which classifies and embraces everything.

It was believed that the soul originated from God and descended the Tree of Life one sephira at a time absorbing characteristics from each as it went. By the time it reached the earth, the soul had become a miniature model of the universe and acquired its physical body. This descent illustrates the Qabalistic belief that man is a reflection of both God and the universe. Once on earth, however, the soul wished to return to God. This involved a hazardous journey back up the Tree of Life armed only for protection and advancement with the knowledge acquired during life to accomplish the ascent.

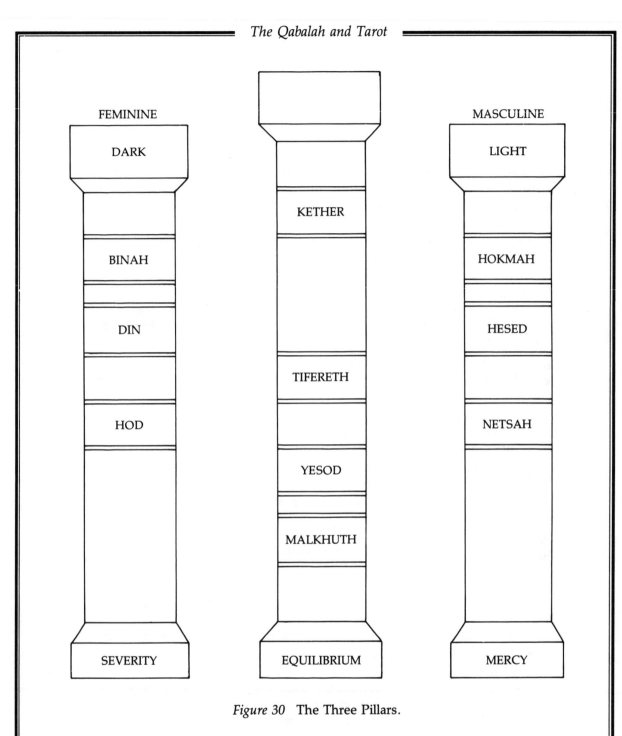

Figure 30 The Three Pillars.

Qabalists sometimes divide the sephiroth into three different groups or pillars in order to gain a deeper understanding of the relationship between the ten sephiroth. The right-hand Pillar of Mercy unites the male, positive, light principles of the universe. The left-hand Pillar of Severity unites the female, passive, dark principles and the centre Pillar of Equilibrium (sometimes known as the Pillar of Consciousness or Soul) attempts to reconcile the male and female pillars and to mediate between the forces of light and darkness.

The names, numbers and a brief description of the ten sephiroth are as follows:

1. KETHER — the Supreme Crown

Corresponds with God. Divinity. The first emanation of the unknowable Godhead. A soul which reaches this sephira reached God. It is guarded by creatures described as follows: 'and everyone had four faces and everyone had four wings'. (Ezekiel Chapter 1.)
Symbol — the point.
For meditation — an old man with a beard in profile, perhaps the Tarot trump card VIIII, The Hermit.

2. HOKMAH — Divine Wisdom

Corresponds with the stars or the zodiac. The father of the Universe and the force behind actions, creativity and changes. Guarded by the Wheels in Ezekiel which moved around and had the spirit of life in them.
Symbols — the phallus, the tower and the straight line.
For meditation — a bearded man, perhaps the Tarot trump card V, The Pope or The Hierophant.

3. BINAH — Understanding

The mother of the Universe, passive and receptive until fertilized and then prolific. It represents slumbering potentiality and all-embracing understanding. It has conflicting attributes of life/death and good/evil. Associated with the mother goddess and with Hecate, the goddess of sorcery and witchcraft.
Planet — Saturn, the planet of stability, old age and fate.
Symbols — female genitals, the oval, the circle, the diamond and the cup.
For meditation — a mature woman, perhaps the Tarot trump card II, The Papess.

4. HESED — Love and Mercy

The builder. The male force which organizes, erects, civilizes and governs. The merciful, loving father, the guide and protector.
Planet —Jupiter.
Symbols — king's sceptre, magician's wand, bishop's crook, the pyramid, the Greek cross, and the unicorn (which represents virility and power).
For meditation — a king on his throne, perhaps the Tarot trump card IV, The Emperor.

5. DIN — Power

Also sometimes known as Geburah. It stands for severity and discipline. It is the force that destroys and which lies behind all wars and hatred. Often believed to be the source of all evil in the world. Associated with a fierce and deadly mythical creature called the basilisk.
Planet — Mars.

Symbols — the pentagon, the chain, the sword, the spear and the scourge.
For meditation — a warrior in a chariot, perhaps the Tarot trump card VII, The Chariot.

6. TIFERETH — Beauty

Christian Qabalists linked this sephira with Christ because of its direct descent from Kether (which represents God) and because the sun, which is associated with Tifereth, also had an early symbolic association with Christ. It represents vital energy.

Planet — the Sun.

Symbols — a lion (the sun), a phoenix (immortality) and a child (mortality).

For meditation — a great king or a sacrificed child, perhaps the Tarot trump card XII, The Hanged Man.

7. NETSAH — Victory and Endurance

It represents the senses, animal drives and passions and is the male force behind nature. Associated with rhythm, movement, colour and the arts. It is linked to Venus, the goddess of sensuality and nature.

Planet — Venus.

Symbols — the wryneck.

For meditation — a beautiful naked woman, perhaps the Tarot trump card XVII, The Star or Crowley's 'Thoth' Tarot XI, Lust.

8. HOD — Majesty and Splendour

It represents the higher qualities of the mind such as intuition, inspiration, insight, reason and logic. A female force. Like the other feminine sephiroth it displays a conflict between good and evil which, in this instance, is wisdom coupled with treachery and cunning.

Planet — Mercury.

Symbols — Mercury was the god of magic and intelligence and the twin serpents from his wand, the Caduceus, form the figure eight and are often associated with Hod.

For meditation — an hermaphrodite, an alchemic symbol for the metal mercury.

9. YESOD — Foundation

Nine is the number of initiation into magic and the occult and Yesod is connected with mystery and magical powers. It is the basis of all active forces of God and stands for creativity (both sexual and mental).

Planet — the Moon.

Symbol — the elephant (which represents strength and intelligence).

For meditation — a beautiful, naked man.

10. MALKHUTH — the Earthly Kingdom, the Earth

Also sometimes known as Shekinah — the Bride of God. The Qabalah strives to unite God (the first sephira) with his bride (the tenth sephira).

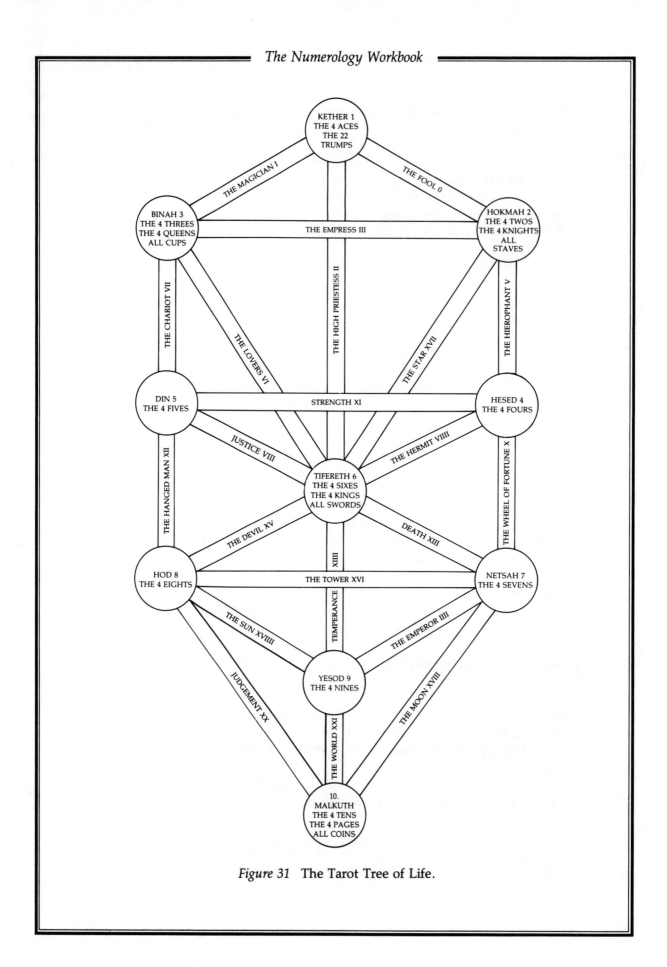

Figure 31 **The Tarot Tree of Life.**

Symbol — the sphinx, which represents the unity of heaven and earth.
For meditation — a young, crowned woman seated on a throne, perhaps the Tarot trump card III, The Empress.

It was the frequent recurrence of the figure twenty-two which first led Alliette, the Barber and occultist, to put forward the idea that the Tarot trumps were somehow linked with a Qabalistic document. Eliphas Levi took this proposal one stage further and successfully linked each Tarot trump with a letter of the Hebrew alphabet and with one of the twenty-two paths of the Tree of Life. Levi's theories of correspondences were greatly expanded by Papus (Dr Gerard Encausse), the English occultist S.L. Macgregor Mathers and the Order of the Golden Dawn. Aleister Crowley, in his work *Liber 777*, listed 194 sets of correspondences between Hebrew names, numbers, Tarot cards, planets, zodiac signs, perfumes, colours, gods of all religions, and so on. And so the Tarot cards became firmly linked with the Qabalah and the Tree of Life in particular.

Joseph Maxwell, the French Procureur-General, made an attempt to apply European numerology to the Tarot cards and to find significance in the numbers given to the trumps themselves. We know that in numerology all numbers are eventually reduced to a single number between one and nine and Maxwell expected to find some overt relationship between cards which reduced to the same number but was unsuccessful in his attempt.

N.B. In ancient times the universally accepted symbolism of both single and compound (double-digit) numbers was shown by means of simple pictures. This symbolism is still to be found today within the cards of the Tarot deck.

Single numbers 1 to 9 denote individuality and character while compound numbers (10 onwards) belong to the more spiritual side of life and show hidden influences which can effect the future and destiny of the individual.

THE TAROT TRUMPS — THE CARDS OF THE MAJOR ARCANA

1. I, The Magician
The Magician signifies the first stage of conscious existence. He represents the conscious mind and the establishment of self-awareness. When linked with one of the four Personal Numbers, this card indicates a pioneering individual who is prepared to use his intellect to set the world to rights. A person who's never satisfied with things the way they are and is always seeking to find fresh alternatives or new solutions to age-old problems. He has boundless energy and needs to see, understand and experience everything in the course of his lifetime. He needs to be free to do as he pleases and fights back hard against personal restraint in any guise. Second best is never good enough for him and he needs to rise to the top in whatever field of endeavour he becomes involved in. He is certainly never afraid to take responsibility — however grave it may appear.

THE MAGICIAN I

In his negative aspect, he can appear as the Juggler, a rather tricky individual who never lets his right hand know what his left hand is doing. He experiences great difficulty in facing up to life and all its attendant problems and is rather a weak-willed character, sadly lacking in courage and moral fibre.

When the Magician exerts only a passing influence on life this can point to the beginning of an important new phase. It indicates a time to do and dare, when you will be given the opportunity to alter the whole course of your future if only you have sufficient courage to take the reins in both hands. You must be prepared to stand up for yourself and to have the courage of your own convictions because no one else will fight your battles for you. Be more independent, and learn to take responsibility for yourself. This could also be a time when you will have to make some important decisions. You should avoid acting impulsively and make sure that you allow yourself sufficient time to realize the full implications of these decisions and the far-reaching consequences a rash decision could have.

2. II The High Priestess

The High Priestess is symbolic of a bridge between the conscious and the unconscious minds, which are represented by the twin pillars behind her throne. She is believed to inspire dreams and visions and is sometimes referred to as 'Divine Inspiration'. The Book of Wisdom lies open in her lap.

THE HIGH PRIESTESS II

When linked with one of the four Personal Numbers this card indicates a shy, gentle and rather retiring person who tends to live his life through the deeds of others rather than through his own first-hand experiences. He is a person who likes to follow while others lead and who likes to remain very much in the background of life never wishing to play a leading role on life's stage. This does not necessarily indicate a dull and boring personality however, as people who fall under the influence of this card possess an innate sense of beauty and have extremely creative imaginations. They are able to see detail whereas many other people might only be aware of shape or form.

From a negative point of view, the High Priestess can so easily become the *femme fatale* who finally destroys her friends and lovers with her little tricks and illusions. She represents the combination of creativity and destruction which turns her into a cunning and deceitful woman.

When the High Priestess exerts no more than a passing influence on life, this can indicate some minor problems arising which could so easily have been avoided with a little forward planning. This is not a period when any major steps forward can be made. It is a time to collect your thoughts and to become aware of yourself and of your inner feelings. Co-operate more with those around you and try to become one of a team working together towards a common goal. Learn to be more tactful and to think before you speak; it could save a great deal of unpleasantness and embarrassment at a later date.

Remember too that if you want to keep a secret you must never tell anyone no matter how sympathetic or trustworthy their outward appearance may be.

3. III, The Empress

The Empress represents feelings, emotions and intuition — an aspect of the subconscious mind. She is the concept of womanhood with all its implications. She symbolizes harmony and an end to tension. This is the card of birth, maternal instincts, domesticity and growth.

THE EMPRESS III

When linked with one of the four Personal Numbers this card indicates an individual with many interests and natural talents — perhaps too many to perform them all to the best of your ability. You are a restless, gregarious spirit who needs to drift from one place to another and from one circle of friends and activities to another. Travel is of the utmost importance to you and in order to fulfil your desires and ambitions you may well choose a career which keeps you on the move and which also prevents you from putting down any permanent roots until much later in life.

The negative face of the Empress is an obese, self-indulgent woman who finds it impossible to resist any pleasure of the flesh whether it be sexual or in the form of overeating or over-imbibing. She is essentially a superficial person and is treated as such by those around her.

When the Empress exerts only a passing influence on life, this indicates a time for growth and the establishment of concrete plans for the future. This can be a particularly enjoyable period of your life when old problems and difficulties can be ironed out and finally forgotten. Lady Luck will also be smiling favourably on you and you could find yourself on the receiving end of a small windfall or two, perhaps from a lottery or a bequest.

Birth and growth which are both represented by the Empress could take a literal form and indicate marriage and children during this period, or they may mean the development of your talents and the birth of new ideas and concepts to work towards.

Travel is also a possibility under the temporary influence of this card and although this could be for business it is more likely to be for the sheer physical pleasure of the whole experience.

4. IIII, The Emperor

The Emperor represents the soul under the control and discipline of will-power. He is reason and, because of his association with the number four, concrete organization. All his decisions are based upon instinct, hard facts and logic and when armed with these weapons he knows just what to do and when to do it.

THE EMPEROR IIII

When linked with one of the four Personal Numbers, this card indicates an organized life coupled with personal security and comfort. People who come under the influence of the Emperor are life's builders and what better to build with than the cube, the symbol of the number four? They are hard-working, efficient, law-abiding people who base all their judgements on sound reasoning. They have been born with the quality of perseverance and this should help them to reach their goals.

A negative manifestation of the Emperor is a very immature person with little or no drive and ambition. He is always ready to give in or to allow someone else to usurp what little authority he has. He usually turns out be one of life's failures at the end of the day. Occasionally the characteristics of the Emperor become exaggerated or 'larger than life' when we behold a stern, forbidding, tyrannical figure who is totally obsessed with work and personal ambitions.

When the Emperor exerts only a passing influence on life, this indicates a phase when you will be in a position to gain further knowledge through experience. Now is the time to use your creative energy to the full and to build yourself a reputation for being a conscientious person who can produce results. You should also gain materially from your efforts if you are prepared to shoulder extra responsibilities and to tackle any obstacles you may find in your path. A new relationship, which could in time become permanent, seems likely during this phase of your life.

5. V, The Hierophant

The Hierophant represents an instrument by which to maintain an acceptable code of behaviour within our society; he upholds the moral standards by which we should all live. He is a man who is capable of producing exciting new ideas which are not only acceptable to everyone but will also fit in with any way of life without causing major problems.

When linked with one of the four Personal Numbers this card indicates the need for personal freedom at all levels. Your mind needs to be allowed to explore ideas and theories at will and for as long as it takes you to reach a conclusion, without being constantly interrupted or having other demands made upon it. At the same time your body needs to be able to come and go as it pleases; wherever and whenever it chooses. In order to learn you need to experience and sample everything life has to offer. Your life could become one long and continual search for that personal 'grail' which you may never find, or indeed recognize, in the end.

The reverse, negative, face of the Hierophant shows an unhelpful person who deliberately distorts the truth in order to mislead others. He can also be a very physical man who seeks his pleasures in bodily comforts such as drugs, alcohol, food and amorous encounters.

When the Hierophant exerts only a passing influence on life this indicates fairly major changes in your lifestyle — possibly a change of job, residence, partner, or all three. Some of these changes and alterations you will make voluntarily but it will seem that others have been almost forced upon you against your will. All in all, this will be a restless and unsettled period of your

THE HIEROPHANT V

life when it will be difficult to know what to do for the best. Some people who fall under the temporary influence of the Hierophant may seek comfort and advice through religious involvement while others may console themselves in a series of love affairs and brief relationships to prove their physical attraction.

6. VI, The Lovers

The Lovers are symbolic of strain and ambivalence. The card/number represents a stage which everyone must reach in life when they break away from their roots and learn to stand alone on their own two feet — it is the moment when independence is asserted. The parting of the ways.

When linked with one of the four Personal Numbers this card indicates an artistic person who likes to be surrounded with beauty and comfort. A person who is every inch the home-maker and one who puts his home and family before all else. These people will go to any lengths to make their partners and children happy. They are loyal, protective and parental. People influenced by the Lovers prefer to be at home then anywhere else and gain their satisfaction from improving their home surroundings.

From a negative point of view, they can become over-protective towards their loved ones and tend to stifle any attempts they may make to gain independence or personal freedom within their home environment. They also tend to do too much for their families and become taken for granted or treated like a drudge. The appreciation they crave is never forthcoming. Occasionally they seem unable to make a choice because they want to have their cake and eat it too.

THE LOVERS VI

When the Lovers exerts only a passing influence on life, this indicates a domestic slant during the period in question. Anything and everything remotely domestic can, and probably will, happen. This could cover such major issues as marriage, childbirth or a move of home, or more minor matters such as the purchase of a new car, an extension to the house or a major redecoration scheme. The accent can also fall on artistic/creative projects during this period when you may decide to put your undoubted talents to better use. Your intuition could also help you find the answer to a long-standing problem which has hitherto seemed insoluble.

7. VII, The Chariot

The Chariot signifies unity within complexity. This man has gained complete control of himself and has harnessed his animal instincts. He has learned to accept the rules and restrictions laid down by society and knows how to deal with any obstacles in his path. He also knows how to turn a situation to his own advantage while still operating within the rules by which he has agreed to abide.

When linked with one of the four Personal Numbers, this card indicates a person who is able to rise above life's obstacles in order to achieve his ambitions. His success will be neither inherited nor won, it will have to be earned the hard way — one step at a time. He will achieve the triumph he so

THE CHARIOT VII

justly deserves but not so quickly nor so easily as others seem to do. Some people ruled by the Chariot seem to rise completely above material matters and develop a philosophical attitude to life; occasionally some will even have clairvoyant or other psychic abilities which they should not ignore. These should be developed so that they can be used for the benefit of others.

The reversed face of the Chariot shows a callous person who will deliberately ride over the personalities he encounters. He is a ruthless individual who cares nothing for the feelings of others and is only concerned with his own interests.

When the Chariot exerts only a passing influence this indicates a good time to take a break from what you are doing. Stop trying to live your life on a head-on collision course with everyone else. Try to take a short holiday if at all possible but at least take a few days off to relax and let yourself unwind a little. Yoga or meditation might help some of you under this temporary influence, while painting, listening to music or simply daydreaming could be of more benefit to others. A short period of enforced rest and relaxation now could have a long-term benefit on your health and physical well-being generally.

8. VIII, Justice

Justice represents the voice of our conscience telling us that it is time to adjust the balance of our lives and finally decide upon some definite course to follow if justice is ever to be done to our existence. Everything should be weighed in

JUSTICE VIII

the balance if we are to proceed fairly. Eight, which is the number of this card, was sometimes called the number of Justice by the Greeks because it is composed of equal divisions of even numbers which provide it with balance.

When linked with one of the four Personal Numbers, this card indicates those who will undoubtedly be called upon to play an arbitrary role at some time in their life. Your sound judgement will be required to settle disputes or to cast the deciding vote in some important moral dilemmas. As an individual, however, you may not feel quite so sure of yourself as others think and occasionally the faith they place in your decisions could be a heavy responsibility to carry and one you might sometimes wish to put down.

When the scales are weighed down on the negative side this produces an individual who is anything but fair. He is prejudiced, biased and inclined, on occasion, to wonder what is 'in it for him' rather than what is right and proper. These people will have to make some major adjustments if they want to achieve a balanced view of life.

When Justice exerts only a passing influence on a person's life, this indicates a period when legal matters could be the focus of your attention. It could quite simply be the reading of a will or some rather complicated conveyancing on a property deal, but on the other hand it could also indicate criminal proceedings with the querent playing the starring role.

A very testing and challenging period for you from all points of view when you will certainly need to have your wits about you if you are to emerge from it unbeaten and unscathed. Be prepared for quick decisions brought about by unexpected events.

9. VIIII, The Hermit

The Hermit represents the seeker of truth with only a lamp (his intuition) to guide him and his staff (his unconscious wisdom) to lean on. He presents a courageous, if somewhat pathetic, figure treading his lonely road through the unknown.

THE HERMIT VIIII

When linked with one of the four Personal Numbers, this card indicates a person who thirsts for spiritual knowledge and wisdom. This is not an easy influence to live under and your innate sympathy and compassion will be needed in order to show understanding to all the various people who will turn to you for assistance. You are a generous, charitable person who is always willing to give up your free time to the service of others although people tend to pass through your life rather than remain in it permanently. They draw from you the comfort and guidance they need and then move on again refreshed and renewed by the experience.

Unfortunately the negative face of he Hermit is not quite so charitable. Here is a person who wouldn't lift a finger to help anyone else in need. He is quite prepared to turn his back on anything he finds distasteful and is suspicious of others, fearing some dark, ulterior motive behind their apparent friendliness. His attitude tends to alienate him from people and he becomes a loner through circumstances rather than personal choice.

When the Hermit exerts only a passing influence on a person's life this indicates a transition period from one stage of development to another. This is a time to forget the past and wipe the slate clean again, ready for a fresh phase. The number nine represents the end of a cycle and so does the Hermit as he sets out in search of himself. You should make an attempt to tidy up all those loose ends, terminate any relationships which have become stale and unfulfilling and put your affairs in order generally. It could even prove beneficial to change jobs if yours offers few, if any, prospects for the future. Then sit back and wait for the wheel to turn and for the arrival of the next stage in your development.

10/1. X, The Wheel of Fortune

The Wheel of Fortune is the tenth of the Tarot trumps. Ten is the first of the compound numbers and together they herald a new beginning. The ancients

THE WHEEL OF FORTUNE X

believed that ten was a perfect number; and the wheel is also symbolic of perfection because it is circular. This trump represents change, the continuous movement of life and the inevitability of death — it endorses the fact that nothing in life can ever be truly constant or permanent.

When linked with one of the four Personal Numbers this card indicates a personality who can accomplish almost anything when sufficiently motivated; a person who can recognize and understand the needs of others and who has total confidence in any decision he might make and any undertakings he might give. This is a fortunate card to be ruled by as most of your plans and ambitions are likely to be carried out in the fullness of time. Chance can also play an important part in some of the unexpected turns your life will almost certainly take.

The negative side of this card shows a fixed and stubborn character who is unwilling and unable to adapt to different situations. New ideas are of no interest to him; he prefers to be a stick-in-the-mud who wants everything to remain exactly the same for all time. Change is a concept which he simply cannot accept.

When the Wheel of Fortune exerts only a passing influence on life this indicates a period when your affairs are likely to take a turn for the better and this beneficial upswing is likely to be caused by events over which you have no personal control. Destiny is a strange process and sometimes takes quite a while to manifest itself fully. Luck will be very much with you during this phase and any speculative ventures you become involved in stand a very fair chance of paying dividends. A problem which has been worrying you for some time could also be solved through a rather strange set of circumstances. This is generally a very remunerative period for anyone who falls under the temporary rulership of this card. It is the time to reap the rewards, so rightly deserved, for past efforts.

11/2. XI, Strength

The Tarot trump Strength represents danger and vulnerability. Only by defeating the lion (the darker, animal side of his personality) can the hero reconcile his animal instincts with his conscious mind. An ominous card.

When linked with on of the four Personal Numbers, this card does not indicate an easy life. Any person who falls under the rulership of Strength will have many difficulties to contend with, and problems to solve. They cannot rely on the help and support of others to see them through these tribulations, as even their most trusted friends could, at some time, prove disloyal and treacherous. However, this does not necessarily condemn them to a life of troubles and hardship. These people are resilient, determined, strong-willed and ambitious; they never give in and simply do not understand the meaning of the word 'failure'. With these qualities they can accomplish anything despite the obstacles and pitfalls they will undoubtedly stumble over on the way.

People who are ruled negatively by this trump will almost certainly fail in life as they don't possess sufficient nerve to seize opportunities when they arise. They seem to display a defeatist attitude right from the start and either end up feeling depressed and sorry for themselves or simply give in to their baser instincts.

When Strength exerts only a passing influence on life, this indicates a time to be courageous; a time to grasp every chance that comes your way with both

STRENGTH XI

hands and to make it work for you. This is also a period in your life when you should settle old scores or reconcile yourself to circumstances as they actually are. This could mean that you should take the trouble to patch up a quarrel but is more likely to refer to an inner conflict. You will need to discipline yourself in order to regain self-control, and so become free of the constant swings of mood which are not only distracting but disruptive too. Now is the time when your chickens could start coming home to roost, when you may be called upon to take responsibility for some past misdemeanour which you thought had been forgotten.

12/3. XII, The Hanged Man
The Hanged Man is symbolic of renewal and salvation. By willingly sacrificing everything he stands to gain an even richer prize — immortality of the spirit and inner peace. The keyword for this card is 'reversal' — by reversing his position the man is able to see everything from a completely different angle.

When linked with one of the four Personal Numbers, this card indicates a unique individual who has the ability to adapt both readily and easily to changing circumstances. These rare people have brilliant, flexible minds and seem to possess an inexhaustible supply of compassion which they are prepared to give unstintingly to others. They are always willing to put aside personal considerations when there is someone who needs their help. People ruled by this card have great wisdom, courage and inner calm.

THE HANGED MAN XII

When negative and reversed the Hanged Man represents suffering and anxiety and indicates a person who is likely to be sacrificed to satisfy the plans and intrigues of others — a scapegoat. It indicates a lifetime of struggle culminating in defeat.

When the Hanged Man exerts only a passing influence on life, it indicates a waiting period which should allow you sufficient time to see matters in perspective — as they really are and not just how they seem to be at a quick glance. As previously mentioned, the keyword for the Hanged Man is reversal and this is quite likely to happen during this phase; something which has been going badly for you could start to improve, and so on. However, there is usually a price to be paid for most things in life and you may have to make a few voluntary sacrifices when influenced by this trump in order to gain other advantages later in life. The balance has to be maintained!

13/4. XIII, Death

Death is not such an unfortunate card as generally supposed. It symbolizes the fact that, although all living things must eventually die, their physical death should be viewed as the beginning of a new state of existence rather than the end of a phase. It represents drastic change and transformation.

DEATH XIII

When linked with one of the four Personal Numbers this card exerts a very powerful influence over the lives of those it rules. There are no shades of grey with the thirteenth trump and people ruled by it have the potential to be either exceptionally good characters or terribly bad. Whichever category they happen to fall into, their lives will certainly never be dull as change will be their constant companion. These people also possess creative imaginations and are able to transform seemingly hopeless situations into success stories almost overnight.

The negative face of the thirteenth trump does not present a pretty picture — it shows a bad-tempered, destructive personality who doesn't care who he hurts so long as he is happy. He is mean, evil and malicious and often finds his pleasures in alcohol, drugs and perverted sexual activities.

When this card exerts only a passing influence on life, it continues to represent change and a totally unexpected major change in personal circumstances is bound to take place during its reign. What's more, this change is likely to be the only possible solution to a prevailing situation however surprising this may seem. Long-standing plans and proposals might also need to be altered, or even aborted, but this is not a bad thing because it will leave you free to take up other, more exciting, offers when they arise. When the thirteenth trump exerts its temporary influence it indicates the commencement of a whole new phase in your life when you must be prepared to forget the past, and all the memories it holds for you, in order to move on and make progress.

14/5. XIIII, Temperance

The word 'temperance', when used in its Tarot sense, refers to the mixing of ingredients in just the right proportions. This card is symbolic of the passage of time as it flows for ever onwards from the past, through the present, and into the future. It can also be said to relate to the concept of reincarnation — the passage of the soul from one existence to another.

TEMPERANCE XIIII

When linked with one of the four Personal Numbers, this card indicates a personal life which will be both harmonious and fulfilling. Fourteen is regarded as an extremely sensual number and the pleasures of the flesh become accentuated under its influence. However, from a business point of view, people ruled by this trump will, throughout their lives, always need to handle people and changing situations with tact, diplomacy and considerable care if they wish to be successful. Caution and prudence are the watchwords here.

The negative side of Temperance indicates the possibility of failure in life due to the constant mishandling of important situations in both the private and business sectors. Such frequent displays of mismanagement will also cause others to lose confidence in your ability to produce results.

When Temperance exerts only a passing influence on life, it indicates a great deal of movement — people entering/leaving your circle of friends, and a number of short journeys — perhaps even a few trips abroad. Financial dealings are also well aspected although the number fourteen carries with it a risk of danger which generally manifests itself through natural occurrences such as floods, earth-quakes and so on, which can cause major disruptions to commercial transactions. The sensual aspect of this vibration has already been mentioned and during a temporary period ruled by this trump exciting sexual encounters are quite likely to occur.

15/6. XV, The Devil

The Devil represents the energy of the inner self — an energy which must be controlled; channelled into a positive use; and steered towards the light. When

THE DEVIL XV

allowed to follow its own path, it leads only to darkness, evil and, eventually, Satan himself. This card reminds us of the need to rise above our baser instincts in order to reach higher levels of consciousness. It urges us to become more civilized and to learn to be more discriminating.

When the Devil rules one of the four Personal Numbers it indicates a person with a remarkably strong, magnetic personality. Very often he/she will also be a gifted speaker in addition to possessing a talent for artistic, literary or musical expression. These people seem to be exceptionally lucky in life and attract all sorts of gifts and favours to themselves from others.

In its negative aspect, this fifteenth trump represents a person who desires power at any cost. Here is someone who would be prepared to use his position in society to further his personal ambitions, an individual who makes little or no effort to control the animal side of his nature and a dangerous person to have as an enemy.

When the Devil exerts only a passing influence on life you could possibly gain more personal freedom and escape from the restrictions previously imposed upon your movements. You could, however, just as easily, become tied down by personal problems and feel trapped and bound by obligations under this card's vibration. Tiredness and strain due to overwork should be guarded against during this phase of your life and if making long-term plans try to allow for the unforseen by adding a few extra days or pounds to your calculations.

16/7. XVI, The Tower
The Tower represents the power of cosmic energy, the flash of inspiration

THE TOWER XVI

which carries with it enlightenment. The devastating impact of the thunderbolt symbolizes a clearing from the mind of out-dated beliefs thus leaving it free to absorb new ideas, conditions and concepts. Its keyword is awakening. The Tower is a rigid structure and stands as a warning that we must remain flexible if we want to survive. Only by constantly bending and adapting will we be able to withstand the severest blows that life can deal us.

When linked with one of the four Personal Numbers this card indicates a lifetime of troubles and thwarted ambitions. The individual will be faced with many disappointments and injustices caused by outside influences over which he has no control. Nature somehow seems to be working against him and every time he appears to have made some progress, fate steps in and pushes him back again. This is not an easy card/number under which to be permanently influenced.

In its negative aspect, the Tower indicates that most of the individual's problems are of his own making and could have been avoided if only he had paid a little more attention to detail. It represents unnecessary suffering and also self-destruction.

When this trump exerts only a passing influence on a person's life, this indicates a degree of personal suffering which it is necessary to undergo in order to achieve further spiritual development. It should be regarded as a warning signal and treated accordingly. Be especially careful when travelling or working with machinery and plan well ahead to avoid possible disappointment.

17/8. XVII, The Star

The Star is a highly spiritual card and is symbolic of the doors of the mind standing open ready to take in knowledge and understanding. The water being poured onto the ground represents the conscious mind and the water being poured back into the pool represents the subconscious. The group of eight stars symbolize higher aspirations and the largest, eight-pointed star, rotation.

When linked with one of the four Personal Numbers this card indicates a spirited person who will fight back when life seems to be treating them unfairly and who will ultimately rise above many trials and difficulties to achieve success. Seventeen is the 'number of immortality' and often people ruled by this card achieve, or create, something which will ensure that their name lives on after them.

People who are negatively affected by the Star are often extremely narrow-minded and find it difficult to accept progressive ideas or modern methods. They are often lacking in confidence in their own abilities as well as those of others. Self-doubt and rigidity of mind are the negative keywords for this trump.

When the Star exerts only a passing influence on a person's life, this indicates a period of good fortune, fulfilment and possible travel. Many good opportunities for personal advancement should arise which will make the immediate future appear more hopeful, secure and happy than it has done for some considerable time. You should be encouraged to broaden your horizons

THE STAR XVII

and look at life, and what it has to offer, from a wider viewpoint than you have previously done. A new lease of life should be yours with sufficient energy to accomplish everything that you desire.

18/9. XVIII, The Moon

The Moon represents rest and recuperation in preparation for the dawn of a new day. Night-time is when we sleep in order to give our bodies time to prepare for a fresh round of experience. During the night physical damage can be repaired, body cells renewed and our brains allowed to enter a world of fantasy and dreams. This card signifies suspended animation and renewal.

When linked with one of the four Personal Numbers this card indicates a person who finds it difficult to cope with reality; a dreamer who prefers to escape into his own fantasies and illusions rather than get on with life and face up to all its attendant problems. These people are extremely emotional and possess vivid imaginations. They often experience particularly disturbing or prophetic dreams and these tend to make them run even away further from everyday life.

People ruled by the Moon are often clairvoyant and some even possess powers of healing. However, they should all treat their bodies with care and respect as self-neglect could have a detrimental effect on both their physical and mental well-being.

THE MOON XVIII

The negative face of the Moon shows us timid, wary individuals who could be frightened by their own shadow. They basically lack courage and, in difficult situations, their nerve usually fails them at the crucial moment. They prefer to remain just as they are rather than risk trying something new which might prove difficult or demanding.

When this trump exerts only a passing influence on a person's life this indicates a period when intuition, rather than reason, should be relied upon to make any headway at all. This is a 'crisis of faith' situation when the only thing you can truly rely upon is yourself. Even when it has only a temporary effect this card can cause attempts to escape from reality by various means which you should actively resist. Also health problems are accentuated under its influence and greater care than usual should be taken to ensure good health if you wish to come through this period unscathed. You must endeavour to slow down the pace of your life and proceed with caution and circumspection. The Moon is a warning against danger from the elements, and treachery and deception from friends.

19/1. XVIIII, The Sun
The Sun represents the pure, unclouded light of the inner self. It has

immeasurable strength and also life-giving powers which are hinted at in its rays which reach down to the earth. It symbolizes the union of consciousness and the unconscious — psychic wholeness.

When linked with one of the four Personal Numbers this card indicates a born leader. A person with an innate sense of organization, direction and management. A vital and magnetic personality full of daring ideas which always seem to succeed against all odds. Here is a person with foresight and imagination and one who so justly deserves the acclaim and approval he seeks. Anyone ruled by this card seems to possess endurance, reason and the ability to overcome any obstacle in his path no matter how great.

THE SUN XVIIII

When the Sun stops shining and goes behind the clouds we behold an entirely different individual who tries to deceive everyone, including himself. He lacks judgement and for this reason his grand schemes inevitably end in failure and ignominy. The occasional success he does achieve has almost certainly been brought about by dubious means and is, therefore, not worth having although he sees it as a wonderful attainment.

When the Sun exerts only a passing influence on a person's life, this indicates an extremely favourable and fortunate period. A time for new beginnings in both your private and professional capacity — in fact love and marriage look well aspected under this particular vibration. Happiness is certainly promised as are success and honour during this phase. Any plans made for the future are also almost certain to succeed. All in all this should prove to be an enjoyable and rewarding period of your life.

20/2. XX, Judgement

Judgement represents a major stage in spiritual development. It is symbolic of the divine discontent that lies within man and which causes him to strive continually to achieve new heights of endeavour — the creative impulse. The keyword here is realization.

When linked with one of the four Personal Numbers this card indicates a

JUDGEMENT XX

person who was born for some great purpose or to fulfil a particular duty during his lifetime. This card certainly cannot be said to indicate worldly success, instead it points to spiritual attainment which can only be achieved the hard way, by overcoming obstacles and by remaining cheerful through times of difficulty. Judgement is the title of this trump and that is what you will have to exercise when confronted with difficult choices that only you can make. Not an easy vibration to live under — you will frequently be called upon to give much of yourself with no promise of any reward during this lifetime although if you believe in reincarnation you will undoubtedly be building up for yourself many 'bonus' karma points to be spent in your next life — if, indeed, there is one.

The negative side of Justice shows us a person who has wasted his life. He hasn't bothered to grab opportunities when they have presented themselves and now feels guilty and bitter because of all the chances he has wasted. He also believes that life is punishing him for his own failure to make something of himself.

When Judgement exerts only a passing influence on a person's life, this indicates a period of 'awakening' when new plans and ambitions can be put into action. However, everything may not run quite so smoothly as you could wish and the odd delay or hindrance is only to be expected. You should be able to achieve a great deal during this phase of your life but your real reward will be the pleasure of accomplishing rather than a monetary one. If your health has previously been causing you some concern it should improve under this vibration and you look all set to enjoy a new lease of life.

21/3. XXI, The World
The World represents the end of the quest when the goal has been reached. Control has been gained over ourself and the environment. It contains the seeds of fresh endeavour which will enable the journey in search of self to start

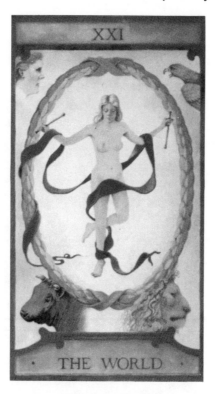

THE WORLD XXI

all over again with the commencement of a new cycle. The picture portrays the never-ending dance of life.

When linked with one of the four Personal Numbers this card indicates a lifetime of struggle and difficulty which will finally be crowned with personal honours and achievement. Anyone who comes under the rulership of this trump will be able to gain advancement but only after a long and necessarily uphill fight which could go on for years. However, if you can remember that success awaits you in the end then this should make the difficult waiting period easier to endure.

When the World brings a negative influence to bear on an individual we see a person who fears change and all that it could bring. He suffers from a loss of momentum and prefers to stand still, do nothing and simply stagnate rather than to drive himself on towards any goal of his own choosing.

When the World exerts only a passing influence on a person's life, this indicates the end of a particular cycle in his destiny. This is a period for tying up loose ends and successfully completing any matters in hand which need to be finalized. A time to put your life in order, ready for a new and exciting phase to begin. Travel is also quite possible under this influence especially if for pleasure. You will need to be relaxed and refreshed in order to face the next challenge life has in store for you.

22/4. 0, The Fool

The Fool is the herald of fresh beginnings and new life. He is the seed of a whole new cycle of experiences which, when planted, grows and develops, experiencing everything and learning a great deal as it does so. The Fool can be

THE FOOL 0

placed at the beginning or the end of the sequence of Tarot trumps; he is 0 or 22. Twenty-two is an ancient numerical symbol for a circle, as well as being a Master Number, and the Fool too is representative of a circle — the circle of life.

When linked with one of the four Personal Numbers this card indicates one of life's dreamers who only seems to wake up and pay attention when surrounded by troubles or dangers. Nine times out of ten this means he has left it too late to do anything positive to solve the tricky situation with which he is faced. This is a sad position for him to be in particularly as he is a good-natured, amiable sort of person who doesn't deserve such problems — but he will insist upon living in a fool's paradise. Throughout life his judgement will almost always be suspect simply because he will allow others to influence his decisions.

The reversed, negative side of the Fool is the Joker who foretells of many major problems arising which will be all of your own making and which could so easily have been avoided if only you had been a little less reckless or impulsive in your choice of action.

When the Fool exerts only a passing influence on a person's life, this indicates a period when you should expect the unexpected because it will greatly affect the final outcome of this phase of your development. There will be challenges to meet which will prove extremely beneficial if handled in the right manner. Important decisions will also have to be taken as a new phase in your life is trying to get under way. Make sure that your choices are realistic as this is not the time to indulge in wishful thinking — both your feet should be kept very firmly on the ground.

THE CARDS OF THE MINOR ARCANA

The Staves (sometimes also referred to as Rods, Wands, Clubs or Batons in other Tarot decks).

23/5, The King of Staves
Permanent Influence: People who come under the permanent influence of the King of Staves possess great moral strength of character, fortitude, courage and generosity. They are extremely loyal and of a passionate nature — in love they can be embarassingly demonstrative of their feelings. They place great store on their family unit and are often vehement traditionalists. Others tend to turn to them for advice or support in times of difficulty and it is not uncommon for them to be asked to act in the role of mediator when a problem arises which is proving difficult to reconcile. These people are friendly and honest to a fault.
Negative Traits: Negative Twenty-threes are unsympathetic and really don't care about anyone but themselves. They are intolerant and totally unwilling to put up with any personal inconvenience, even for a short while. They are

go-getters and they use ruthless methods and dirty tricks to achieve their ends.
Passing Influence: This is a particularly fortunate card which promises successful plans. However, help from superiors in the form of advice might be needed to put these plans into action as too might be the protection of those in high places. Both will be readily available if required. Contracts and travel are highlighted under this temporary influence.

24/6, The Queen of Staves
Permanent Influence: People who come under the permanent influence of the Queen of Staves are good-natured and sympathetic towards the feelings of others. They often possess brilliant minds and have fertile imaginations which they use to benefit the community around them. They are both home and country lovers who prefer to live in close harmony with nature rather than in overcrowded towns and cities which only seem to stifle their loving, generous personalities.
Negative Traits: Negative Twenty-fours are domineering and try to make those around them servants to their will. Some are spiteful and sarcastic while others are incredibly vain. They imagine personal slights where none were intended. Rather unpleasant individuals.
Passing Influence: Another fortunate card which, like the King, promises help and assistance from superiors. Love will be very much on your mind during this period and there is also the possibility of personal gain through a liaison with a member of the opposite sex. This need not necessarily be the person with whom you are conducting a serious relationship — although it could quite well be.

25/7, The Knight of Staves
Permanent Influence: People who come under the permanent influence of the Knight of Staves can be rather startling upon first acquaintance because they are so alive, unpredictable and quixotic. However, the wisdom of their actions can generally be appreciated in retrospect. They are engaging people who are always amusing and fun to be with. Nothing ever seems dull for long when they're around.
Negative Traits: Negative Twenty-fives simply love to cause trouble. They are destructive, disruptive and are quite prepared to go out of their way to cause arguments or to stir up discontent where none previously existed.
Passing Influence: During this period it should be possible to make considerable progress but at a price. You will have to overcome many annoying worries and problems before you can reach your goal. Try to make your road a little easier by using the wisdom gained from past experience as a guide.

26/8, The Page of Staves
Permanent Influence: People who come under the permanent influence of the Page of Staves have an infectious enthusiasm for life; they know what they want from it and also how to go about achieving their ambition. They are human chameleons and can change and adapt their appearance and outlook to fit their current situation. They are stimulating company although some of

their witty remarks can fall rather near the knuckle at times. These people are loyal, faithful workers as well as being completely trustworthy.

Negative Traits: Negative Twenty-sixes are mischief-makers of the worst kind who like nothing better than to pass on a particularly slanderous titbit of gossip. They can never be trusted, particularly with a secret because they will tell it to the world, with a few extra embellishments of their own for good measure, the moment your back is turned. They possess no depth to their character at all and are superficial and totally worthless individuals.

Passing Influence: This is a time in your life when you should tread warily and consider with extra care any decisions or changes you may be about to make. Your immediate future doesn't look too promising for several reasons — some of your friends/associates are really wolves in sheep's clothing and will take advantage of you whenever they have the opportunity to do so; partnerships and speculations could fail because you have been given second-rate guidance; union politics could play a deciding role in your future prosperity. Proceed with caution during this tricky period — it's only temporary and will eventually pass.

27/9, Ace of Staves

Permanent Influences: People who come under the permanent influence of the Ace of Staves have fertile, creative minds. They are original thinkers, inventive, innovative and intuitive. Some individuals ruled by this card are artistically gifted and express their ideas best through this medium.

Negative Traits: Negative Twenty-sevens bear no resemblance to their clever, positive counterparts — these people have barren, sterile minds and seem to be incapable of producing even one vaguely novel idea of their own. Instead they are greedy, physically lustful types who occasionally bring about their own demise through being recklessly over-confident in a potentially dangerous situation.

Passing Influence: This promises to be a particularly fertile phase in your life when seeds sown for the future are sure to take root and grow into success and abundance. It is also a good time to consider entering into marriage or starting a family, should you feel so inclined. During the temporary rulership of the Ace of Staves you should endeavour to convert your ideas into reality — the rewards for a productive intellect could be especially great at this time.

28/1, Two of Staves

Permanent Influence: People who come under the permanent influence of the Two of Staves are progressive and capable, with sufficient determination to see their ideas through to completion. They possess sound judgement coupled with the ability to manage other people fairly but firmly. As they progress through life they gain much of their valuable wisdom from first hand experiences. These people should go to the top of whatever field of endeavour they choose in which to make a careeer and the success which they will undoubtedly achieve is only what they deserve for all their efforts and hard work.

Negative Traits: Negative Twenty-eights are also ambitious but theirs is a ruthless desire and they will stop at nothing to achieve their goal, which is usually power. They are proud, arrogant and sometimes deceitful — these characters don't mind how they come by their money.

Passing Influence: If a period of your life happens to fall under the temporary rulership of the Two of Staves you should prepare yourself for a general feeling of inconsistency and contradiction about almost anything with which you become involved. Great opportunities for future success could be offered to you during this time but you must proceed with caution if you don't want to see them vanish before your eyes. A loss of some kind is indicated, which will probably be monetary although it could be friends or business contracts. Treat anything which appears suspicious with extreme care until this phase passes.

29/11/2, Three of Staves

Permanent Influence: People who come under the permanent influence of the Three of Staves are able, at some time during their lives, to turn their dreams into reality. Their minds are continually overflowing with original ideas which they instinctively seem to know how to promote to their best advantage. These are talented individuals and many artists and inventors are to be found under this fixed vibration.

Negative Traits: Negative Twenty-nines seem to experience tremendous difficulty when attempting to express their ideas or their feelings to others. In fact they find it hard to communicate on any level and prefer to escape into a private world full of fantasies and day-dreams rather than go through the agonizing experience of having to meet people.

Passing Influence: This could prove to be a particularly uncertain period of your life when you would be well advised to keep your wits about you. Friends could show themselves in their true colours during this phase — their treachery and deception will be a great disappointment to you. A member of the opposite sex could also cause you some uneasiness. Provided that you keep your eyes and ears open you should emerge from this temporary period relatively unscathed.

30/3, Four of Staves

Permanent Influence: People who fall under the permanent influence of the Four of Staves are rather civilized individuals who like nothing better than to be surrounded by comfort, beauty and, above all, culture. They possess bright, clever minds and generally choose to wear elegant clothes, no matter whether they are attending the opera or digging the garden! They often become successful inventors or designers.

Negative Traits: Negative Thirties are foppish and affected. They carry their desire for good manners, etiquette and refinement to a ridiculous degree rather like some of the Regency dandies did in earlier times. They are snobs to the core although why they should be so superior to everyone else they never manage to make quite clear. These negative individuals are also decadent.

Passing Influence: When the Four of Staves exerts only a passing influence on life, it indicates that the time is right to put some of your ideas forward for consideration. Your brain should be functioning at its very best under this vibration so you ought to be able to solve some long-standing problems during this period. This number is neither particularly fortunate nor unfortunate so it all depends on you what you make of life during its temporary rule.

31/4, Five of Staves

Permanent Influence: Anyone who comes under the permanent influence of the Five of Staves is not going to have everything handed to him on a plate during this lifetime — he is going to have to fight, and fight hard, every step of the way for each foothold he gains on the ladder of success. However a prize worth having is worth the effort that goes into securing it so you must be determined if you ever want to reach your goal.

Negative Traits: Negative Thirty-ones are often just a little bit too clever for their own good and many could find themselves accused of fraud, trickery or deliberate deception. Their attitude to life could lead to legal complications which could so easily have been avoided if only they had been more reasonable from the start.

Passing Influence: You should choose to spend more time on your own during this period — allow yourself time to think, relax and generally unwind from the pressures of life. This does not mean that you should become a recluse and totally isolate yourself from your fellow men but you should try to set some time aside each day to gather your thoughts. It could prove beneficial to your health.

32/5, Six of Staves

Permanent Influence: Under the permanent influence of the Six of Staves you will always be driven to seek satisfaction from what you do; in fact this will be of greater importance to you than any financial reward could ever be. It should be possible for you to derive this pleasure from your work although you will have to labour extremely hard and come up with some revolutionary ideas if you ever hope to become well known for your achievements. The number thirty-two is usually associated with combinations of peoples and nations.

Negative Traits: Negative Thirty-twos are fearful individuals who always imagine that something dreadful is hiding round the corner just waiting to jump out on them or, if things are going well, they worry about what might go wrong to spoil their pleasure. Some even suffer from persecution complexes and imagine that hidden enemies are plotting against them.

Passing Influence: This should be a very favourable period indeed when you will feel victorious because you will see a major hope fulfilled. Good news is also on the way concerning a matter of a rather personal nature. When dealing with people who seem to oppose your views and opinions, it would be wise to win them round to your way of thinking by diplomacy instead of brute force, especially when under this particular vibration.

33/6, Seven of Staves

Permanent Influence: This card indicates a life of great possibility which can only be realized through courage and determination. This will not be an easy path to tread; there will be others who try to divert you away from your goal, many things will undoubtedly go wrong and you are sure to encounter obstacles. However, success is waiting for you if you are willing to persevere and overcome your trials one by one.

Negative Traits: The negative face of the Seven of Staves shows us a timid person who would probably find it difficult to say 'boo' to a goose. These people usually make up their minds far too late and lose many opportunities because of this weakness. They would sooner run and hide than stand up for themselves and risk the ignominy of defeat.

Passing Influence: During this period you could find you are required to take on extra responsibilities particularly in your private life; one of your children may need your support or an elderly relative could prove burdensome. Under this vibration you may have to make some form of personal sacrifice in order to fulfil all your obligations but this will turn out to be a blessing in disguise. Have courage and don't despair, you are in for a busy and physically demanding time.

34/7, Eight of Staves

Permanent Influence: Yours will most probably be a life of travel both for business and pleasure; journeying overseas in foreign countries will become quite commonplace for you. While success is not actually assured as part of your destiny you should encounter all the conditions necessary to achieve that which you desire during this lifetime and it will be entirely up to you what you make of the opportunities. The number thirty-four rules development and growth and is linked with the mystery of nature.

Negative Traits: In its negative guise this number indicates a person who is over-enthusiastic, energetic and mentally brilliant but who, unfortunately, does not possess any common sense. They try to do too much too soon and inevitably end up burning themselves out long before their real potential can be fully realized.

Passing Influence: Activity is the keyword for this phase. There is bound to be a tremendous amount going on around you with much coming and going of people, ideas and objects. An important matter which has been subject to delays in the past should now speed up and reach a pleasing conclusion. Communications and travel will be highlighted under this vibration so be sure to watch out for important new contacts on the way.

35/8, Nine of Staves

Permanent Influence: If you are lucky enough to come under the permanent influence of the Nine of Staves, you will most assuredly possess great strength of character and a balanced mental outlook on life. Nothing ever seems to shake your calm appearance however disastrous the situation and your attitude is a fine example for others to follow. Your faith will see you through difficulties because you believe that right will triumph in the end. Security is important to you but is something which you should never need to worry about. People under this vibration tend to inherit both power and money at some time during their lives.

Negative Traits: Negative Thirty-fives are narrow-minded, obstinate and unreasonable. They will flatly refuse to give even an inch to effect a working compromise because of the stubborn streak which runs through them. They also find it almost impossible to move with the times, preferring the devil they know to the one they don't. Impatience is also part of their character and delays of any kind drive them almost to the point of distraction.

Passing Influence: When the Nine of Staves exerts only a passing influence on someone's life, this indicates the right time to do battle for what is wanted. Off with the kid gloves and stop defending yourself with excuses! This is the only way that you will ever be victorious. Once you have shown your teeth people will think twice before they try to fob you off with petty excuses again.

36/9, Ten of Staves

Permanent Influence: Once under the permanent influence of the Ten of Staves you become one of life's survivors. No matter what cross you are required to bear or how many obstacles you come up against you will always manage to find the necessary courage to rise above them and carry on. You are a compassionate, understanding person who always has time and sympathy to spare for those worse off than yourself. People like you are the salt of the earth and although you may never scale the dizzy heights, your fighting spirit will prevent you from plumbing the depths of despair.

Negative Traits: Negative Thirty-sixes tell so many lies that they often find it difficult to remember the truth; deceit becomes a way of life for them and they simply cannot resist the temptation to mislead others even when there is no particular need to do so. They weave a very tangled web which usually becomes their own undoing.

Passing Influence: Under this vibration you should expect to encounter a few minor problems which will need to be solved. Some extra responsibilities may also be temporarily placed upon your shoulders for which you should receive adequate compensation. Your health should be particularly good at this time and you should endeavour to channel all your surplus energy into a project which is both useful and creative.

The Cups (Hearts)

37/1, King of Cups

Permanent Influence: People ruled by the King of Cups are born diplomats who use their skill in dealing with others to fulfil their own desires. These are powerful individuals well versed in the ways of the world and quite capable of turning any situation to their advantage, using their mental agility and persuasive conversation. They seek, and frequently achieve, a position of power which, although it gains them respect, hardly ever makes them loved.

Negative Traits: Beware of a negative Thirty-seven! He will inevitably bring people he associates with into disrepute. He has no moral sense whatsoever and is treacherous, dishonest and very often violent too.

Passing Influence: The number thirty-seven, which has a marked potency of its own, is frequently associated with partnerships of all kinds. Under this temporary vibration you can expect a particularly happy, easy-going phase of your life when friendships could play a fairly major role in your affairs. Business partnerships look promising while your romantic life is well aspected with perhaps marriage taking place at the end of this period.

38/11/2, Queen of Cups

Permanent Influence: This is a particularly spiritual vibration and those ruled by the Queen of Cups often appear to be 'miles away' in another world. Many are artistically gifted and most are intuitive, imaginative and sensitive. Their moods are easily influenced, particularly by their surroundings or the company they happen to keep. They are rare individuals whose happiness does not depend upon money or success but is to be found in the simple pleasures of life.

Negative Traits: Negative Thirty-eights seem incapable of coming down to earth for more than two seconds at a time. They drift dreamily through life like butterflies going from flower to flower on a summer's day. They can never be relied upon because they are inclined to wander off in pursuit of an idle whim rather than getting on with the task they have been set.

Passing Influence: When she exerts a temporary influence on our lives the Queen of Cups promises love and romance which might even develop into a more lasting relationship in the fullness of time. She can also make dreams come true, so during her rulership some of your dearest wishes could quite possibly become realities. This could prove to be one of the happiest periods of your life so enjoy it while you may.

39/3, Knight of Cups

Permanent Influence: Many of the people who are permanently influenced by the Knight of Cups are artistically gifted but unless their interest is constantly stimulated they tend to lose interest and often abandon projects whch have only been partially completed in order to pursue some new idea. They are sociable individuals who usually have a great many friends. They almost always create rigid codes of conduct for themselves which they occasionally find almost impossible to live up to.

Negative Traits: How innocent and trustworthy those negative Knights appear when they promise you not only the moon but the stars as well and how angry you feel when you find out how badly they have let you down. Unfortunately that is the black side of the Knight of Cups. They delude everyone including themselves because they will insist upon ignoring the dividing line between fact and fiction. Eventually they forget that it exists at all.

Passing Influence: The suit of Cups is often associated with matters of the heart and under the temporary influence of this particular card love is once again the prime concern. There is also a holiday feeling about this particular period and foreign travel is highly likely. Generally this should be a happy time which you should spend in the company of your family, friends and loved ones whenever possible.

40/4, Page of Cups

Permanent Influence: People who are permanently ruled by the Page of Cups are, generally speaking, educated, well-informed individuals who always seem to know exactly what to do and when to do it. And, what's more, they never seem to mind passing on the benefit of their immense store of wisdom to anyone who cares to ask for their advice. They always give a great deal of thought to their plans, rarely making a move that hasn't been carefully considered first. They like everything to be just so — second rate simply won't do for them.

Negative Traits: Negative Pages appear to know a great deal about a wide variety of subjects but closer examination usually reveals how shallow and worthless their fund of knowledge really is. Unlike their positive counterparts these people are selfish and really only interested in themselves.

Passing Influence: The Page of Cups heralds a period of successful planning prior to the start of a new venture of some kind. This could point to the opening of a business, perhaps the purchase of a new property or, on a more personal level, marriage and parenthood. Look after your money during this phase, your enthusiasm could cause you to overspend.

41/5, Ace of Cups

Permanent Influence: The Ace of Cups represents fertility — those permanently ruled by this card have either fruitful minds or fruitful bodies and, in some cases, both. They are usually at their best when engaged in doing something useful because they simply cannot bear to idle away their time unproductively. They are loyal and faithful in marriage and friendship, almost over-protective of their loved ones and primarily concerned with the comfort and general well-being of their families.

Negative Traits: Negative Forty-ones can best be described as barren in both mind and body. They seem to have no interest in anything or anyone and when they do finally enter into a relationship it soon withers and dies from lack of stimulation. While they may not actually be unable to produce children they might just as well not bother as they usually pay little attention to any they do have.

Passing Influence: You should be feeling extremely happy and confident under this vibration. Many people choose to marry, set up home or start their families under the temporary influence of the Ace of Cups while others change job or move home. The three most important keywords for this phase are change, happiness and love, in any order.

42/6, Two of Cups

Permanent Influence: People ruled by the Two of Cups are natural peacemakers, they have the ability not only to see both sides of an argument but to make the two warring parties see each other's point of view. These are honest, trustworthy characters with tremendous personal charm. They love and live life to the full. They are understanding and sympathetic and consequently their broad shoulders are frequently cried upon by friends in trouble.

Negative Traits: Negative Forty-twos should be avoided whenever possible because they can cause all sorts of trouble. The list of their bad points is almost endless; they are deceitful, irresponsible, loose-tongued, spiteful, jealous and treacherous. They are seldom happy in their private lives, often marrying more than once with disastrous consequences each time.

Passing Influence: As a temporary vibration, the Two of Cups counsels caution. Don't do anything precipitous on the spur of the moment. Instead you should allow yourself time to think matters over carefully before reaching a final decision, especially where contracts are concerned. Marriage is also a contract and it should be considered with extreme caution during this period.

43/7, Three of Cups

Permanent Influence: The Three of Cups is indeed a fortunate card to be permanently ruled by. It promises a life of comfort, ease and good health. People under this influence are well-balanced individuals who probably experienced particularly happy, problem-free childhoods. This accounts for the way they tackle life as adults. These people can be relied upon in any situation. A large proportion of those who come under this vibration are usually found to possess the gifts of healing and clairvoyance.

Negative Traits: Debauched is the only word which adequately describes a negative Forty-three. They are selfish, self-indulgent, sexually promiscuous and lustful. Many put on weight because of their gluttony and a small minority of them abuse their bodies with drugs, tobacco and alcohol.

Passing Influence: Now is the time to harvest the fruits of your labours. All your hard work will finally pay dividends and you should be well rewarded for your efforts. Once you have finished celebrating your success you should endeavour to relax, because this is what your body needs after all the pressure it has been under lately. Try to get away for a while if at all possible.

44/8, Four of Cups

Permanent Influence: People who are permanently influenced by the Four of Cups are steady, cautious individuals who plan every move they make well in advance. Adaptability is one of their strong points. They seem to be able to cope with any situation, no matter how difficult or unfamiliar it may be, because they are practical and possess more than the average quota of common sense. Definitely the type of person you would be pleased to have around in an emergency.

Negative Traits: Negative Forty-fours do everything to excess, usually to the detriment of their health. These people seldom reach old age because their bodies have usually been irreparably damaged by their over-indulgent lifestyles long before they get old.

Passing Influence: During this period you should be able to sit back a little and really enjoy your achievements. You could always use this breathing space to plan what your next move should be. Your private life should also settle down under this influence and the need to be continually proving yourself to your partner should gradually fade away, leaving you a more relaxed person.

45/9, Five of Cups

Permanent Influence: Many people permanently influenced by the Five of Cups marry early and often tend to have large families. Those who do not follow this pattern seem to go to the other extreme; they prefer to withdraw within themselves caring nothing for the company of others or worldly possessions. Both need to achieve a more balanced outlook or they could miss out on so much that life has to offer because of their restrictive family lives or insular existences.

Negative Traits: Bad luck seems to dog these unfortunate Forty-fives continually, leaving them feeling helpless and depressed. They seldom experience a time free of worries and problems and when the rare occasion does occur then they worry about what might go wrong to spoil matters.

Passing Influence: When the Five of Cups exerts only a passing influence this indicates that it is time for a major reassessment and the formulation of new plans, probably brought about by a general feeling of dissatisfaction with life. Remember to learn from past experiences — don't go making the same mistakes all over again. Also, try not to be in too much of a hurry to put your new ideas into action because there are many alternatives to be explored and your first choice may not necessarily be the best.

46/1, Six of Cups

Permanent Influence: This vibration tends to bring out the leadership qualities in those it embraces. They are strong-willed, positive characters who, at times, can seem bossy or dictatorial. They achieve some of their best results when they wear kid gloves and try the more gentle approach to problems. These people know what they want from life and generally get it. However, they are quite happy to share their success with their loved ones in acknowledgement of the love and support so freely given.

Negative Traits: Negative Forty-sixes tend to live in the past, preferring to reminisce about what has been rather than looking forward to what could be. They stubbornly refuse to adapt to the technology of the present century and continue to do everything the hard way simply because that's how it was always done when they were children. The march of progress has made a detour round these individuals.

Passing Influence: The Six of Cups promises happiness as a reward for something done in the past. In fact, this card is very much concerned with what has happened before and how it will affect you both now and in the future. During this period an old idea will be reborn making a much greater impact the second time around because of some slight modifications you will choose to make to the original concept. A happy period although there could be that feeling of *déjà vu* about it all.

47/11/2, Seven of Cups

Permanent Influence: If you come under the permanent influence of the Seven of

Cups you will frequently find yourself in situations where lesser mortals would fear to tread. These tests of character are designed to keep you on your toes and to push you to the limits as though you were being singled out to perform some great task. This could well be the case because forty-seven is, after all, only a higher vibration of the master number eleven.

Negative Traits: Negative Forty-sevens see life through rose-tinted spectacles. They refuse to see things as they really are, preferring to hide behind their mask of delusion and fantasy. In their world pain, ugliness, poverty and misery simply don't exist.

Passing Influence: Choice is the keyword here but it's up to you which opportunity you decide to pursue. There are sure to be several alternatives to choose from but one holds more promise than all the rest put together. Will you make the right decision? You would do well to examine your motives carefully to ensure that you make the right choice.

48/3, Eight of Cups

Permanent Influence: People influenced by the Eight of cups usually want more from life than the material side has to offer. They seek their fulfilment on a spiritual level through meditation or religion, which need not necessarily be of the orthodox variety. They are sensitive people with high ideals who are often attracted by the arts or sciences. Although they sound very serious there is also a streak of mischievious humour running through them all which seems rather out of character with their rather sober appearance.

Negative Traits: Negative Forty-eights are only different from their counterparts in that they lack mental stability. When absorbed in some deep, profound idea they tend to lose their grip on reality, becoming disorientated and vague when addressed. They are dissatisfied with life which makes them restless and hard to please.

Passing Influence: The temporary influence of the Eight of Cups tends to make people want more from life than they have found already. Established pursuits and relationships tend to lose their former attraction and the search begins for something new and altogether more fulfilling at all levels. This quest for new experience is a beneficial move which should evoke many rewards in the rather more distant future.

49/4, Nine of Cups

Permanent Influence: The Nine of Cups rules many happy, well-adjusted people whose almost perfect emotional stability provides a source of inspiration to others. They are kind, generous and warm-hearted, radiating a glow of friendliness wherever they go. Many choose to follow careers where these special qualities can be used to their best advantage, perhaps in marriage guidance or maybe even the diplomatic service.

Negative Traits: Negative Forty-nines devote too much of their time to the service of others and are often taken advantage of, because they are so willing to help. They just don't know how to say no and in consequence they frequently suffer from overwork and strain. They mean well but their inability to refuse a cry for help makes them their own worst enemies at times.

Passing Influence: During the temporary influence of the Nine of Cups you should experience a period of particularly good health. You will be feeling on top of the world when no task will seem too onerous. However, you should try to resist the temptation to push yourself to the limits as this could have serious consequences at a later date. A wealthy marriage is also quite possible under this vibration for those of you prepared to put financial security before love.

50/5, Ten of Cups

Permanent Influence: If you are ruled by the Ten of Cups you should never have to worry or want for anything during your life. Comfort and security are the keywords of this card and that is just what you can expect. The heart is the only area in which you may experience a few problems and disappointments because true love is the one thing which money cannot buy. However there will be so many other pleasant distractions in your life that you'll soon forget your emotional troubles.

Negative Traits: Negative Fifties are social climbers who will use anyone and anything to claw their way up in the world. They are the most outrageous snobs who do not like to be reminded of their roots or of the company they used to keep. Manipulation is the name of their game — and there are no rules.

Passing Influence: Love and changes for the better are both indicated under this vibration. This should prove to be a particularly busy social period when there is much to be done and not nearly enough time to do it. Your family will probably choose to be especially supportive during this period if you're not too stubborn to accept their help. Change is in the air and this could be of environment, occupation or both. A new and meaningful relationship is also almost certain to flourish.

The Swords (Spades)

51/6, King of Swords

Permanent Influence: The number fifty-one has a powerful potency all of its own representing as it does the spirit of the warrior. People under this influence should gain swift advancement in life in whatever career they choose to follow, particularly if it happens to be in one of the armed services. These individuals find it easy to handle life or death decisions and are frequently found in the legal and medical professions. They not only have complete control of themselves but are also able to instil courage into others when faced with difficult situations. They are born commanders who are not afraid to see that justice is done.

Negative Traits: Negative Fifty-ones are sadistic and deliberately cruel. They like nothing better than to see others suffer but when the boot is on the other foot they are the worst imaginable cowards. They are often evil characters who should be avoided at all costs.

Passing Influence: Legal proceedings or a brush with authority are possible when the King of Swords is in power. This is when you will need to muster all your fighting spirit if you wish to emerge victorious at the end of the battle. Justice will be done but you must put your case to its best advantage. Divorce proceedings come under the heading of legal matters so be prepared for disputes and arguments to flare up on the home front.

52/7, Queen of Swords

Permanent Influence: People who come under the rule of the Queen of Swords are extremely intelligent individuals with many wide and varied sides to their personalities. They absorb knowledge like a piece of blotting paper and very often they can sense what is going to happen long before the event actually takes place. They are versatile, creative and sticklers for detail, but totally dependable.

Negative Traits: Negative Fifty-twos are dangerous adversaries who are difficult to fathom because they possess such brilliant, cunning minds. Deceit is second nature to these people and you would be very lucky indeed to catch them out at their little game. They are as slippery as an eel and also deadly.

Passing Influence: During this temporary phase you should try to get away from familiar surroundings in order to stimulate your mind with new experiences. This is a necessary period of personal growth when a few days spent entirely on your own would also prove beneficial to your outlook on life. Allow your mind to wander where it likes and be sure that you make a mental note of everything you see and do for future reference.

53/8, Knight of Swords

Permanent Influence: The permanent influence of the Knight of Swords creates some powerful individuals who are mentally and physically strong. They are afraid of nothing and appear at their best in a difficult situation when their courage becomes particularly noticeable. These people really do know how to look after themselves. However, they are rather inclined to begin a project with great enthusiasm only to give up when it is only half finished.

Negative Traits: Negative Knights are rather inclined to go looking for trouble as there is nothing they enjoy more than a good scrap. Many mercenary soldiers come under the negative influence of this card. They are headstrong people with a cavalier attitude to life.

Passing Influence: Under this temporary vibration many challenging situations will crop up when least expected. You will need all your courage to deal with them. Keep a firm control of matters as once you lose this your opponents will be able to take the upper hand. Troubles will be your constant companions during this period but don't despair too much as they will all pass, leaving you a stronger character for the experience.

54/9, Page of Swords

Permanent Influence: People permanently ruled by the Page of Swords are quick-witted and alert. It never seems to take them long to find the solution to a difficult problem or to come up with a quicker way to get a tiresome task completed. They have the gift of the 'gab' which they should put to good use whenever possible. From a career point of view they would make excellent negotiators, politicians, diplomats or even, at the other end of the scale, street traders.

Negative Traits: Negative Fifty-fours are tricky customers. They are devious, cunning, foxy characters who seem to have a finger in a great many rather dubious pies. They can always spot a person's weak point and quickly turn it to their own advantage.

Passing Influence: During this temporary cycle you should endeavour to be alert and ready to take action at even the slightest hint of trouble so that any problems can be dealt with before they have time to get out of hand. You should also be vigilant for colleagues and friends who may be working against your interests at this time, although don't over-react and imagine that everyone is your enemy. Important messages can be expected under this vibration which may be of a confidential nature. It's up to you to ensure that they remain so.

55/1, Ace of Swords

Permanent Influence: The Ace of Swords indicates success, victory and triumph despite difficulties. Anyone under its permanent influence is almost certain to get on in life. These people spend a great deal of time considering their next move and once launched on a particular course they are virtually unstoppable. Tireless and undaunted, they always seem to reach their goal.

Negative Traits: Negative Fifty-fives are 'vandals' who destroy things for the fun of it. They nearly all carry chips on their shoulders believing that life has been unkind to them in one way or another. They often have extremely violent tempers.

Passing Influence: As a temporary vibration, the Ace of Swords promises substantial progress in a project for which you are solely responsible coupled with some form of personal reward in recognition of all the long hours and hard work you have invested in the scheme. A major change in your lifestyle is also indicated during this period which will be necessary if you wish to build a more secure future for yourself. Some of the restrictions which you have been under in the past should now lift allowing you more personal freedom and ample time to enjoy it.

56/11/2, Two of Swords

Permanent Influence: People ruled by the Two of Swords will not have an easy time during their early years. However, as they mature they should find that the lessons they learn will furnish them with invaluable experience. Their success will only come later in life but they will have earned it. No one makes a more loyal or honest friend than a person permanently ruled by this vibration.

Negative Traits: Negative Fifty-sixes seem to take great delight in causing trouble. They are born with a wooden spoon in their hands which they use to stir up discontent and arguments at every possible opportunity. They are often sly, dishonest, deceitful and selfish.

Passing Influence: The keyword here is balance. Friendship is well aspected and it should be possible to find amicable solutions to old quarrels and arguments which can now be viewed in a different light. This should prove to be a particularly pleasant and harmonious phase of your life.

57/3, Three of Swords

Permanent Influence: This is not an easy vibration to live under although the Three of Swords does indicate a happy ending. Strife and conflict could be your constant companions until well into middle age when your situation should begin to improve after one last major upheaval. Once this necessary disruption has passed it should be possible to establish a far better, and more peaceful, pattern of life.

Negative Traits: Negative Fifty-sevens are often suspected of being mentally unbalanced — one minute they are reasonable human beings and the next they fly into an uncontrollable rage for no apparent reason. It is virtually impossible to gauge with any accuracy the moods of these people because they are so changeable and totally unpredictable.

Passing Influence: Disruptions and disagreements are likely under this temporary vibration. During this period few things will go smoothly. Be prepared for delays, cancellations and a great deal of wasted time. There could also be some problems in your private life which will need careful handling if you wish to continue in your present relationship, as this card indicates separation. Fortunately a positive outcome is also quite likely when something much better and longer lasting can be established.

58/4, Four of Swords

Permanent Influence: People who come under the permanent protection of the Four of Swords possess the ability to recuperate speedily from any blow, however disastrous. They are buoyant individuals who are never down for long and seem to bounce back again with greater determination than ever to succeed. They always remain calm when faced with a difficult situation and, for this reason, many people turn to them for advice or guidance when in trouble themselves.

Negative Traits: Negative Fifty-eights are often cowardly. They are the first to turn and run at the slightest hint of trouble, preferring to hide behind others for protection and comfort.

Passing Influence: Now is the time, under the temporary influence of the Four of Swords, to take a back seat and let the world pass you by for a while. Rest and relaxation are what you need and if you are sensible you should see that you get them. Nothing is that important that it can't wait just a little longer before it is attended to — your health must come first. Visits to the doctor, possibly even a stay in hospital, can all be avoided if you apply the brakes now.

59/5, Five of Swords

Permanent Influence: Under the rulership of the Five of Swords, it will be necessary to fail several times in life before finally rising again to achieve great honours and victory. This preliminary, and necessarily difficult, period should be regarded as a test of character which requires courage, staying-power and determination if you hope to pass with honours. However, once these hurdles have been cleared there is nothing else to stop you achieving success in whichever direction you choose to take.

Negative Traits: Negative Fifty-nines take far too long to make up their minds. This inability to make quick decisions often means that they miss many good opportunities as a result.

Passing Influences: When exerting only a passing influence, the Five of Swords indicates that this would be an appropriate time to swallow your pride. There are some facts in life that we all have to accept no matter how unpalatable, and this is what you must do now. Avoid being defiant and learn to bow to the inevitable. Once you have regained self-control you will see that there are other avenues open for you to explore.

60/6, Six of Swords

Permanent Influence: The Six of Swords indicates an itinerate lifestyle and not an easy one at that as each fresh move seems to lead from one set of difficult circumstances to another. However, progress can be made by those willing to tackle their problems one step at a time in some semblance of order. People who come under this vibration are generally cheerful, friendly and full of self-confidence which often gets them out of tricky situations. Whatever degree of success they manage to achieve, it will be hard won.

Negative Traits: Negative Sixties will rebel against anything. They simply cannot bear to be told what to do and usually decide to do the opposite out of sheer bravado. They seldom make full use of their undoubted talents because they give up too readily when progress becomes a little slow.

Passing Influence: After a long period of difficulties some headway can now be made because a major obstacle will no longer stand in your way. Travel and/or a move of home may be necessary before even further progress can be made. But this is a matter for careful consideration and not to be made on the spur of the moment.

61/7, Seven of Swords

Permanent Influence: This card indicates the possibility of success which can only be realized through courage, determination and the occasional use of cunning. The path is narrow and there are many dangers and pitfalls on either side but you should reach your goal in life if you plan your moves with care. Never make a move until you are certain it is safe to do so and even then proceed with the utmost caution.

Negative Traits: Negative Sixty-ones lack stamina, although their intentions are good. They always seem to run out of steam at the last moment thereby failing to achieve what is almost in their grasp. On the rare occasions they do see a project through to completion they seldom sustain their efforts and lose any ground they have managed to make.

Passing Influence: The keyword for this temporary vibration is inspiration and the way you handle your personal affairs during this period should be truly inspired. You know what you want from life so now it's up to you to set about finding the right, and most expeditious, way to achieve these desires. However, remember to spare a thought for other people's feelings if you want to avoid hearing a few home truths during this period.

62/8, Eight of Swords

Permanent Influence: People ruled by the Eight of Swords will need to create their own luck in life if they wish to realize their full potential. Opportunity won't come looking for them at home — they must go out into the world to seek their fortunes. They should be prepared to accept any challenge which presents itself, no matter how daunting; to work long hours and to put every ounce of effort into the task they are performing. Only then will they find the success they are seeking. These individuals have all been born with one particular, special talent which they should not ignore.

Negative Traits: Negative Sixty-twos are inclined to put a tremendous amount of time and effort into enterprises which everyone else can see, at a glance, are doomed to failure. They never learn from past mistakes becoming gradually more and more depressed and frustrated when their hard work repeatedly goes unrewarded.

Passing Influence: Under the passing influence of the Eight of Swords you are almost certain to acquire a few extra responsibilities from which you can expect no immediate release. These may tend to cramp your style but when the burden is finally lifted it should herald the beginning of a new and improved phase of your life. Be patient and try to rise above these temporary restrictions.

63/9, Nine of Swords

Permanent Influence: This is the number of the martyr and under the permanent influence of the Nine of Swords your faith will frequently be put to the test. It is a necessary stage of your karmic development to experience this vibration and the many trials and the personal suffering you will experience during this lifetime will all serve to develop the tremendous strength of character which has been lying dormant and untested within you for so long. Passivity and resignation are your keywords.

Negative Traits: Negative Sixty-threes allow life to get the better of them. They are, quite simply, unable to cope and in consequence their lives become wasted. They spend most of their time bemoaning their lot instead of fighting back in an attempt to overcome their problems.

Passing Influence: Your best advice is to keep a low profile when under the temporary influence of the Nine of Swords. Keep your head well down and do nothing. If however you decide to ignore this warning, you should be prepared for disappointment, failure, interference and ruined plans.

64/1, Ten of Swords

Permanent Influence: The Ten of Swords represents 'the turning point' and consequently people under this permanent vibration often experience a particularly hard and difficult period early on in their lives. However, having started out at the lowest point on the scale matters can only improve. These people should never lose hope, because if armed with sufficient determination, they can steadily climb the ladder of success right to the very top.

Negative Traits: A negative Sixty-four lives in a fool's paradise constantly pretending that life is rosy when in reality he has made a terrible mess of things. Sixty-fours seem unable to see the folly of their ways and so chaos and muddle continue to dog them throughout their lives.

Passing Influence: This is not a particularly favourable influence to be temporarily under. It indicates that your affairs have probably reached an all-time low and that you could possibly be feeling very angry and bitter about it. Take heart though as it also promises that matters will begin to improve almost immediately, although whether you ever reach again the dizzy heights from which you recently fell is really up to you.

The Coins (Pentacles, Diamonds, Discs)

65/11/2, King of Coins

Permanent Influence: Sixty-five is a success number. All those under this influence should experience it to some degree during their lives. They have the gifts of wisdom and patience, both of which they will frequently use, plus a love of order and tradition. These people are practical, salt of the earth types who are more skilled with their hands than with their brains although this does not necessarily mean that they are dull or boring — quite the reverse in fact.

Negative Traits: Negative Kings are the dull ones. They are slow, brutish and totally ummoved by beauty or sentiment. They have no minds or wills of their own and for this reason they are easily manipulated by others. These sixty-fives are inflexible, weak and malleable.

Passing Influence: As a temporary vibration, the King of Coins indicates advancement, material gain and assistance. Careers in particular should prosper under this influence, especially if someone influential chooses to put in a good word for you. Your financial affairs should also take a turn for the better — it may even be possible to put something away for your old age during this period. However, this King also indicates a slight element of risk and you would be very unwise to do anything foolish no matter how well things seem to be going for you.

66/3, Queen of Coins

Permanent Influence: As a permanent influence, the Queen of Coins indicates common sense and a life of ease. The people she rules are honest, ordinary individuals who put their homes and families before all other considerations. They have a down-to-earth attitude towards life. So long as they are well fed and comfortable they are perfectly happy and seldom, if ever, crave for fame and riches.

Negative Traits: Negative Sixty-sixes are extravagant, although only with themselves; everyone else can go without as far as they are concerned. Whatever they do is done for the effect it creates rather than for the pleasure it gives. They crave for luxury on an overwhelming scale and judge people by their possessions rather than by who they are. They are really nothing more than spoiled children in need of correction.

Passing Influence: As a temporary influence, the Queen of Coins indicates a particularly happy and trouble-free period of your life when you can afford to relax and simply enjoy what life has to offer. Your family and friends will play an active role in your affairs during this phase when there should be many social functions to which you will be invited. The keywords here are entertainment, enjoyment and friendly company.

67/4, Knight of Coins

Permanent Influence: People who fall under the permanent influence of the Knight of Coins are rather like the chivalrous knights of old. They have a personal set of standards to which they adhere rigidly. They defend what is morally right, respect law and order and believe that tradition should be upheld. These characters seldom reach the rank of 'commander' in life but many make fine 'lieutenants'.

Negative Traits: Negative Knights tend to cling to the past, resisting progress and fighting against any proposed changes and improvements simply because they will outmode existing methods. These Sixty-sevens are rather short-sighted individuals.

Passing Influence: When ruled by the Knight of Coins you could be faced with a difficult decision which will involve a moral issue — unfortunately your standards may be rather higher than the accepted norm and this is where your difficulty will lie — should you be true to yourself and miss a golden opportunity or should you turn a blind eye and accept the offer? Only you can decide so don't rush to give your answer.

68/5, Page of Coins

Permanent Influence: People permanently ruled by the Page of Coins generally find that their success lies in the business world, particularly if they are cast in an executive role. They make conscientious workers who are not afraid to take responsibility; they perform their duties with care taking pride in the smooth running of their particular operations. These people are particularly careful with money and seem to be able to get the best possible results with the least expediture.

Negative Traits: Negative Sixty-eights are power-mad tyrants who like nothing better than to terrorize their subordinates into action while they remain idle. They are unpleasant individuals who are widely disliked by one and all.

Passing Influence: As a passing influence the Page of Coins promises new avenues to explore for those of you willing to try something hitherto unknown and untested. You will need to be extremely flexible during this period and should be prepared to alter existing plans at the last moment without becoming flustered. Opportunities to travel could also come your way under this vibration although your movements will, in all probability, be restricted to your own country.

69/6, Ace of Coins

Permanent Influence: The rule of the Ace of Coins indicates a life of emotional contentment coupled with almost certain material success. Love and security are the two things most people desire and under this influence you should be able to enjoy the benefits of both.

Negative Traits: The reverse side of the Ace of Coins does not paint quite such a pretty picture. Negative Sixty-nines are so avaricious and greedy that they often beome infatuated with money and the power it wields. They pursue it relentlessly without a thought for anything else. The possession of a vast amount of money becomes their only goal in life — an end in itself.

Passing Influence: Under the temporary rule of this Ace life should be full of rewards for past efforts plus the chance of lucky accidents thrown in for good measure.

70/7, Two of Coins

Permanent Influence: The Two of Coins points to a busy, interesting lifestyle with never a dull moment and possibly success at the end of the day — certainly happiness. People permanently ruled by this card usually have a light-hearted attitude to life, are seldom depressed for long and seem able to cope adequately with most problems. A career in communications, the media or one involving travel would suit their personalities admirably.

Negative Traits: Negative Seventies seem incapable of sustained effort. They tend to flit from one interest to another and never really do anything properly or indeed ever complete the tasks they have embarked upon. They are inconsistent, foolhardy and lack self-discipline.

Passing Influence: Business opportunities and travel are well aspected under this temporary influence. Stimulating developments should take place in your career which could result in several short trips, probably abroad. These should prove to be a great success provided that you get your facts straight and always play by the rules. If not — watch out! Some form of partnership also seems likely and this could mean a new romantic attachment for you.

71/8, Three of Coins

Permanent Influence: This is the number/card which represents skill — either as the craftsman using his hands, the merchant selling his wares, or the businessman controlling his empire. It also indicates that rewards can be earned and admiration won by exercising your innate skills in the most appropriate ways.

Negative Traits: Negative Seventy-ones never bother to develop their skills and so their potential is wasted and they seldom accomplish little of any worth in life. They are also stubborn individuals who refuse to listen to advice no matter how sound and well-intentioned it may be.

Passing Influence: This vibration indicates expansion and the opportunity for personal advancement. Now is the time to think a little bigger than usual, to push yourself and your ideas, and to climb a few rungs higher up the ladder of success before this fortuitous period ends. You may need to work harder than normal but the rewards should prove adequate compensation for all the extra effort required.

72/9, Four of Coins

Permanent Influence: The Four of Coins indicates the opportunity to establish an empire provided that you begin early enough — complete material security should be within your grasp. Commerce and business are in your blood and even if you start out as a small-time dealer with very limited capital you could end up as a wealthy and influential pillar of local society. Your success story could be a source of inspiration to others.

Negative Traits: Negative Seventy-twos have no business sense whatsoever. Money runs through their fingers like water and any financial dealings in which they become involved are almost bound to fail. These people can go from riches to rags in one generation — theirs!

Passing Influence: Increase is the keyword for this temporary vibration. Now is the time to double your money and really make a financial killing provided that you pay attention to detail and don't allow over-enthusiasm to get the better of your good sense — and money. Material gain through skillful manipulation of your resources is definitely on the cards at this time.

73/1, Five of Coins

Permanent Influence: This will not be an easy vibration to live under for those who tend to give in to despair, as once they have lost hope they have lost everything. Money worries will always cause hardships, and financial insecurity, poverty or unemployment are just three of the ways these troubles could manifest themselves. However, there are still many things in life which money cannot buy, such as good health, and an excess of these blessings should help to balance the scales rather more in your favour.

Negative Traits: The negative aspect of this vibration is only marginally worse than the positive. In this case hope has been removed completely and a life of extreme hardship is almost certain, probably culminating in ruin. Not a pleasant prospect at all.

Passing Influence: The sooner this influence passes the better because it points to only one thing — difficulty (probably of a financial nature). You should try to practise economy whenever possible under this vibration and store away any plans for the future until matters pick up again and your circumstances improve.

74/11/2, Six of Coins

Permanent Influence: A balanced, if rather uneventful, life is promised by the Six of Coins. You should be capable of running your own affairs smoothly so that expenditure never exceeds income and should also be able to find sufficient time to help others less well organized than yourself to put their affairs into better order. People born under this influence are natural philanthropists who really care about people. They have a humane and benevolent approach to life.

Negative Traits: Negative Seventy-fours are selfish. They will never lift a finger to help anyone else if they can possibly avoid doing so. All they want out of life is personal pleasure and very often they spend far more money than they can afford in its pursuit.

Passing Influence: When the Six of Coins exerts a temporary influence this indicates a period when balance can be restored; when life can get back onto an even keel and when financial problems can be resolved. A surprise windfall perhaps as the result of an inheritance, a gift or even a lucky win should go a long way to solving any problems.

75/3, Seven of Coins

Permanent Influence: The Seven of Coins indicates growth provided that a sustained effort is maintained to see projects through to completion. Inertia or complacency will only lead to disappointment. Good results are always possible under this influence provided that hard work has been poured in to the projects in question.

Negative Traits: Negative Seventy-fives bring all their troubles upon themselves through their inability to complete tasks which they undertake. Promising opportunities always end in failure because they will not apply themselves to the job in hand. They often have money worries because they give in too easily when the going gets a little hard and consequently are seldom paid for their incomplete work.

Passing Influence: A period of unremitting hard work is almost always indicated when the Seven of Coins exerts a passing influence. However, financial rewards are also promised when the task has been completed. You should try to remain calm and patient when annoying set-backs occur and don't be too proud to accept any help that may be offered no matter how much you suspect the motives behind such a proposal — many hands make lighter work!

76/4, Eight of Coins

Permanent Influence: Many extremely talented people come under the permanent influence of the Eight of Coins. Success is there waiting for them provided that they are prepared to develop their talents and put them to good use instead of treating them simply as a hobby. It takes a certain amount of courage to go it alone but for those who are willing to accept the challenge the rewards, both financially and personally, are boundless. Don't stay an amateur all your life — turn professional and reap the rewards your abilities can command.

Negative Traits: Negative Seventy-sixes tend to misuse their talents or to ignore them altogether which should be regarded as a punishable offence. Many unfortunately do not look far enough ahead and because immediate recognition does not occur they lose heart and give up altogether.

Passing Influence: Under the temporary influence of the Eight of Coins the opportunity could arise to use your talents to the full and even possibly to develop them even further by embarking on a training scheme of some kind as a private pupil or even as part of a group of like-minded individuals. Whatever transpires you should try to remain level-headed — if you allow matters to go to your head you could lose friends and possibly even make a few enemies by your change in attitude.

77/5, Nine of Coins

Permanent Influence: People who come under the permanent influence of the Nine of Coins should never know more than a moment's worry, discomfort or anxiety during their lifetimes provided they have the good sense to look after themselves and to take care of the assets they will undoubtedly be born with. This is a particularly good vibration which practically guarantees all the comforts of life as well as love, happiness and health for good measure.

Negative Traits: Negative Seventy-sevens are silly enough to want more than they already have and for this reason their financial security never lasts for very long. Because of their extravagant and over-indulgent lifestyle they lose not only their money but occasionally their loved ones too. Some negative Seventy-sevens do manage to prosper but this is usually accomplished by rather dubious means.

Passing Influence: Good fortune is the keyword which can manifest itself in various ways. It may come about as the justly deserved reward for hard work; it could come in the guise of a gift; or it could come out of the blue as the result of some happy accident of fate. However it does come, money will not be in short supply and you should enjoy this temporary period of affluence while it lasts. Try to put something away for a rainy day if you possibly can.

78/6, Ten of Coins

Permanent Influence: The Ten of Coins indicates that your happiness and prosperity depend very much on your close family, perhaps even the family name or the achievements of one of your ancestors. It could mean that you will become an integral part of an existing family firm or business but if this is not the case then perhaps family money will be invested in your future. Two things are certain, your material security is not only assured, it will also be connected, either directly or indirectly, with your family.

Negative Traits: Some negative Seventy-eights suffer from a crisis of identity caused by adoption, illegitimacy or by being orphaned at an early age. Others know only too well who their relations are and just what a drawback they can be, while the odd few feel bitter and disappointed because they have either been disinherited or have somehow been denied their birthright. To negative Seventy-eights their lineage is a distinct disadvantage which should be forgotten rather than an asset which can be used to their advantage.

Passing Influence: Under the temporary influence of the Ten of Coins family gatherings are indicated and as happiness is also highlighted during this period these get-togethers will most probably be weddings, christenings or anniversary parties. Your private life should be so stress-free and settled at this time that you may even feel inclined to start making new, rather ambitious plans for the future.

GLOSSARY OF TERMS

Analogous Numbers — a group of numbers which are either all odd, or all even.

Arithomancy — an ancient method of numerical divination believed to have been used by Pythagoras.

Arrows, The — a system of sixteen arrows, indicating specific directions, used when interpreting a Birthchart.

Birth Number — a term used by some numerologists to describe the Date of Birth Number.

Birthchart — a grid, like the one used in the game of noughts and crosses, which is used to analyse the Date of Birth.

Business Numbers — the numbers 2, 4 and 8.

Colour Number — the numbers 1-9 inclusive are in harmony with certain colours/gem stones and the Colour Number is used to find the 'right' colours for a particular individual.

Compatibility — is determined by comparison of the Date of Birth Numbers of the parties in question.

Composite Numbers — are numbers which are divisible not only by themselves and unity but also by some other number such as 9, 15, 21, 25, 27, 33 and so on.

Compound Numbers — the numbers from 10 onwards, sometimes also referred to as double-digit numbers.

Conflicting Numbers — a mixture of both odd and even numbers in a group.

Consonant Numbers — found by adding the numerical values of the consonants in a name and reducing the total to a single number. It represents the 'outer personality' or the face we show to the world.

Date of Birth Number — found by addition and reduction of the full Date of Birth. It represents the lessons to be learned and is of importance when considering which career to choose.

Deficient Numbers — are numbers which have the sum of their fractional parts less than themselves.

Destiny Number — a term used by some numerologists to describe the Whole Name Number and by others to describe the Date of Birth Number.

Double-digit Numbers — the Compound Numbers from 10 onwards.

Eternity, The Number of — *see* The Sacred Number.

Even Numbers — are numbers which can be divided equally and are regarded as being indefinite, feminine, passive, receptive and introvert. There are six classes of even numbers — evenly-even, evenly-odd, oddly-odd, superperfect, deficient and perfect.

Evenly-even Numbers — are all in duple ratio from unity; thus — 1, 2, 4, 8, 16, 32, 64, 128, 256, 512 and 1024. A perfect evenly-even number can be halved and the halves again halved back to unity — $\frac{1}{2}$ of 16 = 8, $\frac{1}{2}$ of 8 = 4, $\frac{1}{2}$ of 4 = 2, $\frac{1}{2}$ of 2 = 1. It is impossible to go beyond unity.

Evenly-odd Numbers — are numbers which, when halved, are incapable of further division by halving. They are formed by taking the odd numbers in sequential order and multiplying them by two. The following odd numbers produce the evenly-odd numbers which are shown in brackets — 1(2), 3(6), 5(10), 7(14), 9(18), 11(22) — every fourth number is evenly-odd.
Expression Numbers — the numbers 3, 6 and 9.
External Image Number — a term used by some numerologists to describe the Consonant Number.

Fadic Numbers — a term used by Cheiro to describe the four Personal Numbers.
Figures — represent quantities.
Four-month Periods — there are three four-month periods which can be numerologically analysed in each Personal Year.

Gnomones — a means of representing numbers with dots or pebbles, employed by the Pythagoreans.
Golden Number — believed to be a sort of 'universal module'. It has no occult significance. Its value is 0.618 and is expressed geometrically in a rectangle the proportions of which constitute the 'Golden Section'.
Group Numbers — there are three numerical groups of numbers — the Mind Numbers (1, 5, 7), Expression Numbers (3, 6, 9), and the Business Numbers (2, 4, 8).

Incomposite Numbers — are numbers which have no divisor other than themselves and unity such as 3, 5, 7, 11, 13, 17, 19, 23 and so on.
Incomposite-composite Numbers — are numbers which have no common divisor, although each of itself is capable of division, such as 9 and 25. 9 is divisible by 3 and 25 is divisible by 5 but neither is divisible by the divisor of the other — they have no common divisor.

Karmic Numbers — *see* Missing Numbers.

Lemniscate — the symbol for infinity, represented as an eight on its side, a lazy eight.
Life Mission/Lesson/Path Numbers — are terms used by some numerologists to describe the Whole Name Number and by others to describe the Date of Birth Number.

Magic Number — seven.
Master Numbers — eleven and twenty-two.
Middle Life Number — is found by adding the unreduced Date of Birth Number to the unreduced Full Name Number and reducing the total. It represents the talents we should have developed, or the skills we should have learned, by the time middle life is reached (between 30-50 years of age).
Mind Numbers — the numbers 1, 5 and 7.
Missing Numbers — represent characteristics which we should try to develop during this lifetime.

Namechart — a grid, like the one used in the game of noughts and crosses, which is used to analyse the name.
Numbers — represent qualities. Number is the term applied by Pythagoras to all numerals and their combinations.
Numeromancy — is an ancient method of numerical divination believed to have been used by Pythagoras.

Oblong Numbers — are even numbers expressed as gnomones.
Odd Numbers — are numbers which cannot be divided equally and are regarded as being definite, masculine, active, creative and extrovert. There are three classes of odd numbers — incomposite, composite and incomposite-composite.

Oddly-odd Numbers — cannot be halved back to unity but are capable of more than one division by halving — $\frac{1}{2}$ of 12 = 6, $\frac{1}{2}$ of 6 = 3.

Onomancy/Onomomancy — an ancient method of name analysis.

Outer Personality Number — is a term used by some numerologists to describe the Consonant Number.

Peak Numbers — represent important stages reached on the Pyramids of Maturity.

Perfect Numbers — are numbers which have the sum of their fractional parts equal to themselves. Perfect numbers do not occur very often, in fact there is only one Perfect Number between 1 and 10 and this is 6, only one between 10 and 100 which is 28, only one between 100 and 1,000 which is 496 and only one between 1,000 and 10,000 which is 8128.

Personal Months — these are sub-divisions of the Personal Years (as are the Four-Month Periods).

Personal Numbers — there are four Personal Numbers which are as follows — the Date of Birth Number, the Vowel Number, the Consonant Number and the Full Name Number.

Personal Years — our lives are believed to consist of recurring nine-year cycles and the nine various stages of this cycle are the Personal Years.

THE SIEVE OF ERATOSTHENES

The Sieve is extremely simple to use once the odd numbers have been inserted (see line 4). It then becomes apparent that every third number from 3 onwards is divisible by 3 (see line 3); every fifth number from 5 onwards is divisible by 5 (see line 2); every seventh number from 7 onwards is divisible by 7 (see line 1); and so on. Incomposite numbers are also sifted out (see line 5).

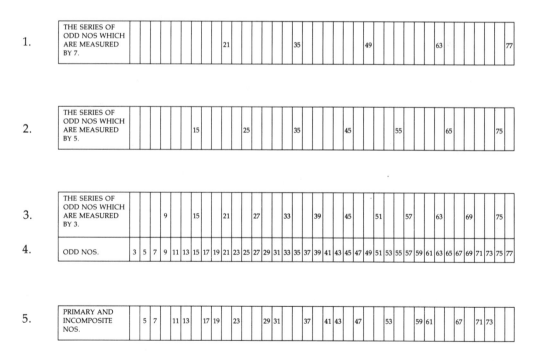

Figure 32 The Sieve of Eratosthenes.

Place Numbers — is the number which rules a particular place such as a country, county, city, town and so on.

Prime Numbers — a Prime Number is a number having no integral factors except itself and unity (2, 3, 5, 7, 11 and so on).

Pyramids of Maturity, The — are a system used when analysing the twenty-seven year period of maturity.

Recurring Numbers — are numbers which occur frequently in numerological calculations.

Ruling Number — is the number which governs, influences or 'rules' a person/object/place/period of time.

Sacred Number, The — is 142857 which contains the full range of numbers from 1–9 when it is calculated by dividing the number one, with as many noughts after it as you care to chose, by seven.

Secret Self Number — is a term used by some numerologists to describe the Vowel Number.

Shemhamphorash — the supreme name of God which contains seventy-two syllables.

Sieve of Eratosthenes, The — a mathematical contrivance used to divide odd numbers into three general classes — incomposite, composite and incomposite-composite (see page 221).

Single Numbers — are the numbers from 1 to 9 inclusive, each of which has been ascribed with specific characteristics.

Soul Number — is a term used by some numerologists to describe the Vowel Number.

Square Numbers — are odd numbers expressed as Gnomones.

Superperfect Numbers — are numbers which have the sum of their fractional parts greater than themselves.

Tetragrammaton — is the secret name of God.

Triangular Numbers — are numbers which are expressed in a triangular shape such as the Pythagorean 'Tetraktys'.

Vowel Number — is found by adding together the numerical values of the vowels in a name and reducing the total to a single number. It represents the 'inner you'.

Whole Name Number — is found by adding together the numerical values of all the letters in a name and reducing the total to a single number. It reveals what must be achieved during this lifetime and how to go about it.

INDEX